Hineni – Here I Am

by
Rabbi Herman Schaalman

KTAV Publishing House, Inc.
Jersey City, NJ

Copyright © 2007 Herman Schaalman

Library of Congress Cataloging-in-Publication Data

Schaalman, Herman E. (Herman Ezra), 1916–
Hineni = Here I am / by Rabbi Herman Schaalman.
    p. cm.
Includes bibliographical references and index.
ISBN 978-0-88125-954-4 (alk. paper)
1. God (Judaism) 2. Faith (Judaism) 3. Spiritual life – Judaism. 4. Holocaust
(Jewish theology) 5. Judaism – Relations – Christianity. 6. Christianity and other
religions – Judaism. I. Title. II. Title: Here I am.
BM610.S314 2007
296.3'11 – dc22
                    2007006974
Manufactured in the United States of America

Published by
KTAV **Publishing House, Inc.**
930 Newark Avenue
Jersey City, NJ 07306
(201) 963-9524
FAX (201) 963-0102
www.ktav.com
bernie@ktav.com

Typeset by
Raphaël Freeman, Jerusalem Typesetting,
www.jerusalemtype.com

Contents

Introduction

"Of the writing of books there is no end," so the adage goes, and despite the enormous volume of electronic communication, the flood of books does not seem to diminish. So, why this book?

The first and immediate answer is "Anita." It was Anita Rifkind's wise, intelligent, persistent devotion that made this book possible. It was her questions, the subtle turnings of her inquisitive mind, that produced so much of the content and format of these pages. This acknowledgment of her part in it is a totally inadequate tribute to her initiative and work.

The other part of my gratitude, insufficient and never really enough, is due to my wife, now of sixty-five years, Lotte, who for years urged me to write down some of my thoughts. She knows, as do so very many others, that I almost never have notes when I speak publicly or teach. Somewhere there are a few dozen essays and such, but primarily, almost without exception, I have used my voice without notes, speaking extemporaneously. If there is any value in these pages, Lotte is somehow deeply hidden in it.

Part of my reluctance to use the written word regularly, or at all, is my recognition that the written word is somehow so defenseless. The author is not present to the reader, and thus readers can do with the written word whatever they wish and are capable of. The spoken word is ephemeral, heard and gone, and the speaker is usually there to interpret and, when necessary, to defend it.

It took me a long time to overcome my reluctance to write and to produce a book. Now that it is finished, at least for now, it is entrusted to the reader. May it experience a good reception.

Hineni, "Here I am," is a partial record of decades of wrestling with what to me have been basic questions about God, about us humans, about me as a Jew, about other mysteries of existence and our inadequate attempts to respond to them. This book is not a systematic theological treatise. Rather it is a partial summing up of decades of teaching and dialoging with Jews and Christians, and trying to answer their questions and to respond to their quandaries. It is the incomplete record of a long life as a rabbi – buffeted by doubts, inspired by flashes of insight, and driven by a never-ending need to explore further.

Chapter One
Foundations

I will make of you a great nation.

(Genesis 12:2)

There were many years, a whole part of my life in fact, that I lived as a sleepwalker. I operated on the accumulated intentions, motivations, and impulses implanted in me from the time I was a baby by my parents, who in their own way were very pious, very observant Jews. I did not for a long time get to a self-critical examination of my own thinking. First of all, I came out of a tradition that has existed for millennia, and its historicity was enough. And not just enough, the traditions were so good, so proven, that I did not feel a need, or even think I had a right, to challenge them. Second, I was comfortably running on the accumulated energy and motivation of my early life and on the training I received afterwards in the rabbinical seminaries. So I was really not compelled to ask the tough questions. I certainly did not do it from within myself.

The oldest of three sons, I spent my youth in Bavaria, raised in a way that was typical for Jews in Germany at that time, attending school, reading and playing sports in my leisure time.

We learned to ski. We studied Torah. As a young Jew preparing for bar mitzvah and thereafter, I knew that I was expected to live a certain kind of life. I grew up in a fairly observant household, though intellectually very open, and in that regard, very modern. My parents, like nearly all Jews in Germany at the time, kept kosher. There were only a couple of small Reform congregations in Germany, one in Berlin and one in Hamburg. They were so marginal to Jewish life that virtually no one paid any attention to them.

I have always had a sense of the reality of God, a sense of the awe of the creature over against the Creator. I do not claim by this statement to have been graced in any fashion. Rather I credit the impact of my father, who seemed to embody the human response to what he would have called "his God." My father was very pious in this sense. He was a mathematician and a physicist.

I always say that I was raised by people who were born in the nineteenth century. My father was born in 1890. The youngest of eight or nine siblings, his parents died when he was quite young, so I never knew my grandparents. My father's family traced their ancestry back to 1519 in Bavaria, when the Jews were expelled from Regensburg. He belonged to very simple people living in a small Jewish community in a village of a few thousand people. Typical of German men at that time, my father was a man of few words. He fought in the First World War as a sergeant, was wounded and decorated.

My mother was born in 1893 in a village in Ukraine. She lived to be ninety-three. Her family fled to Germany to escape a pogrom when she was six months old. My mother came from an intellectually curious family. Two of her brothers were doctors, and she was one of the rare women students at the university. She was also a woman of deep feelings and sensitivities about other human beings.

Right after World War I, she was studying either biology

or botany. She attempted to continue her education even after I was born, bringing me with her to class. One of my earliest memories, at about three years of age, is of going with her to the university. She left me near a fountain and told me not to move from there while she was in class. I was totally reliable in that regard, except that a big black dog came over to me, and I was absolutely panicked. A man happened along and lured the dog away, or I don't know what might have happened to me. But that was the end of my mother's going to class.

In addition to the influence of my parents, as a teenager I was part of a youth movement that held Martin Buber in high respect. After school we would meet in the youth group to discuss his theology. To me he was already an "elderly" man. I remember one particular gathering with him when he was teaching Isaiah to us. I can still see him sitting on a bench with his beard fluttering in the breeze, all of us sitting at his feet.

So my basic upbringing instilled in me the foundations of Judaism, especially the two classic key events defining both the Jewish experience and the Jewish community, the Exodus from Egypt and the theophany at Sinai. It was only much later that I understood that these were unique events, never to be repeated. Never again did God rescue the entire people. Never again did God speak to the entire people, at least according to the way we tell our story and have written it. So it is extraordinary that the entire foundation of the Jewish belief structure and the whole identity of the Jewish community rests on the foundation of two events that have never been repeated and are unrepeatable. In addition to being a profound puzzle about God, it is also an enormous insight into the nature of being a Jew. Somehow we are willing to rest our whole identity and destiny, our whole vision of life, world, history, time, on two events that at least so far have not been repeated, and need to be considered to be inherently unrepeatable. This means, at the very least, that what God did then is most probably not to be expected again. Eventually I learned that we Jews have existed to this day on the accumulated impact of those unique events.

Jews as an identifiable entity have been on the stage of the world's drama for better than thirty-five hundred years, although this number is subject to controversy. Beginning with Abraham, we have lived under every conceivable condition of life, and in virtually every corner of the globe. As individuals or in groups, we have lived under the most inhuman pressures, persecutions, and even wholesale murder. We have been sovereign in a land of our own, have lived as barely tolerated strangers in other people's environs, have created some of humanity's greatest works and institutions, and have been hounded even unto death as incompatible aliens. We have brought the world insight into the uniqueness, the singularity of God, and have lived in this belief, in this "faith," in unbroken continuity for better than 150 generations.

"Faith" is an easy word to use when we talk about religious life, and especially when we talk about it in a somewhat theological framework. In fact, it is the one word that seems to come almost instinctively into the vocabulary of a modern person. It is a word, however, that has both history and baggage. It occurred to me to look closely at the word when I recently went over a passage in Exodus, just before the great Song at the Sea. That passage, in translation, essentially reads that after having witnessed the great deeds of God in Egypt, and especially at the sea, which according to the story split and let the people pass through unscathed and became a deadly trap for the pursing Egyptian army, the people "*had faith* in God and in His servant Moses." The Hebrew word for what is usually translated as "had faith" or "believed" is *ya'aminu*, which has the same root as the very commonly used word "Amen." However, I think that a better, truer translation would be that the people "trusted" in God and His servant Moses.

There is a difference between faith and trust. Trust inescapably represents mutuality – it is interactive. Trust is "between," a response to something that rises in one and extends to the other. Faith, belief, on the other hand is totally solipsistic, within oneself. It is a total expenditure, a gift on the part of the self. There is really no inherent compelling need to be faithful or in a faith posture for anything that exists or that happens outside of oneself. Faith is the capacity of human beings, as it is imputed that the church father Tertullian taught, to believe in what is not rational, in what is not in any manner present to us as sentient, that is, sense-dependent, human beings. "*Credo quia absurdum est* – I believe *because* it is nonrational." It has always seemed to me that this formulation is not only pithy but also so on target that it actually represents and identifies the essential quality of faith as being the nonrational, perhaps even the irrational.

Trust, on the other hand, seems to be based on the perception of some reality, of something that is given or experienced, some stimulant, some occurrence beyond me. Trust needs to be confirmed, reaffirmed, reconstituted by the participation of the one or the thing with whom or with which one has the relationship.

So when I use the word "faith," as I do almost unthinkingly when it seems to fit the context, I have increasingly become aware that I am using a word that carries its own consequences and overtones which I believe are frequently not what the Hebrew text really wants to express. In other words, the biblical Hebrew word, the noun *emuna*, and its verbal base, *l'ha'amin*, is, like many other terms in the biblical vocabulary, relational, dialogic, something that happens between two. Thus I come back to what in other contexts is so very clear to me, that at the heart of the Jewish response to reality is the basic relational term of "both/and" rather than "either/or." In conventional logic and therefore also in so much conventional philosophic thinking, either/or is indispensable. It is basic.

The biblical wording seems to me to be pointing to another truth, perhaps even a deeper truth: all being is relational. If this sounds very much like Buber, so be it. We will talk more about this later, because that concept has not only had a profound influence on my life and thinking, but it has penetrated into such diverse areas as psychology, sociology, art, and philosophy. It is not without justification that the little book *I and Thou* has sometimes been recognized as one of the most profound literary and thought creations of the twentieth century. Basically, Buber develops the idea that all life is dialogical, is question and answer, is stimulus and response. Therefore, the deepest insights into the nature of being human are really both the willingness to "hear" and the subsequent capacity and willingness to respond.

Faith as a concept is much more needed in the Christian world because the beginning of the Christian story demands, really, the surrender of reason to a mystery that is beyond reason. The Christian religious perception starts in the willingness to make a faith declaration of oneself about the nature of the Christ and with it to accept scriptural passages that are clearly framed in the same fashion.

I am not saying that Judaism and Christianity are totally different from each other in their basic assumptions, but the story of the Christ, and the affirmation of Christ as the single most important component of Christian life, is far more intense and central to Christianity than any affirmation that I know of that Jews would make about God as the Creator or Liberator. The only such assertion a Jew must make is that God is singular, *echad*. Therefore, a Christian needs a faith capacity and a faith commitment to a degree that a Jew does not. The only statement that a Jew really has to finally affirm – and it is an affirmation, a declaration – is the singularity of God. Everything else is either derivative or sometimes, perhaps, even secondary.

Jews are invited to begin with the literal biblical text as the necessary first step. If, however, one gets stuck at the first step, whatever meaning the text intended to convey is lost. According to the Pharisaic schema, there are four levels to the text: literal, allegorical, homiletical, and mystical. That there are four levels is of itself an inescapable invitation to interact with the text. If the text is taken literally, then there is no interaction; it simply has to be accepted, period. The person is not involved anymore; the believer has to commit the act of faith that this is so. The grandeur of the Pharisaic concept is not only that the text is therefore alive and malleable, but the insistence that each person hears the word specifically as that person can and does receive it.

Nevertheless, the affirmation of a singular God may ultimately have equal force as a faith statement. Furthermore, the rabbis instituted that one has to say the *Sh'ma* three times a day, which could be considered an indication that by itself the affirmation does not promote its own acceptance. It has to be stated over and over again, it has to be driven home by sheer repetitiveness, and has to be pounded into Jewish self-awareness in a way that indicates in a profound sense how difficult and near-impossible that statement really is. Clearly, this is a statement that needs a faith commitment.

Throughout the long history of living in this faith, the Jewish people have not lived in isolation. Jews have encountered virtually all of the great cultures and religious systems, ancient or modern, long dead or still vibrant to this day, and in these encounters they have received often decisively different ideas and inspirations, and, as well, have frequently given profound, even revolutionary impulses to other civilizations and religions. It was Jews and their Judaism out of which grew both Christianity and Islam, links that are still alive and creative to this day. Although the number of Jews has always been relatively small compared to most other peoples, our impact upon the world has been vastly disproportionate to our numbers. This small community has borne witness to its trust in God and the personal and moral demands flowing from such trust in joy and exultation, as well as in pain and sorrow.

At bottom, Judaism is less a systematic structure of interlocking theological propositions than a way of life. From birth through death, from awakening to going to sleep, at work or at the table, singly or in family and community, authentic Jewish life is held in a web of *mitzvot*, commandments. These commandments are accepted as flowing from a revealing God whose intent it is to sanctify virtually every aspect of human existence. Thus in the preparation of food, as in sexual relations, in the treatment of strangers as in the treatment of family and friends, as employers or employees, as citizens or outsiders, child or parent, aged or young, female or male, Jews find guidance and direction for their lives in the 613 commandments that can be read out of Torah, the Pentateuch, as taught and interpreted by the rabbis of old and of today.

The *mitzvah* system of life cradles the Jew securely and time and again points the "way to go," the *halacha*, the law. And while over the millennia of Jewish existence, some of these commandments may have been altered or suspended, and while there are at times wide differences of interpretation among the authorities, producing the diverse strands of living Judaism, all authentic Jewish life is rooted though not exhausted in an interpretation and acceptance of tradition and traditions. Some of these differences and variations stem from major cleavages, such as Ashkenazic and Sephardic or rationalist and mystic, and are at times shaped by the interplay with major influences in surrounding cultures. But all share a basic reference and commitment to God, Torah, and the Jewish people. These three are the invariant common elements no matter how each may be understood or interpreted.

The great problem is how a belief system based on the revelation of God's words, which are immutable and whose content and intent are known, fits into a highly experimental and open society that prides itself on its capacity to absorb new discoveries and not only to encourage them but to be poised to look for them. So it is a question whether to be afraid of the new rather than to be excited by the acceptance of the new or at least by an open confrontation with it.

There was a famous rabbi in Hungary in the nineteenth century who made the categorical statement that "anything new is forbidden by Torah." This was a radical position vis-à-vis liberalism, but it is also an indication of the deep fear of those who tried to keep whatever they knew to be the tradition intact and protected against what they defined as the corrosion of modernity.

Nevertheless, despite these differences, and despite the minor recognition extended to systematic theology and the clear preference for "telling the story" as the major source of truth or truths, most Jews would accept a tripartite construction for the Jewish perception of God. Not the least reason for this principled ordering is the liturgy, which teaches us to see God in three primary roles: Creator, Revealer, and Redeemer.

From a Jewish point of view, the main emphasis is on creation. God as Creator is the most important of the three major categories by which we try to schematize our understanding of God. As Creator, God is seen as the ground of all existence – of the world and all it contains, including emphatically ourselves. As creatures we are linked inseparably to the Creator aspect of God by the haunting phrase, "God created humankind in His image" (Genesis 1:27). This universally shared quality of being human is unavoidably extended into a whole series of moral commands ranging from "Be loving to him [the sojourner] as one like yourself, for sojourners were you in the land of Egypt" (Leviticus 19:34) to the radical "You are not to murder" (Exodus 20:13). It is God's creatorhood that makes morality inescapably central, not derivative or elective, in the monotheistic belief assertions of Judaism. By contrast, in polytheism gods and goddesses are available for every conceivable human emotion and need, with obvious negative consequences for a consistent system of ethics.

Each week the Sabbath celebrates the creatorhood of God. It is the day on which we emphasize, relive God's creation. The fact that this is the single most important religious moment, rhythmically reappearing week after week, year after year, is intentionally the moment toward which the Jewish understanding of our prime relation with God wants to aim.

It is easy to be under the misapprehension that the Christian idea of Sunday is just Sabbath postponed by a day, mostly for political and organizational reasons, by the Council of Nicea. However, Sunday is basically a weekly reenactment of resurrection, a salvational day, a redemptive day. This understanding is utterly different from what the Sabbath is for the Jew. While Christianity has stressed the redemptive, Judaism has remained focused mainly on the divine creatorhood.

For instance, in the daily traditional liturgy, in the morning prayers, we read that "God repeats the work of creation every day." So creation is not a one-time event but is, in fact, an ever-repeated, continually unfolding, and never-finished process in which we believe God is involved. This is an enormously important insight toward understanding the kind of world in which we live, which surrounds us, and of which we are a part. At the same time, the question of the unbroken involvement of God in reality contradicts the Aristotelian notion of God as the cause of initial action and thereafter uninvolved.

This is not to say that we do not believe in God as Revealer. Torah, either in whole or in part, is linked to God's commanding Presence. Torah is the assertion that divine grace teaches and instructs us how we are to live with God, and with each other, in God's world. Revelation is the ground out of which grows an encompassing set of values represented in moral and ritual elements. It is indispensable for Jewish life set into the relationship that we call covenant, and that we understand to be unbreakable for God, no matter how well or how badly we live up to it.

Torah, the prime text of the Revelation, is a two-track system consisting of the written text and the oral tradition. The former is linked to Moses and the prophets, the latter is primarily linked to the Pharisaic rabbis and their students. The former is Scripture, *Tanach*; the latter, the Talmud, responsa, and codes. The former is the unchangeable text; the latter is the ever vibrantly evolving interpretation. Neither is complete or can exist without the other. Together they constitute a sacred heritage that is traced ultimately to God as the Revealer.

The traditional Jewish view is that God has ceased communicating directly. The Pharisaic movement established the position, and defended it successfully, that whatever the oral tradition was, it came from the same time, same event, and same source as the written tradition, namely Sinai. With that the rabbis established their authenticity, and their claim to authority, and successfully implanted this understanding in the Jewish tradition and lifestyle. The whole methodology which they developed, the minute inquiry into the meaning of the words of the sacred texts, the freedom to expand and investigate every word, to find novel connections between them, and also to have conflicting opinions deriving from such efforts, is the hallmark of the rabbinic movement and mind.

This tradition has allowed Judaism to avoid the curse of fundamentalism. There is no fundamentalism in Jewish tradition per se, even though sometimes ultra-traditionalists come close to maintaining that there is only one way of hearing the texts and interpreting them. But by and large, Jewish life has been spared fundamentalism. The Talmud says that if, according to Torah, there were 600,000 males twenty years old and older at Sinai, then there would be 600,000 different versions, because everybody would have heard what happened there in his own way. Another rabbi says that a servant maid at Sinai would have understood what was said more fully than the most learned scholars hundreds and hundreds of years later. These are examples of the creation of a climate that makes it clear, first, that history and culture play a role in interpretation, which is a basic safeguard against fundamentalism, and second, that they lead to a development and appreciation of a keen intellectual capacity because one is invited to challenge, to find one's way into the text, and then to test it against the findings of others.

Even though, from time to time, women managed to penetrate the purposefully constructed wall, this study and interpretation was originally restricted to male adults and children. And that is certainly one of the major defects of that part of the past. Those of us who are not traditionalists have accepted that a major revision is in order, and efforts are being made today to remedy the exclusion of the female. The basis for making these revisions is simply to understand that the prohibition against female participation was cultural; there is no other justification.

Torah traditionally is the text of the revelation issuing from an encounter between God and Moses. Jewish tradition insists that the relationship of Moses with God was unique, unrepeated, and unrepeatable. All the other prophets had visions or dreams, but they were more passive as recipients of divine impulses. Some of the prophets described it by saying that they were seized, overwhelmed, captured by the divine, compelled by the divine to speak. This is a different type of response than was granted and experienced by Moses, whose relationship to God is depicted as unique. Later revelations, to Samuel, Isaiah, Jeremiah, and others, have to be judged against the revelation at Sinai for their validity. It is generally assumed that none of these prophets taught anything that was not already either explicit or implicit in the text presumed to derive from the Sinai event.

The question is, what happened at Sinai? Here there are

stunning possibilities of description and of interpretation. Most traditionalists believe that the entire corpus of the Pentateuch, the five books, was the immediate result of Sinai. On the other hand, some rabbis have been convinced from the very beginning that only the ten words (also spoken of as the Ten Commandments) were given at Sinai. As expected, there are all kinds of variations on this idea.

There is a rabbinic opinion that the people were so frightened and overwhelmed that they fled from the revelation, and for that reason only heard the first sentence, "I am Adonai your God, who brought you out of Egypt, the house of slavery" (Exodus 20:2). There is another opinion that as soon as they heard the first word "I," they were already so unsettled that they fled. And finally, there is a stunning opinion that says they only heard the first letter of the Hebrew word for "I," which is a silent letter, the aleph. So we have the paradox that respectable opinions say that the initiation of the revelation occurred without humans being capable of understanding it. Finally, according to the story written in the book of Exodus, the people put Moses forward in a place which was supposed to be God's concentrated presence, so that in a very real way it was only Moses who "heard" (Exodus 20:18). And later, in his deuteronomic review before his death, Moses speaks of himself as the purveyor of the divine message. In the end, there are many different opinions, and they can all be read out of the multifaceted text that deals with the single most important event in all Jewish history which has had an incalculable impact on so many of our world's religions and cultures.

There is a difference particularly between Christianity and Judaism with regard to revelation, in that in Christianity the possibility of interaction with God, especially by direct word, direct appearance, is not only desirable, but considered to be factual and continuous. Christians believe that God continues to interact with humans, that people can be visited by God, hear voices or have personal revelations of God, and the like. In Christianity it is assumed that anybody can have direct contact with the divine, and such contacts are often claimed. Not only a Joan of Arc, but many hundreds of thousands, even millions of people, some of them living right now, I am sure, claim to have had direct inspiration or revelation from God.

In Jewish mysticism, the immediacy of God's presence is of a different character. An awareness of the Divine's infusion into everything is certainly a large part of Jewish mysticism, but not in an active sense where God materializes through voices or through direct interferences. On the folk level, and we need to make this distinction, there are all kinds of stories indicating that at least some individuals may have this special ability or special grace bestowed upon them. On the official level of Jewish religious thought and tradition, the issue of direct communications is at the very least so shrouded that it does not become active, however. An important element of Jewish tradition says that the last time God spoke to any Jew is to Malachi, who was a prophet around the year 500 B.C.E.

Finally, in Judaism, redemption is corporate, not individual. In contrast to Christianity, personal salvation is not a focus. Redemption is for the community, for the people, for the world eventually. The Jewish point of view is that "saving" pertains to society. The classical origin, the basic Jewish ideas about God as Redeemer, comes out of the Egypt experience. Redemption can have different meanings, something very simple, such as being free from foreign domination, becoming independent again, having a land, a ruler of one's own. Since Jewish history in ancient times was very frequently a struggle for independence and survival as an independent entity, redemption often meant victory over an enemy, a return to self-determination, to secure possession of land and destiny.

Such visions, hopes, and needs converge on the idea of Messiah. For most Jews they powerfully intersect with the mes-

sianic expectation and vision. It is a part of the historical experience of the absence of the Messiah that has been maintained
over all this time, because some of the expectations linked to
the Messiah simply have not been fulfilled. This leads to the
notion developed in some traditional circles that the Messiah
waits at the command of God. The coming of the Messiah is
seen as an act of God, a saving act of God. With the appearance of the Messiah, God will reestablish the redemptive relationship between a demanding God and a sinful people. In this
perception, God will clearly be seen to have forgiven the people.
In that act of forgiveness, God will send the Redeemer so that
whatever has befallen the people, and has so painfully pursued
them, will then be removed and changed into well-being, into
shalom. While this certainly is not all of the messianic construction, it is a major part. It flows from the perception of God as
a Rewarder and a Punisher.

Traditionally, whether Creator, Revealer, Redeemer, whether
explicitly or implicitly, God was depicted as omnipotent. God
was the supreme, unchallengeable power from Whom, through
Whom, by Whom, everything proceeded. All reality, all existence, all history were the immediate or mediate products of
Divine Power. In its purest form, this belief and proclamation
of omnipotence allowed for no other cause for any effect in the
universe, including in human life. Sin, therefore, was the always
ultimately futile attempt to thwart, contravene, or evade divine
omnipotence. And, it was believed, always to be followed by
punishment whether immediate or delayed.

Covenant is the key to the profound understanding of
the relationship between the Jewish community and God. As
tradition teaches it, it is my obligation to live up to the terms
of the covenant. It must be understood that the covenant is
not necessarily just an individual responsibility. Individual
responsibility flows out of one's membership in the covenant
community. Judaism starts with the communal, the corporate,

and individuals develop as part of the community. It does not start with a conviction of some kind, or a deliberate step, or an unfolding within a single individual. It starts with the fact that one is born into Jewish contexts, a Jewish family, a Jewish community, the Jewish people. (Of course, room is made for proselytism.) Growing up in this environment one evolves into a Jewish individual. This is one of the clear differences between Church and Synagogue: Christianity is a confessional system to a much greater degree than Judaism. One can be a Jew without ever knowing that there is a theology, an underlying reasoned system of thought, because if you practice your religious obligations, then you are a legitimately functioning part of it. Whether that practice must be undergirded by a detailed or even a subtle understanding of the theological terms involved is something that can be debated. It can even be omitted.

To a nontraditionalist Jew, the formulations of the *mitzvot* are time-bound and culture driven. Tradition says that there are 613 commandments in the Torah, but whole blocks of them, perhaps even the majority of them, are no longer operative. For example, anything that has to do with the land of Israel is understood not to be operative for those not living in the land of Israel, and the *mitzvot* that pertain to the king or to the priests are not applicable to anyone who is neither. According to a traditional colleague, a very observant traditional Jew could observe between 200 and 250 of the *mitzvot*. Of course, the 613 biblical commandments do not include the rules established by the rabbis, who did not hesitate to formulate their own *mitzvot* as though they were speaking on God's behalf, or just used the *mitzvah* formula to introduce their own interpretive or novel ideas.

Taking this into account, those Jews who are basically nontraditionalist need to review and sort out *mitzvot* that they are able and willing to observe. Martin Buber made the point that he wanted to perform those *mitzvot* that spoke to him, that elicited from him a response at a given moment and occasion in his life. Of course, there is also the approach of Franz Rosenzweig, who held that he was "on the way" to performing the *mitzvot*, but had not yet reached the whole panoply of *mitzvot* that he hoped someday to perform. For him, it was a process with progressive stages.

All of this discussion is predicated on a theological understanding of the relationship between God and humans as expressed in traditional vocabulary, especially in the liturgy, of Master to servant, King to subject, and the like. In other words, it is a relationship of obedience. It is an understanding that the traditional Jewish relationship with God is expressed primarily in the *mitzvah* system, and that the *mitzvot,* the commandments, are to be fulfilled by me as a faithful Jew. To be a member of the covenant community meant that all of us were obligated to this performance of the commandments, which traditionally were believed to have come from Sinai. There are three central pieces to this: the *metzave*, the One Who commands; the *mitzvah,* the commandment; and the *metzuve*, the one who is commanded. This triad is central to the covenantal relationship. To this day, it is the pattern for most Jews. But it is also a pattern for most Christians and Muslims, especially Muslims, since the very name Islam means "submission" to God.

This view of God had the unquestioned advantage of so ordering and structuring existence as to provide clearly definable guidelines and commandments. It wove an always reliable, secure armorlike vestment for human life, its decision, crises, and hopes. It was a most comforting, though at times uncomfortable, harness directing humans from birth through life to death and beyond.

Until the Shoah.

Chapter Two
Assimilation

Go forth from your country, and from your relatives, and from your father's house, to the land which I will show you.

(Genesis 12:1)

I graduated from high school at the end of April 1935, having spent the customary nine years in the Maximilian Gymnasium in Munich. I had a classical education, studying both Latin and Greek. Since my bar mitzvah at age thirteen, it had been my desire and even decision to try to study for the rabbinate and to become a liberal rabbi in Germany. And so, immediately after graduation from the Gymnasium on May 1, 1935, at nineteen years of age, I went to Berlin to enroll in the Lehranstalt für die Wissenschaft des Judentums, a storied Jewish seminary that had been downgraded by the Nazis from a *Hochschule* to a *Lehranstalt*, thereby decreasing its academic standing. I enrolled in what was known as the preparation section, which was to last ten weeks.

About halfway through, a notice appeared on the bulletin board that a scholarship was being offered to five students of the Berlin seminary by the Hebrew Union College in Cincinnati, Ohio, in the United States. The president of the Berlin seminary, who had known my late father, challenged me to apply for the scholarship, and in a sequence of events I finally did and was eventually selected as one of the five. The number five was not a sacred number, but was the counterpart of the five members of the faculty of the Cincinnati seminary who had studied in Berlin in the 1920s. The scholarships now being offered were a sort of return reward for the hospitality the five had enjoyed earlier.

There were initially six candidates, but at the last minute, when one of the six was unable to go, I became the recipient of a scholarship. Most of the rest of my classmates who did not receive scholarships perished in the Shoah.

Being chosen was not directly related to intellect or merit. One of my brightest classmates in Berlin and a lifelong friend, intellectually superior to those of us who were chosen to come, was Emil Fackenheim. He was arrested on Kristallnacht and spent three months in the Sachsenhausen concentration camp. He was then allowed to emigrate to London, where he initially attended school, but when the war broke out, the British interned him because he was a German national. He was sent to a prison camp in Canada and held for twenty months. He then returned to school, and after the war remained in Canada, becoming a professor of philosophy at Toronto University. He eventually moved to Jerusalem, where he died in 2004. He was the outstanding Jewish philosopher of the second half of the twentieth century.

And so, at the end of August in 1935, we five students boarded a British ship for the United States. Leaving family and home was not easy. I was young, just at a point in my life where my father's guidance was sorely needed. I spoke little English. On the way over aboard ship, I remember the waiter asking me if I wanted cereal for breakfast. I didn't know what that meant, so I said no, but proceeded to order "Poofed Wheat."

We arrived in New York on Labor Day. Of course I knew nothing about what Labor Day was. A very distant relative picked me up at the ship and decided, because Coney Island was to close for the season the next day, to take me there in order to show me America. My first impression was total shock. There was a huge mobile advertising sign for Sunkist Oranges, and as it moved it also displayed a Yiddish inscription. I was not just amazed, I was scared out of my wits, because having come from Nazi Germany, where everybody tried to camouflage anything that pertained to Jewish identity, to see a public display of Hebrew letters was frightening. The people who had picked me up sought to console me, explaining that this was totally natural and there was nothing to it. They had not even noticed the sign. It was normal for them. To me it was total culture shock.

Another example of the enormous cultural differences occurred a day or two later. The five us had to meet at what turned out to be a travel agency in Wall Street to pick up our tickets for the train trip to Cincinnati. I had never seen a skyscraper, and so I did not go into the agency but stood outside looking up at these huge buildings, the like of which there were none in Europe at the time. All of a sudden I saw a truck a pull up to a door in the building. Two men jumped out, drew their guns, and went in. A moment later they came out dragging a bag, threw it into the truck, and sped off.

I ran into the travel agency and called for my companions to come out because I had witnessed what I had always expected to see in America – a brazen robbery in broad daylight. What absolutely threw me was that nobody seemed to care. Nobody even seemed to notice that this had happened. I had witnessed what our imagination of the United States had prepared us to expect – crime in the streets as so normal that it totally passed by the many people who were walking past. It was a Brink's truck, of course. But it took me years to understand that it was just a normal delivery or pickup from the bank.

The changes I encountered in the seminary were as difficult and less humorous. It truly became a matter of survival. Prior to leaving Germany, I had lived within a familial web of relationships that were close, tightly knit, and deeply mutually interactive. Having been torn out of this, and now totally reliant on my own nineteen-year-old resources, in retrospect achieving ordination at the age of twenty-five looks like a minor miracle.

None of us had any idea of what we were getting into when we arrived at Hebrew Union College. Reform Judaism was a form of Judaism that was totally strange to us, totally unknown. Nor was there any intention in the culture to which we belonged to take time to prepare us. We were considered budding adults, we were supposed to be able to take care of ourselves, make our own way. So all of a sudden, from one week to the next, we were in a totally new environment. Nor was the environment particularly supportive. It was radically different from the way I had lived. There was no *kashrut*, no ritual restrictions on the food one ate. The prayers were in English almost without exception. I was used to only Hebrew prayers and barely spoke English. Everyone prayed bareheaded. Never in my life had I even known that Jews would do such a thing. I continued to use a *kippah* to cover my head until I ran up against the school authorities, who forbade me to continue. From their perspective, it was just simply not the way things were done in Reform Judaism in America.

So my choice was to conform or leave, because I was a scholarship student, totally dependent on the good graces of the giving institution. I survived the experience, not by an in-depth examination, but by a smooth and mostly painless adoption of the new environment, the new system of thinking, into which I had been plunged.

I had promised my parents that I would only stay away for two years. So in the summer of 1937 I returned home to attend the bar mitzvah of my youngest brother. Things were bad in Germany by then, and I became very conscious of the stupidity of having returned. I was lucky to get a second student visa to return to school in Cincinnati. But at the time, I was also very comfortable, happy to be back home, if only for a visit.

Although I returned to Cincinnati, the rest of my family remained in Germany. My father was arrested on Kristallnacht, November 9, 1938, and was interned in Dachau. For two days my mother and my brothers heard nothing from him, did not know where he was, whether he was alive or dead, whether he would return or not. It was an awakening for my family, but one that almost came too late. My father expressed it this way. He said that during the few months he was interned, he learned that he was not "beloved" by the Germans despite his family's long German lineage and his military service. This convinced him that it was necessary to leave. My father was told that he and the others would only be released if they could show that they had made final arrangements for emigration. My mother had a brother in Brazil, and through convoluted actions my aunt was able to get immigration certificates for them. They got to Brazil just a week before the war broke out in August 1939. It is an unbelievable story. So neither I nor my immediate family were, strictly speaking, Holocaust survivors. My immediate, nuclear family was very blessed.

After I returned to the seminary in Ohio from my visit home, I realized what an opportunity was being given me in America and what an incipient hell was growing in Germany, which I could see much more clearly than my parents. It would be ten years until I saw any of my family again.

Much was made a few years ago of the term "old Europe." In my opinion, it is a totally correct perception. Over and over again, and I won't tire of saying it, the United States is indeed a New World. We are radically different from much in Europe. The Old World, as organized, structured, and self-identified, is radically different from, and opposite to, the structure and identity of the United States.

To most of Europe the past is everything. They are overwhelmed by it, first of all, because nobody moves. Everybody stays put. Most are living in houses, in surroundings, in a landscape that has been unaltered and unchanged for hundreds and hundreds of years. They have monuments all around them that are linked to the past for which for many of them yearn, which, without their knowing and identifying it as such, has simply imprinted itself on them to such an extent that they and their past are in total harmony.

On the other hand, we have virtually no past here. If something is fifty years old, we tear it down because it is obsolete. We are all future oriented in this country. And groups that have a past are often demeaned or, worse yet, exterminated. I am talking, on the one hand, of such groups as the Daughters of the American Revolution or the Mayflower descendants, and, on the other, of the native American Indians, with whom we dealt in a most brutal, genocidal way.

The sense here is that we each began anew, that almost everything American is something new. The very fact that we are still taking in millions of new people each year, and therefore are ingesting new cultures and new impressions and new values in a stream that is unabated, makes us radically different from everybody else. We ask only that the children go to school and learn English, so as to preserve a basic ethos.

As a nation, we are basically reconciled to the fact that we are country of immigrants. When President Kennedy spoke the words "*Ich bin ein Berliner*," he wanted to indicate that he fell in with the whole configuration of values, thoughts, memories that represented the Old World. Nobody would come here and say "I am a Chicagoan" who doesn't live here, because it wouldn't mean anything. Americans are all "on the way." Europeans are settled, rooted.

The Jewish people have always also been "on the way." For Jews, by and large, past experience has taught that claiming a particular geographic space, except the land of Israel, is illusory. Historians say that in the first century every fourth person in the Roman Empire was Jewish, which is something like eight to ten million people. If that community had been allowed to lead a normal existence comparable to others, we would today, two thousand years later, be as numerous as the Chinese instead of barely as large a population as we were then.

The cost of survival for Jews has been enormous, the pain of it, the loss of life and talent. The question rises: is there another way, a landless way, of enduring? Not by giving up and attenuating to a point where there is nothing any longer that is characteristic and specific and exacting, but by finding ways to amalgamate whatever is necessary and good to endure with the new cultures and settings in the unfolding human drama. The question really is whether clinging to tradition is sufficient and an effective enough instrumentality to survive or even to endure all these enormous and very often violent changes in the condition of existence. The issue is still in question, though up to now it seems to have worked to the extent that there are still living Jewish communities. But the cost has been enormous.

I think of the rabbinic movement in the first century and beyond as an extraordinarily creative and in some ways daring attempt to adjust to radically new conditions, to understand that the loss of the land, of the city, of the altar, while assumed to be temporary, might really not be temporary in any graspable or predicable sense. I believe very strongly that the underlying epochal thrust and experimentation of the ancient rabbinic movement goes unnoticed or is ignored by those who call themselves the guardians of the tradition.

The prime model was formed in the Babylonian exile in the sixth century B.C.E., an experience that lasted only sixty to seventy years. Actually, it was only fifty years until permission was given by the new Persian emperor for those who wanted to return to Israel, and a minority of the exiles did. A similar experience was hoped for in 132 C.E., sixty years after the defeat of the Jews by the Romans that ended in Masada in 73 C.E., when the second horrendous war against Rome was launched. I speculate, without any documentation to support it, that our ancestors may have viewed this sixty-year time span as a test of whether God was ready to undo what the Romans had done to them, as tradition had interpreted what had happened in Babylon. They were led by a messianic figure. Bar Kochba, "Son of the Star," is a mysterious appellation, indicative of the fact that he was believed to have, somehow, a divine commission to do what he did. To his supporters, this certainly would have meant that he was sent by God, that his actions were permitted by God. Therefore, his leadership was somehow hoped to be an indirect signal of God's readiness to forgive and restore, as was the interpretation of what had happened when the Babylonian exile came to an end. Instead, the actual result was that the second Roman war was an even worse catastrophe in terms of loss of life than the first. Not only was this a most horrendous defeat, but it became necessary for the rabbinic leadership to come to terms with the fact that there was to be no repetition of the Babylonian model.

From that point onward, the Jewish people have had to adjust to a radically different condition of life. Their communities spread all over the globe. There is no longer a central authority, nothing either visible or concrete to be the center and hold the people together. Everything now becomes text, word, feelings, and hope. This is utterly different from being able to look out the window and see the Temple standing on Mount Zion, or to know that all you have to do is get on the donkey and ride a couple of days to Jerusalem, any time you want or need to be there.

To understand what the rabbis had to do is a clue to what is at the heart of what Judaism is now, in terms of the search for and capacity to find new ways of living and expressing one's Jewish self. Reform Judaism is right in line with that basic impulse and capacity, and this makes me believe that we are really the true heirs and continuation of the rabbis' innovative, creative impulse.

At this point, it is necessary to discuss the importance of the Greek influence on Judaism. First of all, for its historical meaning; second, because it seems to have been so very massive; and third, because it demonstrates, without any challenge possible, the fact that Judaism never was hermetically sealed off from the surrounding culture, never was self-created and self-sustaining. On the contrary, from the moment the Jews entered the world, in any way and according to whatever text and sources we may consult, they were engaged in encounters with other cultures.

The very fact that Abraham is recorded as leaving his own home, background, and civilization, to travel to what to him must have been an unknown and different milieu, indicates that he had to make far-reaching adjustments. Abraham had to learn a lot of new facts, and while in some ways the Canaanite civilization was not radically different from the Mesopotamian one from which he is alleged to have come, still there must have been significant local variations. Local deities, local customs of clothing, of food, of speech, all which he had not known before, now become an unavoidable part of his new existence. Once Abraham settled down in Beersheba and became a land-owner of substance, he had a multitude of relations with those around him.[1]

In fact, Torah itself speaks of these relations in regard to neighboring rulers and his relationship with others who lived in the same space. None of this interaction could have happened in self-imposed isolation. On the contrary, this interaction assumes that Abraham was thoroughly aware of the others, and without question, to a large measure, he needed to fit in to this new culture. The story of Abraham handing over his wife, Sarah, as his reputed sister to the harem of the pharaoh in Egypt is in itself a clear indication that he knew something about the lifestyle of that era and that particular culture. The same thing is true of later similar instances in his life.

Right from the very beginning, the first Jew lives in openness to other cultures, notwithstanding the fact that with regard to his religious practices Abraham is already radically different, since according to the Torah, he is a follower of the singular God. He is no longer a polytheist, as no doubt everybody in his immediate environment continued to be. And what is true of Abraham is also true of his descendants, Isaac and Jacob.

Jacob, for instance, lives with a relative, Laban, in Haran. Jacob enters his household and becomes part of a family configuration that is substantially different from the one from which he has come. The fact that Rachel steals the household gods of her father, the teraphim, is the clearest indication that we are not dealing with consistent monotheists, but most likely with

1. Abraham's journey from Mesopotamia to Canaan raises the question of what language was spoken by the Canaanites and, in particular, whether Abraham or anyone else spoke Hebrew. In other words, who was the first Hebrew speaker? How did Hebrew arise? The fact that the Torah has Abraham and others before him speak Hebrew is clearly anachronistic.

someone who is either a syncretist or an out-and-out polytheist. The very length of Jacob's residence with Laban makes it clear that he could not have been sealed off against the influence of that different environment.

Other examples include the story of Shechem. The horrendous deeds in connection with the enforced circumcision of the male population indicate both contacts with the environment and differences in significant aspects of religious life. Jacob's sibling, Esau, is not known in our sacred texts as a great champion of monotheism, indicating unmistakably that from the very beginning, in the patriarchal phase of our people's origins, openness to other cultures and strong encounters with them were natural and continuous.

Then there is the Egyptian chapter. While tradition tries to create an image of our ancestors as being faithful, for the most part, to the monotheistic traditions of their patriarchal ancestors, in the absence of any specific texts or sources to the contrary, it would have to be assumed that centuries-long living in the midst of the Egyptian culture would have had a powerful influence on our ancestors. Forty days after the Sinaitic event, in the temporary absence of both God and Moses, the people constructed a golden calf. This indicates that they must have had worship patterns in their immediate Egyptian past that would have included calves, bulls, that is, bovines, as symbols of divinity. The great sin of the golden calf was not only the lack of continued pervasive trust in the God of the momentous event at Sinai that only shortly preceded it, but also the clear assumption of a form of worship that Sinai had intended to overcome and replace. The divine proclamation, brought on by another major transgression, that the entire adult population who had come out of Egypt had to pass away before the people's entry into the Land of Promise was apparently predicated on the notion that this generation was so contaminated by Egyptian cultural influences that it could not be faithful to the singular God who was supposed to be the very hallmark of their new identify and purpose.

The Torah record contains continuous warnings, especially in the book of Deuteronomy, against regression to idol worship, against the lure of polytheism. Because legislation is not made in a vacuum, but refers to and tries to answer problems that arise from the lived life, it is clear that regression was a real issue. Hence, the entire pentateuchal record is a clear indication of the continuous, pervasive, seductive influence of other cultures on the formation of this earliest phase of our people's existence. And what was true, according to the Torah, in pre-Canaanite life is heightened once our ancestors are described as having taken hold of the Land of Promise.

Over and over again there is irrefutable evidence in the subsequent biblical texts that our ancestors intermarried with the native population, and had recourse to local shrines and cult practices, most of which persisted despite warnings to the contrary. It is clear that Solomon himself, having dedicated the newly built Temple on Mount Zion to the singular God, does not seem to feel it improper or contradictory to erect and worship idols in the same Temple precincts. This action was quite aside from the fact that many of his foreign wives came with their own retinue of cultic personalities, who then also were given access to the sacred precincts of the Temple, where they performed their rituals.

Further, the prophetic literature is replete with continuous and ultimately futile warnings by the spokespersons for the singular God against the inevitable disastrous consequences of their persistence in turning toward and having relations with polytheistic cultic places, procedures, and beliefs. In fact, Jewish historiography clearly indicates that the Babylonian capture of Jerusalem, the destruction of the Temple and its altars, and the subsequent exile of the leaders of the people to Babylon, was the inevitable divine punishment for those who would not desist from the syncretistic worship of local and other deities in addition to the One Who was the God of the ancestors.

The unavoidable conclusion of all of this is that Judaism has never been secluded from, or protected against, the influences of surrounding neighboring cultures, especially their religious practices. Judaism has always been an affirmation of specific monotheism despite widespread popular polytheistic cultic practices. One can easily speak of the post-exilic period as the beginning of an attempt to cleanse Judaism from such foreign intrusions and components. Ezra not only insists that the people divorce foreign wives, whose influence had easily been pinpointed as instrumental in seducing their husbands and sons from the worship of the singular God, but he also induces the people to renew the Covenant. He reads them part of sacred writ, which so deeply stuns and moves them that they are willing to once again undertake a solemn oath to be exclusive worshipers of the singular God. We have very little source material to know how all this worked itself through the actual lives of our ancestors. Quite apart from this fact, during the latter third of the fourth pre-Christian century, or something like 125 to 150 years after Ezra, events overtake that part of the world which change it radically.

Alexander, later known as the Great, invades Asia, which was then ruled by the Persians, in order to avenge an earlier, failed Persian invasion of the Greek motherland. Alexander not only succeeds extraordinarily well militarily, but also is driven by a dream of amalgamating West and East. Almost literally marrying these two cultures, his military victories bring Greek language, Greek worship, Greek food, Greek art, Greek philosophy, and all that these imply, into an area that, if not altogether untouched by these influences, had never before seriously engaged with them. Now, as a result of the fact that Alexander became the heir of the Persian Empire, and established a huge empire of his own, including vast stretches of Asia, Africa, and portions of Europe, the Hellenistic culture became the victorious, supreme, dominant mode of life in that entire huge area.

Jews who lived in the very heart of this struggle and these events were not exempt from its impact. On the contrary, Greek influence became pervasive and potent in Judaism. We know, for instance, that there were high priests who had Greek names, such as Menelaus and Jason. In the household of Rabban Gamaliel, the young were taught Greek in addition to Hebrew and Aramaic. This is a clear indication that in the top stratum of Jewish society, Greek influences were compelling. We know that Hellenizers in the Jewish community eagerly adopted Greek mores and ways. A gymnasium was established in Jerusalem at the very foot of Mount Zion. We know that in all such athletic events young men participated in the nude, hence the term "gymnasium," which designates a place to exercise in the nude. As a result, circumcision became a matter of embarrassment and derision for young Jewish athletes, and we know that efforts were made to erase all such evidences of the physical covenantal identification.

Altogether, it is easy to trace the pervasive and powerful impact of Hellenism on other aspects of Jewish life. We know that in the city of Caesarea, Jews recited the *Sh'ma* in Greek. Greek names were given to Jewish babies. The city of Alexandria in Egypt, founded by Alexander in 332 B.C.E., became in short order not only one of the great cities of the world but a preferred place for Jews to live. Greek influence on the lifestyle of those who lived there was self-understood. It may even be that the very commission to translate the Tanach into Greek sometime in the last third of the third pre-Christian era, a translation that we know as the Septuagint, may in part have been a concession to the prevailing Hellenization of Jews in Egypt, for surely among them there would have been much interest in a Greek version of the Hebrew Bible, as there may have been among Egyptians and other Greek-speaking peoples.

The Hellenic victory, and the very fact that Hellenic culture, beginning in the sixth century, had risen to a climax in the fifth, fourth, and third pre-Christian centuries, led to one of the most astounding creative periods in human annals. It also left a deep imprint on Jewish life. The very fact that the rabbis organized their material into six rubrics in their great work, the Mishna, quite contrary to the underlying organization or lack thereof in the biblical texts, is in itself evidence of the influence of Greek patterns and methodology. The adversarial style of the talmudic literature is certainly not found in biblical texts, and may well be an imitation of the dialogic mode of Greek philosophic study and discourse.

All in all, it seems clear that in this period, the influence of the surrounding world on the formation and actual life of our ancestors was very noticeable. The building projects undertaken by Herod are themselves evidence of the Roman impact on his life. The enlargement of the Temple that he undertook, making it one of the most notable buildings in the ancient world, was certainly not spurred by inherently Jewish impulses, but was a consequence of his upbringing during his formative years in the Roman world as a hostage for his father's loyalty. What is clear is that in these first fifteen hundred to two thousand years of the Jewish people's struggle to find its own identity, foreign influences are not only notable, they are unavoidable and ever-present.

Most especially, Greek philosophy created a new way of looking at reality. Greek philosophers were interested in the absolute. What is the absolute truth, the absolute component of reality? This became so intriguing a search that it is also found in some of the rabbinic modalities – for example, in the attempt to encapsulize Jewish teaching, to bring it down to three formulations or even one. While this modality can also be explained as a pedagogic measure that made it easy for prospective proselytes to capture the essentials of Judaism, it is certainly not found in Torah texts. It may well be that the very search for the ultimate interpretation of given legal and ethical maxims, as culled from biblical texts, reflects the philosophic methodology that was introduced so powerfully and overwhelmingly by the victory of Greek culture over its Asian and African victims.

The influence of other cultures on Judaism is a field that needs more study, particularly because it has always been taught, thereby creating a false impression, that Judaism has been able to ward off and wall itself against foreign influences. But the very fact that the quest for isolationism became both a mode of living and a cherished value is indirect evidence that the lure and influence of other cultures was a permanent shadow on the Jewish experience. The circling of the wagons so reflective of certain aspects and groups in Jewish life, and a widespread commitment to this very day, is clearly a response to the threat perceived by encounters with non-Jewish cultures.

The perennial question about such encounters is whether they are, in fact, not only advisable but also fruitful. In reviewing the history of the Jewish people over a long stretch of time, one could make the point that both views are true. There are always certain incompatibilities, but there is also a remarkable amount of fructification. Take a figure like Maimonides, who in his *Guide to the Perplexed* tried in some ways to inoculate his Jewish readership against the lure and power of Muslim philosophy and theology, and yet was also deeply influenced by them. Jewish thinkers have always been influenced by and open to the thoughts of thinkers who are not of their own community. The very fact that it became necessary to translate the Bible into Aramaic and into Arabic indicates that there was a need to make sacred texts accessible to people who were no longer primarily Hebrew speaking. The very fact that segments of the Jewish community of sufficient importance and numbers needed translations of the Tanach into the vernacular languages which they were using is a prima facie evidence of other cultural influences penetrating most deeply into the texture of Jewish life. Language is one of the most obvious evidences of such influence.

While there is a need to be on one's guard when confronting other cultures and their products, it is both inadvisable and, in most instances, virtually impossible to isolate oneself from them. A marked example of the impact of such confrontations exists in the religious life of contemporary American Judaism.

American Judaism has four main divisions, some with subdivisions. On the right wing, there is Orthodoxy, which I prefer to term the Traditionalists. Then there are the Conservatives, who hold a central position on the spectrum, and Reform, which is the left, or liberal, wing. The fourth is a fairly recent group that is still rather small, but one that is certainly significant, the Reconstructionists. If one were to place this group in perspective, it could be placed between Reform and Conservative.

It is interesting to think about the origin of these various movements. As I understand it, both Traditionalists and Reform are part of the response by Jews, essentially in Central Europe and perhaps even specifically in Germany, to the possibilities offered as a result of the emancipation of Jews following the French Revolution in 1791. When the Napoleonic armies swept over Europe, they brought with them more than their significant military power; they also became champions of "Liberty, Equality, Fraternity," the great slogan of the French Revolution. As a result, in many places, notably Prussia, the government emancipated the Jews and gave them the same freedoms and equality that the French Revolution had so radically injected into the fabric of Western civilization. In some instances, Jews were actually given citizenship.

However, after the defeat of Napoleon, there was a powerful reaction by Central European power structures, not only against Napoleon personally but against what they saw as the dangerous notions of the French Revolution. A massive retrenchment took place. Jews were confronted with the need to adjust, and to calculate accurately and properly what Western civilization was all about. To put it differently, they needed to find out whether that civilization could be trusted. To a great extent, Jews came to the conclusion that Western civilization could *not* be trusted, and four major ultimate responses were fueled by this distrust.

One response was Orthodoxy. The Traditionalists said that we must preserve our identify against all the blandishments of Western civilization, which is only superficially willing to accept Jews as human and perhaps equal, but really deep down has no such intention.

Another response was a total escape from Judaism. Those who chose this path believed that they would never again submit themselves or their descendants to the taint of Judaism. Whatever they had experienced as a possible liberation would be permanent; thousands of Jews converted to Christianity, predominantly to Protestantism, but some also to Catholicism. As an aside, legislation that the Nazis enacted in 1936, the so-called Nuremberg laws, designated someone as a non-Aryan who had a Jewish grandmother, which meant really a Jewish great-grandmother, which took them right back to the first half of the nineteenth century, when there were all those mass conversions of Jews hoping to escape the unreliability of Western civilization and obtain the possibility of living normal lives.

Socialism became another attractive alternative because it viewed religion as a private matter, totally irrelevant to public life and public policy. Religion had no place in the texture of society. Many Jews felt that this was the ideal solution, because it seemed that socialism was a blend of high ethics and radical religious privacy.

Zionism needs to be understood in the same vein. Theodor Herzl, the founder of political Zionism in the 1890s, witnessed the ugly fury of the anti-Semitic mobs that threatened Jews in connection with the infamous Dreyfus affair. He came to the conclusion that Western civilization could never be trusted by Jews, and would never accept them as equal human beings and citizens. Herzl therefore proposed that Jews should be physically removed from Europe to a state of their own.

These were the four basic responses to emancipation: Orthodoxy, total assimilation, socialism, and Zionism, all born from a distrust of Western civilization. There was really only one response that gave sufficient credit to the possibilities of Western civilization's invitation to Jews to trust it, and that was liberalism. Among other things, this response led to the formation of Reform Judaism as first pioneered in Germany. The early reformers were sometimes quite radical in their reassessment of religious practices and theological positions, as contrasted to traditional Judaism – so much so that many Jews felt that the reassessment had gone too far. Basically, the struggle within Reform Judaism over how to respond to the culture and ethos of any given moment in the development of Western civilization is still ongoing. In fact we like to say that "Reform" is a verb, meaning that there are few permanent Reform positions on any issue. On the contrary, the Reform movement is basically a posture of willingness to reconsider, reshape, and reform as may be necessary.

Those who felt that the early reformers were too radical and had been too insensitive to traditional values formed a group that was eventually called Conservatism. The Conservative movement also surfaced in Germany in the 1860s.

It is noteworthy that the Reform and Conservative positions

in modern Judaism, especially Reform, have flourished in the United States, to which they were brought by immigrants, more than in Central Europe, where they began. Reform, as understood and practiced in America today, never really took hold in Central Europe, whereas Conservatism did in Germany and other European countries. For example, the Great Synagogue in Munich, where I grew up, introduced certain modifications of traditional practices. Women were seated in the balconies, and the main floor was reserved for men. However, the women were no longer hidden behind a curtain or a barrier, so that one could easily make eye contact or even use gestures. There was also the introduction into the liturgy of a few prayers in the vernacular. By and large, however, the modifications were relatively modest. Once Conservative Judaism was transplanted into the United States, it underwent the same changes that the alchemy of the culture of the United States made it impossible for Reform Judaism to resist.

So both Reform and Conservative Judaism were shaped into the recognizable forms with which we deal today right here in the United States toward the latter part of the nineteenth century and increasingly in the twentieth century. And it is indicative of both these positions that they are not frozen into a definite state, but that they experience major and minor revisions. Sometimes, in each group, there are severe tensions between those who tend to be more resistant to change and those who are more avid for change.

"Orthodoxy" is a very contentious word because it means literally "the only true doctrine." However, even Orthodoxy has undergone and is undergoing many stresses and changes here in the United States. It is subdivided into divergent positions held together, sometimes uneasily, under the same umbrella. "Observant," as the Orthodox use the word, really means adherence to the *mitzvot* derived from biblical sources and interpreted over many centuries of rabbinic thought and teaching.

There is a genuine, strict discipline in this position. In fact Orthodoxy is unthinkable without an individual's acceptance of the pervasive discipline of observance. This goes not only for the liturgical life, but for *kashrut* and aspects of family life and purity. Frankly, Orthodoxy is much more all-encompassing of a person's being, one's relationship to God and to others, than any of the other variants of Jewish life, where there is much greater freedom given, and thus a much greater readiness to accept individual decisions and choices. While there is still an expectation of discipline, it is much reduced in scope and intensity. This is an advantage, in that it comports much more with individualist perceptions of being human in our culture. It is also a disadvantage, in that it introduces a whole host of difficult questions and problems, for the simple reason that it is much more difficult under these circumstances to have community, to experience that sense of community which results from the enforcement of certain observances or modes of behavior.

Reconstructionism is primarily a result of Mordecai Kaplan's published work in the mid-1930s, *Judaism as a Civilization*. This book proposed an alternative which has attracted any number of academically trained people who were drawn to it by its sociological approach to Jewish tradition and its application of Jewish tradition to contemporary life.

The differences between Reconstructionism and Reform Judaism can be quite nuanced. I was a student at the Hebrew Union College at the time of the publication of Kaplan's book. We became totally captivated. It seemed to us a contemporary, intelligent, sensitive treatment of Judaism. It put the peoplehood at the center, and everything radiated from the centrality of Jewish ethnicity. It dealt not only with liturgy and theology, it also went into such areas as art and cooking. It was an all-encompassing reconstructing of Jewish life, and the impact of the sociological terminology and understandings, and the sensitive regard for tradition left a deep impression. I would think, though this is not perhaps true of all times or all aspects, that the main difference between Reform and Reconstructionism is the greater emphasis on "theology" in Reform Judaism, especially when it takes itself seriously, which it often does not, and also on the role of the rabbi.

The whole question confronting American Jewry is whether it is possible to have a significant and authentic Jewish life within the framework of the kind of freedom that modern general culture not only produces but elevates as the single most desirable component of human existence. Extremist segments of the Orthodox division of Judaism will not allow their children to go to university, assuming that higher education will introduce values, and thus problems, that it might not be possible to accommodate within their Orthodox framework. Some very extreme communities have developed their own little enclaves in a self-contained atmosphere to reduce exposure to the surrounding culture. When it comes to political issues, those who are Orthodox and those who are Reform will quite regularly be found on opposite sides of an issue.

Ultimately, one has to have the confidence that the verities of Judaism, as interpreted, taught, and refined over the centuries, have the capacity to be enhanced through confrontation with other cultures. And that from these encounters, time and again, new possibilities arise in such a way that they add vitality, elasticity, and, not infrequently, new shades of meaning to the direction and commitments of the Jewish religion and Jewish life.

Chapter Three
Crisis of Faith

> But Moses said to God, "Who am I, that I should go to
> Pharaoh and bring the Israelites out of Egypt?"
>
> *(Exodus 3:11)*

When I returned to Cincinnati from my visit to Germany in 1937, I knew that this was going to be my life and that I had better try to come to terms with it. But I struggled. I had some really rough times at the seminary. It was lonely, especially in the summers. Everybody else went home, everybody had family. I was alone. Even the fellows I had come over with had made attachments in this country.

Finding Lotte knitted my whole life together. Perhaps you could call it a coincidence or an accident. If so, then it was an astounding accident. If, however, you think that there is some kind of "hand" working somewhere or somehow, you could surely make a case for that in how we met. I simply cannot imagine being alive without her. Quite apart from any of the other influences on my existence, her grace, her capacity to understand, her total capacity to forgive, these are aspects of her character at which I sometimes just marvel. She changed me, enormously. The only credit I take is that I was changeable.

After we were married, we left for our first congregation in Cedar Rapids, Iowa. It was the first time I really became acquainted with American culture, and it was an experience I will always treasure. The reason I was sent there was that I had no one in this country to speak for me. I was a scholarship student at the seminary, and the president did not care for some of my values anyhow. So, in essence, this was the congregation to which he exiled me. He probably thought I was not going to be heard from again, which easily could have happened. We loved it there.

When I came to town Temple Judah had just thirty-three families in the congregation. But among them were people who had been educated in some of the finest eastern schools, and some really well-to-do people. Clouds of war were already beginning to obscure the horizon. My first salary was $2,000 a year, $38 and some cents per week. After two months, a small subsistence was added because it was clear that we could not make it. Lotte's mother was living with us, so we were three adults.

The wealthiest man in town was Howard Hall, a famous industrialist. He had two major factories, a foundry, and a road-machinery factory. He was married to the daughter of the man who had founded Quaker Oats. President Hoover had slept in their home. Alice Longworth Roosevelt had been their guest.

About two months after we got to Cedar Rapids, on September 1, 1940, the scrap dealer of the city, one Esak Cohn, died. Cohn belonged to the local synagogue, not to the temple where I was rabbi. But I had met him once because his children belonged to the temple. When he died, despite the fact that the synagogue too had a rabbi, the children all insisted that I had to do the funeral. This was my first funeral. I got the information from the family, delivered the eulogy, and performed the service. As I come down the steps afterwards, there stood the treasurer of my congregation, a rather hefty woman. Before I could say anything, she says, "Rabbi, you made him out like a plaster saint. He was such a son of a gun." I hear that woman every time I prepare a eulogy to this day. I learned something that I have always observed since then. Eulogies have to have a total integrity; the words used to describe the deceased must be true to fact and not lead the hearers to become incredulous or even derisive. Eulogies are an opportunity to be truthful, and it is better to leave things out if they cannot be said in an atmosphere of reverential memory.

Two days after the funeral, the oldest son, who was now the head of the family, called me, all excited. "Get yourself dressed up, Howard Hall wants to see you." Because Esak Cohn was a scrap dealer, he had done business with Howard Hall, and Howard had been at the funeral. So off Harry Cohn and I went to one of Hall's factories. Howard had a huge office. He was guarded by two German shepherds because he and his workers were not on the best terms. Whenever he walked through the plant, he had these dogs with him.

When we came in, Howard was sitting way over yonder behind a huge desk. Harry Cohn, totally overwhelmed, had taken off his hat and was wringing his hands. He was not just dumbfounded, but overcome. Howard Hall greeted me very cordially and handed me a picture. He had a pet lion on his estate, and he'd had himself photographed with his head in the lion's mouth and had inscribed it, "From one lion tamer to another." He gave me the picture and told me what a wonderful eulogy I had given. He had never heard a eulogy like it.

About a week later, there was a ring at the door of our home. A chauffeur took off his cap and handed me an envelope. I opened it. "Margaret and Howard Hall desire your company next Sunday at their country cottage." Lotte was behind me; I showed it to her. We told the chauffeur "Yes, thank you."

Come Sunday, a Cadillac drove up. Only this time, there was no chauffeur. Howard Hall was driving himself, his two dogs sitting in front, Margaret sitting in the back. She motioned for us to get in.

We had not yet met her. She turned out to be an absolutely wonderful lady. We drove out of town about a half an hour to their "cottage" on the Cedar River. Everything was absolutely perfect, everything hand-made. Floors laid with wooden nails. Copper ceilings. After we got out of the car, Howard said, "We told the servants to take time off." So turning to his wife he says, "Margaret, you prepare the steaks. I'm going to take the rabbi for a spin on the river."

There was about a mile of river between the cottage and the rapids and we rode up and back in this large Cris-Craft. After a few minutes, the conversation took a turn. Howard said, "If it weren't for those God-damned Jews who stir up the working people, then we wouldn't have those God-damned labor unions, and this would be a better country."

Here I was in a boat with the most powerful man in Iowa. I said, "Mr. Hall, if it weren't for the God-damned steel barons who don't treat their workers right, there wouldn't be any unions."

I'm sure he had never been contradicted, certainly not in his own Cris-Craft. And certainly not by a twenty-five-year-old Jew who had just come to town.

We became good friends. He became the biggest contributor to the congregation, in fact to whatever Jewish philanthropic fund we had. Whenever he had a famous visitor, he would call me, "Herman, come over. I want you to meet my friends." He also had the only swimming pool in town. And we were permitted in the summer, on two or three occasions, to bring our child to swim in the pool, which was quite a privilege.

Howard Hall died in 1950, the year after I moved to Chicago. Lotte and I had just come back on a Sunday from a trip to Israel, and I was exhausted. The phone rang, late Sunday afternoon. It was Margaret, "Herman, Howard died. The funeral is tomorrow. We are holding the time. I am sending a plane for you. We want you to give the eulogy." I had to refuse. I was just too jet-lagged to go. So their Presbyterian minister did the eulogy.

The very fact that Howard Hall took such a shine to me opened the whole city to me. I was asked to join the Kiwanis Club. First I was asked to give a speech, and the speech went over quite well, so they asked me to join. It got so that whoever came, the senator or the governor, whoever came and spoke, there would be a chorus typical to those kinds of organizations, "Oh, sit down, we want Herman." I became vice-president of the YMCA. I became vice-president of the War Allocations Board.

I had never known what a Methodist was, I had never heard of an Episcopalian. I knew there were Lutherans and Catholics, nothing in between. They asked me to join the clergy association, no Catholics, only Protestants and I, because this was before Catholics were acceptable to the Protestant reigning stratum in that forum.

In 1943 I was invited to speak at the chapel at Cornell College in Mount Vernon, Iowa, about half an hour out of town. I'll never forget the dean of the chapel, Roy Albion King, introducing me. The peroration was, "…and so, ladies and gentlemen, my fellow faculty and students, I give you Rabbi Herman Schaalman, a truly Christian gentleman." This was the highest accolade he could bestow.

As a result of having spoken at Cornell, I was invited in the fall of that year to become an adjunct professor of non-Christian religions. And I also taught at Coe College in the adult education program. I started a radio program called *Three Men on a Limb*. The three of us were the president of Coe College, the editor of the local newspaper, and I. The newspaper had originally been edited by Vernon Marshall, the founder of the

America First movement. He tried to keep America out of the war, was pro-fascist. He was finally put away because on one occasion on the stage he took off his coat and threatened to beat up a protester. We lived in the heartland of America.

It was quite clear that we had become part of Cedar Rapids, and we were happy.

About six years after becoming a rabbi, I underwent a profound crisis. I was living in virtual isolation from other rabbis and Jewish scholars, forced to be self-reliant. However, I had the opportunity to attend a small workshop with twelve or fifteen other rabbis, including, as it turned out, Emil Fackenheim, the brilliant fellow student from my Berlin days. I had not seen him since then, and was not even aware that he had survived. At that time, he was at the University of Toronto. During the course of the workshop, he and I wound up in a debate, with me defending positions that were considered more congenial by the rest of the group. But after I returned home, the more I thought about the discussion, the more I realized that I had not previously come across positions and thoughts of the kind Fackenheim had been expressing. The longer I thought about it, the more convincing his arguments seemed to me, and the more shallow and untenable my own positions became, to the point where my whole belief structure seemed to crack open and virtually disappear.

One night, I sat in my small study at home, brooding, questioning whether I had the right to be a rabbi. I thought seriously about quitting the rabbinate because I thought myself theologically unfit to lead a congregation. It had struck me that I was caught in a theological stance, in a religious life, that simply could no longer withstand the facts of Jewish experience and history. My whole theological structure had collapsed.

As I sat there, my eyes fell on a small book that I had read as an adolescent but had not read since, Martin Buber's *I and Thou*. As teenagers in Germany, we had arrogantly thought we could understand Buber. I pulled it out on impulse, and I read it again that evening and into the night. As I read, it was as though a curtain had rolled away. The philosophic foundation for belief became so whole, firm, and clear that I have never again faltered. In terms of the basic structure of my faith, there have been only modifications, not radical revisions, more refinements and additions.

From that book, an entirely new possibility of rebuilding my belief structure emerged. Buber's principle insight is that we approach the world in two basic "words": I-Thou and I-It. And if we understood the character, content, and meaning of these basic words, I-Thou and I-It, then we can hammer together the structure of life. That night, I became aware of the fact that I was living nearly exclusively in the I-It.

I had been given an education, given a tradition, and I was accepting it mostly uncritically. Obviously, the transition from the "liberal" German Jewish environment in which I had grown up to the Reform Hebrew Union College in Cincinnati had been a clash and culture shock of considerable magnitude requiring some alterations in my worldview. It is clear in retrospect, because mostly it was not a conscious process, that at the time all I really wanted was to survive this transition: to adjust to the demands and possibilities that were given me without any in-depth critical examination. Ultimately, however, mere survival was not enough.

This questioning is not only true for me alone. I am just one human being, struggling in the last half of the twentieth century and now at the beginning of the twenty-first, with what I came to understand as profoundly difficult demands on my thinking and on my believing. In no way was my struggle unique; on the contrary, it is where most of us who think of ourselves as believers need to pause or at least to pass through. Although this questioning may be seen initially in personal terms, it is really a prototype of a universal crisis, and of the subsequent need for clarity and new decisions. All living is a question to which we are called to give an answer, so taught Martin Buber.

Buber's formulation of the idea that all living is dialogue is one of the most important he developed. In addition to theology, it is an idea that has also worked its way into such areas as education, psychology, social work, and art. Dialogue always assumes that there is an "other" who is somehow capable of giving and requiring a response. It is the capacity for that response, both given and received, that is vital; whether or not the response will be adequate is not the point. The basic assumption is that one is not dealing only with an "it," one needs to be open to dealing with a "thou."

From this point forward, these ideas began to illuminate the landscape of my despair. The dialogic nature of reality became for me a fundamental truth. It is the key to unlocking the puzzle of reality on two levels. First, it opened me to the possibility of reaching toward God in a way I had not consciously done in the past: God as the Thou. And second, it gave me insights into human relations that are fundamental to my whole outlook and being. I am not anything of what I could be and should be unless I have an "other." The other is the indispensable means of my being me; my *I* depends on the *Thou* of the other, and vice versa.

This needs to be emphasized: the other is not only the indispensable ingredient in fulfilling oneself, or of becoming the optimum self; the other is also the ultimate risk. Whether "other" is written with a lowercase *o* or a capital *O* does not really matter, because in either case the word points to the very same mystery. The other is not to be controlled, not to be used, not to be manipulated, because if that happens, then the self is diminished. This is the world of the I-it, where true dialogue becomes impossible. There are several reasons why the vulnerability of unconditional openness is such a risk. Chief among them is the fear of what the other might do to us if we do not seek to tie up the other, to control the other. We then diminish the other's capacity to unfold and respond, to be a true self, and we become a diminished I.

Much of traditional religion is manipulative. God punishes and rewards, and therefore needs to be propitiated either by gifts or prescribed behavior. All intention to control arises from an instinctual or perceived weakness in the one who wants to control. The very fact that we need to abjure any intention of controlling the other and instead to be totally open and defenseless to the other, is an enormous risk, because if the other is not the right kind of other, one whose response will enhance us, we might end up being controlled, damaged, bound up, limited, hurt.

It was Emmanuel Levinas, the French Jewish philosopher, who elevated the other even beyond where Buber had taken it. For Levinas, the other was the entity from whom one could learn what one ought to be. The other is totally indispensable for the constitution of the root of one's own self.

Reality is, in a sense, the product of our capacity to accept it, understand it, and define it, but defining the other is to be avoided. Definitions are a self-protective device, because if we have the power to set limits for someone else, then we are in power to control and manipulate. Thus it is wrong to try to define God, just as it is wrong to define the other. The other needs to be received in openness, because if we are not changed, or capable of being changed, or even wanting to be changed as a result of our contact with the other, our response to the other, our lack of vulnerability to the other, evades the inherent possibilities of finding the other. Rather, we should simply retire into a self-defensive kind of assertion that says, "I'm good enough as I am." In other words, the recognition of the other is immediately a confession that we are not yet what we could be, and ought to be. This takes much courage. It is a genuine, profound risk, and uncomfortable to boot.

All dialogue requires of us to be as unconditional as we can possibly train ourselves to be, and this requires that we both be self-critical and have a reasonable image of how far we can stretch, an idea of what we could become. If the other is at all capable of sensing our readiness and responds in a like manner, then a remarkable process begins. This mutual defenselessness, this unconditional being there, this vulnerability, this high-risk living is what then finally comes through. It changes everything in the sense that this unconditional way of being marks our arrival at a stage of self-knowledge that is a sufficient level for achieving the optimal in the human condition. It is also the basis of *emuna,* which translates as "trusting faith."

In a like manner, the dialogue with the divine cannot be limited. The human must be open to whatever the Mystery "wishes" to do, has done, is doing. While we must respond to this Mystery, it is not a question of possessing or being possessed. The individual must remain intact in order to be ready for the "Other," or to be an other for someone else. In the Jewish understanding of the mystic experience of God, there is no annihilation of the self, no mystical union in which the human is absorbed into divinity or the Godhead. On the contrary, the human has to remain human and has to remain intact. Only then is he or she capable of entering into a heightened state of relationship and awareness.

This leads to very important conclusions in terms of ethics, because ethics then is not simply a construct of some kind, but is really a searching for the being, the needs, and the gifts of the other. In this regard, the other becomes the only really authentic basis for morality.

In terms of human relationships, the use of the word "vulnerability" should not suggest an absolute defenselessness in the sense that the other can do whatever he or she wants. Each of us is also an other; we are the *other* to them. The relationship has to be interactive, and it has to finally be based on that indefinable something called trust. If one's defenselessness cannot immediately lead to trust, which comes from an *initial* evaluation of the other, or even be the product of trust because it should be open to development, if that trust is not there, then vulnerability could be self-destructive. We are not to be self-sacrificing, not to be emptied of our own selfhood when we are with the other. Quite the contrary: the other needs me to be an other.

Buber was also a biblical scholar, and as part of the outgrowth of my rereading *I and Thou* at that point, I began to reexamine the biblical texts concerning God in a different light. One of the results of this reexamination was the disclosure of nuances in the texts that I had previously overlooked.

The single most important question to ask in reading the Bible is: What does this particular text say about God? This ought to be the initial focus, perhaps even the main focus, in reading biblical texts. Yet traditionally it is not the focus being taught. Over and over again one discovers that what the text indicates about God is often significantly different from what tradition and the usual understandings seem to indicate.

Looking at the texts in such a different light enables the development of a more intimate relationship to God. Previously the question was: How does an imperfect being relate to a God that is perfect? That is, at least, only a partial interpretation of sacred writ. Quite often it is possible, many times necessary, to hear the text speak of a God who is becoming, who is "learning," who is similar to what we as humans are. Under such revised understandings, the relationship between human and God becomes much deeper, more fulfilling, more meaningful. No longer is the human in the primary stance of obedience, with all the guilt that comes from nonperformance. Now the human is seen in a more mutually relational posture.

Chapter Four
Is God Dead?

> Then the Lord spoke to Job out of the storm:..."Would you discredit my justice?"
>
> *(Job 40:6,8)*

As a result of my awakening to the need to think through and discuss with others a contemporary approach to Jewish faith, I organized several conferences at what became the Olin Sang Ruby Union Institute camp in Oconomowoc, Wisconsin. These conferences, held about twice a year, brought together eight or ten people in the Reform and Conservative movements who were thinking about, struggling with, writing about contemporary issues in Judaism. But after I moved from the Chicago directorship of the Union of American Hebrew Congregations to Emanuel Congregation, I had more responsibilities and less time to organize the conferences.

In fact, I had not really wanted to leave Iowa. In 1946, a former classmate of mine living out west called to tell me that there was a congregation forming in Culver City, California. He wanted me to come and interest myself in that congregation. So I was invited to speak to the biggest congregation out there, and people from the new congregation had come to listen to me. They were very much impressed, and they offered me the job. I said, "Give me a few days to think about it." On the flight back, I said to myself, "This congregation in Cedar Rapids has been so good to me and my family, especially during recovery from a serious automobile accident, I just can't leave this congregation." In those days, right after the war, there was such a shortage of rabbis that I knew they would not find anyone to come to Cedar Rapids. I turned down the Culver City congregation.

By then, the congregation was sixty or seventy families. I went to the board and I said, "You know my family and I are very happy here. We like you, we understand the congregation. Build me a house with a garden and I'll stay for life." They went into executive session and notified me the next day that they had turned down the proposition.

In the meantime, Rabbi Maurice Eisendrath, the president of the Union of American Hebrew Congregations, had gotten to know me, and he had asked me if I would do some part-time work for him in the area, which meant that I would do such jobs as arrange for regional conventions of congregations, and also visit some congregations in places like St. Louis, Omaha, Des Moines, and Milwaukee. So beginning in my fifth year there, from time to time I had begun to travel, which was a very nice addition to my work. I was not really confined to one spot.

The rabbi of Des Moines had come to visit me while I was in the hospital after an automobile accident. He said to me, "You get well, and you come and become my assistant." Des Moines was the big congregation in the area, three or four hundred families at that time. This was a good opportunity, because he was getting older, and being there as his assistant meant that unless things went terribly wrong, I would be his successor. I was overwhelmed by such a wonderful opportunity being offered to an immigrant.

I told the president of the Union about this prospect. He

said to me, "Don't go to Des Moines. That is not where you belong. I'll take care of you." On one of my trips I had also gone to Kansas City, where there was a really famous congregation and rabbi. This rabbi too wanted me to come to be his assistant and potentially to succeed him. I told this to the president of the Union, and he said, "Kansas City is just an overgrown Cedar Rapids. Stick it out. Something will come along. I'll take care of you."

We stayed for eight years in Cedar Rapids, an unheard-of length of time in those days. But we were happy, both of our children had been born there. One day, Eisendrath called me. The person who had been in charge of the Union's office in Chicago wanted to go to the new regional office being opened in Los Angeles. He said, "Herman, I want you to go to Chicago." I said, "Let me think about it for a day or two."

There happened to be a meeting of the congregation's board that night. By that time, Lotte and I had pretty much decided we were going, and I let the board know that I had this offer. They went into executive session and within minutes I was called back in. "You want us to build you this house?" I said, "I didn't tell you about Chicago in order to use it as a lever or some kind of bribe. We have decided to leave."

So we moved. It wasn't easy for us to leave Cedar Rapids. And we maintained relationships with some of the people until very recently, when they now have all died. There were people from there who came to my installation at Emanuel in Chicago and to some of my jubilees at Emanuel.

After I moved to Chicago, Zalman Schacter, Emil Fackenheim, and David Harman organized a meeting of younger Jewish thinkers in Canada, a group similar to those I had brought together in Oconomowoc. There were about thirty-five of us, a bit larger group, since we had been encouraged to bring friends. The conference lasted from Thursday evening over the weekend. Someone had asked a young writer from New York to assist in the Shabbat morning services. As soon as he began to chant the opening prayers, something flowed to me that was deeply gripping. Never had I heard such prayer. I knew that I was in the presence of someone who had something to tell me. His name was Elie Wiesel.

I read *Night* shortly after that, and subsequently everything else he has written. Elie Wiesel has been a decisive influence on the direction my thinking has taken ever since that moment. He pointed me to the profundity of the Shoah, and I woke up to the fact that I had never asked the important questions. Asking those questions has given my whole theological and religious life a new turn. Although not the kind of deeply personal crises I faced in Iowa, this was a recognition that I had never considered, or had repressed, aspects of life and reality with which I had to confront myself, and through which I needed to find my way. I have spent the last decades of my life in that effort.

For a long time after World War II, the overwhelming sorrow and catastrophic after-effects of those events in the Jewish community so dominated the life and thinking of many that it was a long time before there was a fundamental review of what one believed. Those raised with a traditional upbringing were always told that whatever happened was the result of God's judgment; therefore, when bad things happened, it was obviously the fault either of oneself or of others who deserved to be punished. On the basis of assumptions of that kind, it was very easy to develop the reward-and-punishment syndrome by which virtually all of Jewish life was shaped, as was also true for Christianity and Islam, both as history and theology.

If the Shoah were the effect of an omnipotent divine cause, then what could have been the motivation? Was it sheer divine caprice? Was it divine absence, no matter how motivated, divine hiding, or even divine indifference? Was it, as traditionally assumed and historiographically noted, divine punishment for egregious Jewish human sins?

I could not think of anything that the six million Jews might have done or not done that would have justified a divine punishment of genocidal proportions. Particularly when I thought of the one and a half million children under ten who were murdered at the same time, it became impossible for me to put that into a context of divine judgment. For had not some of the prophets already taught that children no longer died for the sins of their parents, that each of us is responsible for our own life and its virtues or faults? On that basis, therefore, the statement of the second commandment that children would bear the consequences of the iniquity of their ancestors into the third or fourth generation (Exodus 20:5) had been declared abolished.

So even on the basis of Jewish theology, because the prophets were speaking on behalf of God as surely as did Torah itself, it became impossible for me to make my peace with a God who would punish by death millions of people, including their children and grandchildren, for whatever they might have omitted or committed. And if I had to think that God could have intervened in the Holocaust but did not, then I would no longer be a faithful Jew, for I would no longer want to have anything to do with such a God.

For me, the Shoah is comparable in magnitude to each of the other major theological events in the Judeo-Christian past: the covenantal revelation at Mount Sinai; the need for revolutionary reconstructions after the loss of Temple, altar, and sovereignty to the Romans; and perhaps even the pain, death, and redemption associated with Golgotha. How can that be?

It centers on God. After the Shoah there is an unavoidable need to reconsider the traditional formulations of God's being, and therefore, also, of the traditional liturgical vocabulary. Traditionally, whether explicitly or implicitly, God was depicted and spoken of as possessed of limitless power. God was the supreme, unchallengeable power from Whom, through

Whom, by Whom everything proceeded. All reality, all existence, all history were the immediate or mediate products of Divine Power. He was the *melech*, the "king." In its purest form this belief and proclamation of omnipotence allowed for no other cause for any effect in the universe and in human life. Sin, therefore, was the always ultimately futile attempt to thwart, contravene, or evade divine omnipotence. It was believed that it was always to be followed by punishment, whether immediate or delayed.

In the decades that have elapsed since the Shoah, the questions about God have not been silenced. The initial searing pain anesthetized us, overpowering our capacity to fully grasp its significance and the details of the Shoah. As the numbness recedes, we return over and over again to the questions concerning God's place in the Shoah, an overwhelming and unprecedented event in the history of the Jewish people as in history generally, because never before were Jews murdered only because of their birth.

Where was God in Auschwitz? How could God permit the slaughter? Why did God not interfere and rescue the covenant people? Is there still a God? Can we still pray to God? What has happened to God?

There are only a few basic answers to these questions. One is to apply the traditional causal connection between human action and divine reaction, and therefore to accept the Shoah as an act of divine punishment. In this view, God was involved actively, deliberately, centrally. Having rendered the judgment that the Jewish people was sinful and beyond other, less radical means of chastisement and correction, God caused the events we call the Shoah to execute the divine degree of justice that falls upon unrepentant sinners.

This is a well-known traditional category of Jewish historiography and theology. "Because of our sins were we exiled from our land." So the Siddur laments, contradicting the psalmist's comforting words, "He has not dealt with us according to our sins, nor has He requited us according to our iniquities" (Psalm 103). The destruction of Jerusalem and its Temple, with its loss of independent national identity, forced our forebears to find a sufficient explanation for the enormous catastrophe that had befallen them. Obviously, they did not question God's place in history. They were compelled, therefore, to see the cause of the disaster in their own wickedness. They saw God's presence in history in their loss, and they justified God's act by assuming full responsibility for having caused divine punishment to befall them. Our sins caused death and destruction; our incomplete fulfillment of our part of the covenantal obligation caused suffering, exile, destruction, and pain. God was just.

This assertion of the unvarying rightness of divine retribution as a consequence of human action is quintessential in Jewish tradition biblically and post-biblically. As the main category of traditional historical understanding, it could also serve as an explanation of the Shoah, and has been used to that end.

There are, however, some serious difficulties with this view. Accepting for the moment that God acts in history by way of reward and punishment, then we need to ask what sins were committed by the Jewish people in the first decades of this century, or even before, to furnish sufficient and plausible cause for the catastrophic effect called the Shoah? What transgression did the Jews of Europe, and of Eastern Europe in particular, commit to bring upon them such stupendous radical destruction? True, the overly romanticized view of the East European shtetl and Jewish life has been revised somewhat by the disclosure of the occasionally seamy and ugly side of the picture. But surely there was nothing so spectacularly different or hideous in the behavior and life style of that Jewry to draw upon it the unspeakable punishment of the Shoah. And if one were to say that the cumulative accretion of a much longer past erupted volcanically, then surely we must assert that East European

Jewry was not different from Jews in other places. In fact, if any accounting of their deeds was to be made, it is safe to conclude that the Jews in Eastern Europe were among the most pious and observant who had ever lived. If the Shoah were to be understood as divine punishment for sins, then surely American Jewry would have been a much more "deserving" target for divine wrath and justice.

Moreover, as noted earlier, the extinction of approximately one and a half million children under ten years of age renders this purported divine retribution so totally disproportionate as to make it monstrous. Even if we invoke and claim divine justice, a proportionate correlation between cause and effect, between sin and punishment, is to be expected and mandatory. This is necessary because otherwise accountability, and with it the whole system of reward and punishment, become untenable.

Thus, despite its traditional rooting, this explanation of the role of God in the Shoah is unacceptable. Furthermore, if on principle God is in history but is entitled to, and wants to, assert the divine will, then how can God gain freedom from being trapped into an otherwise almost compulsory reaction following upon human action? The system of reward and punishment suffers from the defect that it renders God so dependent upon human initiative as to virtually eliminate God's ability to make choices. God is in this way seen as bound to respond to human initiatives. God is hardly, if ever, really free to act independently. A major exception may be the operation of *teshuva* and *selicha*, of human repentance and God's gracious forgiveness. But even here God's freedom is severely limited, for the expectation is stated clearly that God will forgive when we repent. And if it appears that the expected sequence of reward and punishment is not effective in this world, tradition assures us that it will function as expected in the "world to come." This traditional attempt to answer the question of God's role in historic catastrophes is inherently defective in itself and thus unhelpful in furnishing sufficient answers to the question of where God was at Auschwitz.

Another answer is to declare baldly that the Shoah could only occur because God was not there, not involved at all. By inference, and in a radical way, saying that God was not there implies that all history is exclusively a human category. History in this view is always the product and result only of human factors; there is no place for God in it. God and history are two different categories, unrelated and unrelatable. Taken out of context, Psalm 115 could be cited as a biblical warrant for the severance of the two: "The heavens belong to the Lord, but the earth He gave over to man." An extrapolation from this verse might well be that history is man's domain, into which God intrudes only rarely, if at all. Biblical warrant or not, the idea that God has no place in history is widespread today. Human beings are given the sole responsibility for historical events, their causes and consequences; genocide, for example, is "man's inhumanity to man." In this view, the Shoah is *prima facie* evidence of the noninvolvement of God.

This is a simple and radical solution. The end-result, however, is that God is rendered nearly irrelevant to human life. If God is not in history, not in those innumerable events that make up the rich tapestry of history, then there is little that remains of any relations between God and human beings. At most one could assert that God was active in the beginning, at creation, but since then God has withdrawn, essentially leaving human beings to their devices. There is some biblical warrant for this position. Was not the purpose of the creation of Adam – that is, of all of us – to be seen as God's making us agents to fix up the world, which had been left incomplete, flawed at creation?

There is also a well-documented thesis that the biblical texts record a gradual but irreversible withdrawal by God from the human scene. But as an answer to God's place in the Shoah, it becomes irrelevant, because it proposes that God has no place, or no longer any place, in history.

What if God had died? What if Auschwitz is, so to speak, God's grave? The "God is Dead" proposition retains God's presence in history, or at least does not challenge it on principle for the events prior to the Shoah. In this view, the Shoah is perceived as so overwhelmingly evil and potent that it destroys not only millions of Jewish lives, as well as millions of others, but destroys God also.

While it cannot be refuted, this is a radical statement produced by a radical evil. It is no more amenable to universally accepted proof than its opposite, namely, that God is alive. Both statements, God is alive or God is dead, are applicable to God only as metaphoric statements, as statements of belief or the lack thereof. While it cannot be taken literally, the Jewish belief system emphatically declares God to be the source of life, indeed, life itself. In Hebrew the words are *mekor chayyim*, "wellspring of life," and *elohim chayyim*, the "living God." To speak of God as dead is so ultimately, inherently contradictory, even repugnant, to everything that Judaism believes about God that it renders this proposition impossible in a Jewish context.

It is clear that such a position would come close to severing the cord that binds God and humankind. It is therefore a position unacceptable in any form of the Jewish religious system. The heart of Jewish religious belief and life is the faith assertion that there is an unbreakable bond between human beings and God, and between God and human beings. A believing, religiously oriented Jew cannot escape from having to declare on principle that God is in history; the puzzling question is: How?

A variant of the proposition that God was not at Auschwitz asserts that God willed to be absent. This explanation has respectable backing in tradition. The idea of the *el mistater, deus absconditus*, or "hiding God" is a declaration about God, an insight into the Divine Being that preserves God's freedom to act. In this view God is not bound to human initiative in a purely reactive mode. On the contrary, the turning away by God, God's hiding, is the assertion of the freedom of divine action that not only preserves for God an aspect that we humans prize as a most precious characteristic of our own, if not also a definition of ourselves. It is a radical alternative and correction to the feature of the reward and punishment sequence that often reverses the relations of God and human beings to God's disadvantage in that it makes God an appendage to human action and will.

Evil, in this case Auschwitz, can appear in a world created and supervised by God because God has the choice to be present at a given moment or event, or to be absent. That is to say, the Divine Presence is turned toward or averted from a given time and place. It would seem that this is the ideal solution to the question of where God was at Auschwitz. God *histir panav*, averted, turned aside the Divine Presence, and evil erupted and reigned unopposed. God's usual potential presence in history is preserved, and God and history continue to be relevant to each other. The possibility and reality of evil are established as well.

This position is the modern application and version of Ezekiel's declaration: "And the nations shall know that the House of Israel were exiled only for their iniquity, because they trespassed against Me, so that I hid my face from them and delivered them into the hands of their adversaries, and they fell by the sword" (Ezekiel 39:23). For Ezekiel, this was a straightforward and even simple, though terrible, explanation. Israel sins. God averts His face. The enemy triumphs.

Inasmuch as it has already been noted that the sin-punishment category is an unsatisfactory, unacceptable interpretation of the Shoah, there arises a fundamental problem with the prophetic notion of the hiding, willfully absent God. For we need to ask why God would have chosen to be absent at that moment and in those places that coalesced into the Shoah. If we must reject any causal connection between Jewish failures and sins and the hideous triumph of the radical evil of the Shoah, then the question becomes inescapable and painful: Why would God turn away and hide there and then?

In other words, the explanation of *hester panim* does not hold. Rather, it pushes the question one level further. Why hide to make Auschwitz possible? It is not really a validly alternative explanation. It gets mired in the same self-accusatory confession that the Jewish people "deserved" divine punishment. And even if one were to say that God had no good reason to hide, but merely hid to assert divine freedom, acted out of pure caprice, then that answer is monstrous. Then the covenant is ruptured. Then the ancient promise "I will be your God" is broken, for in accepting to be God's people, the implication was clearly also that God had obligations, had to do more than we do. God was always God, and we were always only human.

God's capricious, foundationless turning away does not, cannot fit the covenantal bond that links God and Israel, Israel and God. Much as the covenant obligates the Jew, even more does it obligate God. The covenant sets limits to God's freedom. Moreover, God freely yielded up this freedom because it was God who initiated the covenant, not our ancestors. It was God's *bechira*, God's seeking out of Abraham and his descendants, that is the heart of Jewish identity and destiny. After the covenant, God is no longer free to hide. God never really was.

The prophets and other traditional statements sought to exculpate God and locate the source of evil primarily or exclusively in the human element, but on those terms God either became our prisoner or was totally irrelevant. Thus, despite the roots of this view in tradition, the answer that God hid is also unacceptable.

All of these explanations and more have been proposed

to account for the event of the Shoah in a world ruled by an omnipotent, limitlessly powerful God. Every one of them fails, some from sheer absurdity, others from the horrendous implications about God being hidden or explicit. Nor is there any comfort or profit in retreating to a posture of total unquestioning submission, pleading ignorance of God's will and intentions, and desperately seeking to resume a pre-Shoah liturgical and theological life, as though such a retreat could restore the earlier covenantal assurances, trust, and relationship.

The Shoah shatters divine omnipotence for many Jews once and for all. If God willed or permitted the Shoah, faithful Jews are left in a bottomless void. And not Jews alone! Christians share this horror-filled stare into the abyss, and if they were willing to delve seriously into the issue, Muslims would share it as well.

But what of omniscience? Is omniscience likewise doomed to irretrievable collapse? It is. What could omniscience possibly mean when it is decoupled from omnipotence? What value to believers can a God be who knows all but is either incapable or, in principle, unwilling to act on such totality of knowledge? It would merely be an interior event within God without any consequences for humans seeking answers by which to live in divinely acceptable ways. Seen this way, omniscience is the ultimate isolation of God from human life and history, it is the ultimate absence of God.

Neither omnipotence nor omniscience can furnish the insights into the Shoah or offer the explanations of it that would enable a genuine post-Shoah believer in God to remain faithful. Both are inadequate in principle. Both fail us, and need to be discarded. Biblical and rabbinic texts speak clearly of divine anger, divine retribution, of God being so taken unaware, so surprised, that God flares up. Are these not unmistakable signs of an understanding of the nature of God that is incompatible with omnipotence and omniscience?

The story of Job, while not considered revelation in the same way as Torah, is a story told to probe the nature of suffering, of the infliction of evil. It comes down to the old question of reward and punishment. The book of Job is one of the earlier protests against the reward-and-punishment system. In the story, Job's friends are unwavering proponents of that theory, and they probe and test, plague and push Job to admit that he had to have deserved what happened to him, that there must have been some kind of transgression to cause God so to visit him. Of course, the best part of their argument is that the very fact that Job denies their accusation is evidence of his sinfulness. It is very clever, circular reasoning. Remarkably Job resists it.

The conclusion of the book is not really satisfactory in terms of the problem, because it never goes to the point of saying that the whole construction of reward and punishment is one that is not valid and needs to be replaced by a different kind of understanding of the relationship between God and humans. The book ends with Job being flattened out, as it were, by the power of God, who is portrayed as capable of silencing Job, although Job appears to understand that ending as an endorsement of his own position and conviction that he did not deserve what had happened, that it was not the result of being punished for some sin. The book is an early step towards the repudiation of reward and punishment, and Job begins the process of being a stand-up human.

Philosophic terms such as omnipotence and omniscience are clear evidence of the impact of Greek culture upon religious ideas. Omnipotence and omniscience are the fruits of the Greek philosophical search for the Absolute, an Absolute that is, by definition, beyond human reach, beyond relation. These terms became standard, an unchallenged mode of understanding and expressing the relation of God and humans.

On the other hand, for Judaism, as we have said, the God of the Bible is fundamentally relational, interactive, tied to us as we are to God, mutually dependent, covenantal. If, after the Shoah, omnipotence and omniscience are untenable, nevertheless there is another "omni" that does not share this fate. God's omnipresence can be asserted; indeed, it needs to be asserted as the indispensable basis for a new understanding of God's being.

So where was God? God was at Auschwitz. God had to be there, not as Ruler, not as Redeemer, not as Victor, but as Sufferer. There is the possibility of seeing the Shoah as God's wound, as God's pain and suffering. God was wounded in the Shoah, suffered grievously together with God's first covenant people and all of the others. God is present in human suffering. There is ample precedent in our tradition for such an answer. Recall the Midrash, which depicts God's Presence, the Shechina, weeping over the Jewish people's bloody defeat by the Romans, accompanying the fleeing exiles. It is a classic picture of divine suffering, of theopathy, the identification of God with the pain and catastrophe of His people that God did not, could not prevent. Moreover, Torah is full of instances where the people's acts hurt and anger God, at times to the point of wanting to abandon them, to destroy them. God is not understood to be unaffected by human behavior. Rather, God is shown as suffering because of us, as grieving over our failures even to point where "I regret that I made them" (Genesis 6:7).

At the same time, God is also not able to call it quits and go back to a pre-creation condition. In the act of creating, God assumed a total risk. Creation was the foremost conferral of a dynamic, ineradicable measure of freedom for the human element that was to appear within the creation that God conceded, made possible, bestowed. That transition from Nothing to Something that we attribute to God involved restriction upon the totality, the absoluteness of God. Creation was a partial self-diminution, a giving up of totality by God. The Lurianic Kabbalah calls it *tsimtsum*, "contraction." As long as the created world exists, somehow God wills no longer to be totally power-ful. Omnipotence and omniscience are incompatible with God the creator as described in our sacred texts.

Not that God as Sufferer is altogether powerless or no longer involved in creation. Quite the contrary, *mechadesh bechol yom ma'ase bereshit*, "He renews daily the work of cre-ation" (Morning Liturgy). God remains in creation, active but no longer all-powerful, as a result of the divine decision to become Creator. We have become God's partners, not only by our own decision and will, but also by God's. There often ex-ists an uneasy relationship, full of tensions, between God and humans, between God and us. And so there are times when the creature afflicts the Creator, when the human partners ex-ceed the limit and misuse the freedom that, in creating, God conveyed upon them.

Torah tells that God is bound by the decision to create, by the decision to have human beings with free will appear in the process of creation. Thus, having renounced total power in becoming Creator, God is powerless by His own will to stop human beings who wantonly flout the rules and break the bounds that God as Revealer has made known.

Creation did not set human beings free to pursue any whim, desire, or goal. Revelation set boundaries, statues, precepts. Human beings were no more totally free than was God after creation began. And they are certainly not all-powerful. But they had a large measure of freedom and power, which inevi-tably and not infrequently would clash with God's intentions, which, to the extent that His intentions can be identified or read out of the sacred texts for which the claim of revelation is sus-tainable, fall into the large categories of life, justice, and peace. After deciding to become Creator, God could not be the puppet master, pulling human creatures by divinely controlled strings. Consequently, God suffers – maybe, we even say, because God wanted human beings to be free and even increasingly powerful. God's suffering is an inevitable outcome of being Creator.

Auschwitz, then, is a horrendous example of the interplay between divine surrender of the totality of power and human freedom as it was before creation turned to wanton, cruel license. God was at Auschwitz, God remains in history, but with self-limited power in consequence of being Creator. A curious but perhaps unavoidable question then is: Why did God become Creator? What might have motivated God to such a far-reaching act? Attempting to read God's mind and trying to put oneself within God's own Being is, of course, while enticing, totally impossible. Nonetheless, the question will not be stilled. It urges a response. And so one speculates: Was God lonely? Did God's *shalom*, totality, undisturbed unfracturedness, eventually cause boredom? Did God want, need, an "other"? And are we the result, the answer to God's need?

It is another, most devastatingly painful consequence of that primal act by the Creator that endowed Adam and all his descendants with freedom. When evil produced by human beings erupts, God can be affected by it, as are the victims. The Jewish people and many others are paying what is at certain times a frightful price for this freedom. So does God.

God is wounded. God is hurt and helpless in the face of the exercise of that freedom irrevocably implanted in the first human being and all his descendants. Right along we have traced instance after instance in the traditional texts that inescapably point to the price God had to pay for that original grant of freedom to the human being. Only a God thus tragically involved, and now needing us to help and heal, is tenable. Only such a God, who needs me to love and pray and bring joy, helps and strengthens the retrieval of trust and faithfulness after the enormity of the catastrophe of Shoah.

And if this is so, additional consequences ensue. God is in

need of healing much as are the survivors, primary among them the Jewish people. Many Christians and others also feel this wound. As Jews we have two major tasks, to restore the Jewish people, and to restore God. Our prayers, our care for God, our love for God are more needed now than ever. The God who gave us creation, life, and Torah now needs our help. We now have the opportunity to restore to God something of what we have received so abundantly, so graciously, so undeservedly. Somehow the imagery of the enthroned Majesty commanding its subjects who stand deferentially and tremblingly before the throne ill fits our experience, our post-Shoah condition. No longer do we only implore *rachmanut,* empathy, mercy. We now need to give it to God.

Chapter Five
God in Need of Man – Man in Need of God

What are humans that you are mindful of them?
(Psalm 8:5)

On a Sunday evening in January, 1945, I spoke in a church near Cedar Rapids. The event was over sooner than we thought, and Lotte and I were driving back home on the highway, kind of slowly because it was early. We had just decided we would stop at the house of one of our congregants for a visit. All of sudden a vehicle roared up – I could only see the headlights – and before I knew it we were hit. The car that hit us overturned into the ditch on the other side of the road, the engine smoking. I turned off the engine to my car, and realized that the front left wheel was near my lap. I looked at Lotte. Her face was molded in the windshield. She was bleeding, and I wanted to go to her aid. I opened my door and tried to get out of the car. Instantly I realized that my right leg would not come along, and I fell backwards onto the highway.

A few minutes later I saw a car coming in my direction, and

I waved and waved and waved. I think he stopped about twenty feet from my head. He immediately saw that it was an accident. By this time, the man who had been driving the other car had come over and was berating me. I said, "As soon as I can get up, I'll slug you." The man went back to his car because, as we found out later, the woman who was in his car seemed lifeless. They took her to the hospital, and three days later, she simply walked out. She had been so drunk that she had apparently passed out. She had no injuries at all.

The fellow who had stopped then went to a nearby farmhouse and called an ambulance and a doctor. Again, this was 1945. Everybody who was anybody was in the war, and there were no Jewish doctors in Cedar Rapids. In fact, when we arrived, there had only been one Jewish attorney. The doctor arrived at the accident first, and who was it? Dr. Phil Crew, of whom it was widely known that he was a flaming anti-Semite. He took one look at me and Lotte and said we had to get to the hospital. The ambulance came and took us to St. Luke's hospital, a Methodist hospital, where Dr. Crew was on the staff.

It was quite clear that I had broken my femur. In those days, the best advice was to cast it. So the next morning, Monday, Phil Crew took me to the cast room in the hospital and they cast the fracture. We had a dear, dear friend who was the best dentist in town, and he came early, 6:30 or 7:00 in the morning, to see Lotte, who had lost seven teeth. Needless to say, this accident still has an impact on her.

Lotte and I drove the nurses so crazy, each wanting to know how the other was doing, that they finally decided to put us in the same room, which was unheard of in those days. Fortunately, we had my mother-in-law, who lived with us, to take care of our daughter, Susie, then only one and a half years old. Susie came every day to visit, and would go from door to door, saying hello.

I had a lot of pain. They gave me an opiate of some kind against pain, but by the second day the pain became really intense. I said to the doctor, "I have terrible pain." He said, "Oh, you Jews, you can't take pain." So I asked the nurse to give me a Turkish towel, and I put it in my mouth, and bit it to pieces instead of crying out, because the pain was that intense. By the third day I could not even make it the four hours between shots; by about three hours or so, it began to wear off and the pain became really excruciating. So on the third or fourth day, I said to the doctor, "I don't care what you think about Jews, there is something wrong here. I want you to cut a window and take a look."

So he went and got the instruments and cut a window. He blanched. It was almost gangrenous. He had tied the bandages under the cast too tight, and they had begun to dry and cut into my flesh. So immediately, I was taken to surgery, and I got this device known as a Kirchner wire. This time, they drilled a hole into my bone, put a wire through, and then put on one of those horseshoe devices to which weights are attached. And that is how I was for twenty-two weeks.

The accident happened on the 25th of January 1945. I didn't get out of the hospital until the end of June. Lying flat on my back, I had to have a nurse for everything. At times the only thing I could think of was that I was going to have to lose my leg because it would not heal. And all I could do was lie there. The congregation was without a rabbi. My family was without a father. My wife was without a husband. There were times when the despair was very bad. By my birthday in April, I was so despondent that if someone had left a gun on my night table I think I might have used it.

Fortunately, I was not forgotten. My congregation was totally loyal and supportive to a degree that really is legendary. You need to understand that I had come with only a suitcase in 1935. Neither Lotte nor I had known how to drive. The congregation had given us a car the year before because we had no transportation. The car was a total loss.

I had visitors every day. Everything my family needed was provided. On April 12 President Roosevelt died, and they had a huge memorial observance in the city. And it was unthinkable in those days that anything like that would happen without me. So they rigged a microphone to my bed, and I spoke from my bedside to the assembly. This was amazing to me, because I was still writing out every word I said from the pulpit because I didn't trust my English at all, and despite my poor English, and my accent, and being the only rabbi, they still wanted to hear from me.

Fortunately, the University of Iowa in Iowa City is a really first-class institution, and they had a medical department of international standing. There was a Professor Steiner who had come from Austria, a refugee who was reputed to be the finest orthopedic surgeon in the country and maybe in the world at that time. The pressure was finally brought on Dr. Crew to get a consultation with Dr. Steiner. I'll never forget when Steiner came into the room. I can still see his fingers on my leg. He just bent over and said, "You will be all right. It will take time. But you will be all right."

From that time on, I began to heal, and it became clear to Dr. Crew that things were beginning to show positive signs. But I was still walking with a cane in November 1945.

Incidentally, Phil Crew became a good friend. After this was all over, he became part of a group of members of my congregation who regularly played cards with each other. Our relationship turned him around just about 180 degrees.

An attorney had come the day after the accident, Abe Bass. He said, "If it's okay with you, I'll take care of any legal matters there might be in connection with this." He came back a day later and said, "You know, it's a strange thing. This man who ran into you is a reject from the army, his mother takes in wash in order to make a living, but three months ago he had an automobile accident." There was a law in Iowa that if the damage exceeded a certain amount, you had to take out automobile insurance. So because of this prior accident, he had $5,000 of insurance for which one premium had been paid. It was a national insurance company with an office in Des Moines. The insurance adjuster came from time to time to look at me, because our accident had been headlined in the newspaper, and he would come just to make sure I was still there.

Came the time that I am out of the hospital and Abe Bass said, "Let's talk to the insurance company now." Sure enough, the insurance adjuster makes the date for some time in November, and all that Abe said to me was, "Herman, you are going down to the office of the attorney the insurance company had hired" – the top legal office in Cedar Rapids. He and I wind up sitting in Craven Shuttlesworth's law office with the insurance adjuster. While we were sitting there talking, Shuttlesworth's secretary brought him a slip of paper. He looked at it kind of quizzically, nodded his head, and she left. Finally, the insurance adjuster says, "You realize we have a very special case here. I'm prepared to make such-and-such an offer." My jaw dropped. But the next thing I know, Abe says, "Rabbi, we're leaving." He closes the file. Gets off his chair, and we leave.

When we got out of his office, I said, "Abe, what are you doing to me?" He says, "It was not an appropriate offer on their part." So I went home on the bus. I didn't have a car, obviously, and anyhow I didn't have to go far. Cedar Rapids was a little town then. I had just taken off my coat, maybe a half an hour later, the phone rings. It's Abe Bass. "Herman, come on down. We are signing the contract, and we need your signature." I put on my coat, got back on the bus, went to Abe's office this time, and he has a settlement offer. He says, "This is just right. Now lets go for lunch."

At lunch, Abe asks me, "Do you remember the note the secretary handed Shuttlesworth?" I said, "Yes, but what has that got to with this" He said, "Well, that note was a request from someone whom Shuttlesworth could not identify who wanted to have lunch with him. And Shuttlesworth had nothing else to do, so he had lunch. The man identified himself to Shuttlesworth and said, 'You and I were in high school together. I remembered your name. I don't live here any more. I live in California. I was on the City of Los Angeles train, and as the train slowed down and stopped in Cedar Rapids, almost on an impulse, I decided I'm going to stay and take the next train and see what the 'old burg' looks like. I went to a telephone book to see if anyone I knew was still here, and I remembered your unusual name when I saw the law firm. And here we are.'"

Shuttlesworth asked him what he was doing now, and the stranger said, "I'm with an insurance company." Shuttlesworth says, "What insurance company?" It turns out, the stranger was the national vice-president of the insurance company against which I had the claim. Shuttlesworth tells him of the incident, the negotiations, and says, "I'm trying to get the best deal for you." The vice-president said, "Do whatever is necessary to settle the claim."

It would be an understatement to say that the experience was long and difficult, but because there was some money left over after the bills were paid, Lotte, Susie, and I were able to fly to South America two years later in 1947, to see my parents for the first time in ten years.

Individual suffering is a fundamental theological component in creation. If creation is seen as the work of God, and this surely is one of the main Jewish understandings, it has to be incomplete. Creation is a work in progress.

The creation story is the response to that haunting and ultimately unanswerable question: How did everything begin? Precisely because there is no way that human beings can give an accurate, definitive answer, faith answers: God did it. To say that God began the process we call creation is a religious response to the mystery of existence. The Torah is a human record of encounters with God, most likely written in part by Moses, by others perhaps later. It is a human attempt to express something so extraordinary that we have no other way of talking about it.

"Express" is a good word, implying that we squeeze out from within ourselves words that give meaning to the Torah. There is a saying that if two study Torah, the Shechina, the divine presence, is invoked, is functioning, becomes present. Originally, it was said that it took three persons for the divine to be present, and then later, two persons. Ultimately, it was said that one person alone studying Torah also invokes the divine presence, and is therefore part of the Mystery that by another opaque word we call inspiration. Because it is ineffable and basically inexpressible, Mystery is a more resonant word than spirit. So for me, Torah is the record, first spoken and then written, of the overwhelming encounter of the human with the divine. But Torah is not God's words; it is human language. It is the human account of a message that we believe originates outside of our own mind and being, and wells up within us by a trigger, a presence. "Presence" is a dangerous word, but it reflects, to the extent our human language can, that which we intend to say when we speak of our relationship with God. God becomes present so powerfully that the whole human being can be radically altered and suffused by this experience, this encountering. So Torah can be seen as an expression of the human groping for an understanding, a wording of the relationship between God and humans.

According to that tradition, God created all that we know on this earth, progressing from light to earth, from sun and moon to oceans and dry land, each with all of the uncountable forms of life, and God pronounced all of these efforts "good"

(Genesis 1:12). On the sixth day, Adam is created, and God judges the work "very good" (Genesis 1:12). In this mythlike description, God's intent is now clear. Human beings are to be God's masterpiece. Adam, the earthling, whose name is taken from *adama*, "earth," is the crown of creation. Not surprisingly, then, the text says, "The heavens and the earth were finished, and all their array" (Genesis 2:1f.). And it further says "and He ceased on the seventh day from all His work which He had done" (Genesis 2:2). Clearly, no matter how impressive, how infinite, the results of creation had been before Adam, it is only when a human appears that God is finished with the work.

This is an important point. Apparently no matter how complicated and varied all previous creative acts may have been, God does not rest, does not enjoy Shabbat, until you and I are present. God's Shabbat depends on humankind.

The very wording in the Hebrew texts implies the transfer of the responsibility to the human. The usual translations include: "He rested from all His work which God in creating had made" (Soncino); "God ceased from all the work of creation that he had done" (*Etz Hayim*); "He ceased on it from doing all His work which God had created" (Friedman Commentary); "He ceased from all his work, that by creating, God had made." (Fox, *The Five Books of Moses*). All of these miss the crucial point. Only Kaplan's *The Living Torah* comes close: "…that He had been creating (so that it would continue to function)." The text avers that God's work was done, apparently after the creation of Adam. Implied, or hidden, in the very last Hebrew word of that verse (Genesis 2:3) is not satisfaction with the past, with the grand, glorious story of creation, but rather a hint that after God had finished, what He had created was now to work (*la'asot*), was now to function, was now to be set in motion. And by whom? God was done, finished creating, so now it was up to Adam, the crowing climax of creation, after which God could "rest" to "do it," to make creation work. God's rest, "Sabbath," is bound up with the availability of a human agent who now and from now on is to continue, to work with, to keep functioning God's creative work. This creation was inherently, of necessity, incomplete – perhaps intentionally?

So the creation story unfolds in stately sequence through all of creation to Adam, the first human being, who represents an extraordinary leap beyond all preceding layers of existence. A human being is created, one endowed with consciousness of a high-level, self-reflective, self-critical, and keen type of intelligence. But above all, God has created a being with an irreducible sense of freedom. And just as soon as Adam is created and God pronounces creation "very good," Adam presents a problem to God.

Up until this point, God was in full and unquestioned control. God is depicted as the Shaper and Originator of everything that evolved out of the primal *tohu vavohu,* the formless void. Why not stop there? Why wasn't creation sufficient at that point? Didn't God know what would happen when He created a human being in His "own image"? This phrase, in the Hebrew *tzelem,* is translated "in the likeness." It hints at the possibility that the relationship between God and humans is not static, is not frozen, is not so fixed that there is only one way of looking at it.

There is a perceptive Midrash commentary on the plural construction of "shall we make man…" or "let us make man" (Genesis 1:26). The rabbis tell the story that God consulted His cabinet, the four archangels, for advice when He began thinking of creating a man. In typical fashion, the archangels were deadlocked in their contradictory opinions. God, therefore, ignored them, and just went ahead and created Adam. This story is the rabbinic way of saying that this is not just a simple tale; it is a story touching on ultimate profundities.

The only perfect creation God could have made would have been to duplicate Himself, but God did not do this. He made

something that is other than God, other than *shalom* – unfracturedness – and so it is imperfect. Whether God was aware of
it at the moment of creation we cannot know, but God soon
discovers that in making Adam, He made somebody who has
a will of his own. It becomes clear almost immediately that
there are problems.

"The Lord God said, 'It is not good for man to be alone; I
will make a fitting helper for him.' And the Lord God formed
out of the earth all the wild beasts and all the birds of the sky
and brought them to the man to see what he would call them;
and whatever the man called each living creature, that would
be his name. And the man gave names to all the cattle and to
the birds of the sky and to all the wild beasts; but for Adam, no
fitting helper was found" (Genesis 2:18). Quite apart from its
charm, this is a most astounding passage. After having stated,
after Adam, that creation was "very good," God now says, "It
is not good for man to be alone."

Did God not anticipate this defect in creation? Did God not
know that Adam needed a companion, a human other? This
text tells us that God is learning as His creation unfolds.

Tradition, midrashic commentaries and elaborations insist
that God had the animals parade before Adam in pairs, male
and female. Was only Adam to remain single, nonsexual, while
all the other animals were clearly paired, even if there was no
procreation in Eden? Does God only then "discover" that a ti-
gress or a weasel is not a suitable companion for Adam, and
what does this say about God's omniscience?

Moreover, it is clear from this story that without Adam,
creation was undifferentiated. God apparently needs help in
finishing His creation. The "wild beasts" and "birds of the sky"
existed helter-skelter in an unnamed mass, no identities, no
taxonomy. By bringing them to Adam to be named, God invites Adam to be a collaborator in creation. Names, identities,

definitions, differentiation, all apparently come from Adam, not from God. Perhaps such naming is reserved for humans, is only possible for us as an inescapable consequence of being human. Who else is there in this new reality that would call a giraffe a giraffe?

It is human insight, discrimination, language, that identifies and therefore also orders the chaotic lack of differentiation into cosmos. The structure of the nonhuman biomass, while created by God, only becomes manageable, orderly, after being structured by the human, Adam. The created order derives from Adam. From the very first moments of reality, as depicted in the biblical record, the human is involved radically, indispensably. Even the most obvious and necessary consequences of the divine initiative invite – *need* – human assistance, involvement, collaboration. There would be no world as we understand it without human participation, without human language to distinguish, designate, and thus render creation intelligible.

The world, our reality, is not only God's work, it is the result of a cooperative process, of human participation in an elemental fashion. God only "rested" from creation; there was more work to be done, and God did not do it alone. God does not do it alone now, either. Even the very mystery of creation is not God's solely. We were then, as we are now, indispensable. The fundamental verity of being human is that we are a collaborative event between God and ourselves.

In the end, "no fitting helper" (Genesis 2:21 f.) can be found. God learns that Adam needs a like companion. Woman is created, and from that moment on, Adam is no longer alone. God now also has a companion, and a rather obstreperous one at that, because once Eve is created, Adam becomes fully human. Up to that point, he was just like any of the other entities in Paradise, smarter, but still only a creature. In Paradise there was no time, no birth, no death. But with Eve's arrival, first of all,

Adam is paired. Second, he finds out that he is male and Eve is female: sex enters, and the power to procreate, which apparently had previously not been part of Paradise.

According to the story, God understood that human beings belonged to a different order of being. After all, grasses and rabbits, larks and elephants, were not covered by a divine interdict. Adam is obviously made in such a way that he is capable of choice. God knew that He needed to set limits on the acts of this extraordinary creature. And so God does. "But of the tree of the knowledge of good and evil, you shall not eat" (Genesis 2:17). Adam is free, and it does not take long before his self-assertion results in disobedience. Henceforth, Adam, representing all of humankind, is God's counter-player.

Did God take into account the possibility, perhaps even the probability, of disobedience? Did He plan for the exercise of that freedom of choice, willful and deliberate, the result of careful weighing of the pros and cons of such action which brought the human pair into flaring confrontation with their Creator, even to the point of their expulsion from Eden?

Or was God taken by surprise? Was the swift and draconic punishment evidence of divine anger at having been confronted by the unforeseen? Of course, we cannot know for sure, but the Scripture invites such questions. If God is surprised, then it cannot be asserted that God is omniscient. On the other hand, if God knew that human beings would challenge the divine will, and not for the last time, but did nothing to prevent this occurrence, then it is God's omnipotence that is called into question. In either case, the moment this creature "made in God's image" appears in the sequential unfolding of creation, he becomes a problem not only to God, but also to creation.

This notion of being "made in God's image" is a probing toward the mystery of the fact that between God and the human there is a kind of bonding possible, a relation possible that we don't have with a tree or an animal, or even with another human, even though such relationships may be very similar. It may be also be a hint at the fact that the human-divine relationship is unique, unavailable to other creatures.

Ultimately, in the expulsion of Adam and Eve from *Gan Eden*, the world is turned over to Adam. In Paradise, God was unopposed, and everything happened, one would assume, as God wanted it. But with the coming of Adam, that is, you and me, the original totality and completeness of God's power and rule was radically diminished. God was taking an ultimate risk with this new creature, particularly as God hands over the created order to Adam and Eve and their descendants – us.

The first human family was by no means an adornment of creation. The problems for God continued. He accepts Abel's offering and not Cain's, apparently without understanding what would happen afterwards, that His action would anger Cain to the point of committing murder. This is not the action of an omniscient God. The alternative, that God did know that His action would cause Cain to murder Abel, is monstrous. Who would have any use for such a God? Rather than a fulfillment of the inherent purpose of the creation of the cosmos, both Adam's disobedience and Cain's murder are severe interferences with, and tests of, the created order understood as the result of God's will.

Nor is that the end of it. Almost immediately, humans seek to invade the divine realm. They are pictured as building a huge tower whose design and intent is the invasion of what is pictured as the region in which God dwells. God is surprised and alarmed by this invasive act, and takes drastic action to thwart the overbearing intentions of the human race. The clear implication is that if human beings had known the divine power and authority, and accepted it without question or challenge, they would not have been building the tower. The question arises again. Did God not anticipate the challenge? An omniscient deity would have acted to arrest this development before it became virulent, threatening.

Be all this as it may, Scripture makes it abundantly clear that God derives little joy and satisfaction from the creative act that brought forth Adam and his progeny. The early chapters of Torah are virtually an unbroken record of God's increasing failures with his human creatures and the concomitant disappointment and pain. It is barely ten generations from the appearance of the first human beings to the time of Noah, by which time human beings have become so hopelessly corrupt that God decides to make an end of them, save Noah and his immediate kin. This is the greatest disaster that befalls God, because He must destroy virtually His whole created order.

From the report in Genesis that God looked at creation and thought it good, we can assume that God's intent was for the created order to be a continuous source of satisfaction, even joy. Instead, and in a relatively short time, the creation turns sour, becomes corrupt, is full of evil. So God takes the drastic action of destroying much of what He has done and calls forth a replacement in the hope that it may be more successful than its predecessor.

One may conclude from these stories that the freedom inherent in the human being is capable of such deviation from God's will and hope that reconciliation is questionable, that only the most devastating exercise of power can cope with human self-assertiveness. Was all of this divinely programmed? Hardly. It is incontrovertibly obvious from these early texts that the human and the divine are in collision, that there is a basic, inherent conflict between the two. To put it boldly, God's original intent in creating Adam was misconceived; it is impossible to work out the relationship to God's satisfaction. The whole conception of the human role and place within creation does not work, and apparently cannot. The "sixth day," in the language of the traditional story, is essentially fatal to everything called forth before it. The flood is a macabre, brutal confrontation of the failure of the human being to exist within the parameters of God's original creation.

What choice did God have? In the beginning, there might have been a radically different order of being, so utterly other than what we know as human that we cannot even imagine it. Short of that, God could try again, destroy much of creation, and afterwards have different expectations, no longer expecting all human beings to obey and respond acceptably to God's hopes and wishes for them.

When read in this way, the early biblical texts portray an image of God fundamentally at odds with the much later constructions formulated in absolute terms as a result of Greek philosophic influences. Read in this way, the image of God is radically relative, interactive with humans. It is not the image of an absolute monarch, or of the equally foreign "First Cause." Nor does the image have anything to do with omnipotence or omniscience. In fact, it is just the opposite. This image is of a God who is becoming suffused in the unfolding fabric of reality, of existence, of life. It is "God with us," *imanu-el.*

All of this is proof, if such is still necessary, and perhaps it is, that the Bible is not a book of philosophy, of theology or belief. Rather, from the opening chapters and onward, it is the story of how humans learn of God, a God who may not be encased in formulae devised by humans, but whose presence floods reality, the omnipresent God. This is a God who is becoming, who is "learning," to use that word with all sorts of quotation marks around it. This God needs human beings because giraffes and earthworms were not enough.

So it is clear to me that the very word *la'asot* is the direction in which the future is to be seen. Work is to be done, and the work is to be done now, not by God but by Adam, and by all of us who are Adamites. If this is a possible, perhaps correct, understanding both of the text and of what the creatorhood of God might imply, then suffering is no surprise. The incomplete nature of the created order, in itself, implies and directly leads to such defects in the human experience as pain, suffering, and ultimately death. And so there is no radical surprise in finding that even though we attribute the existence of the world to the creator God, it is thereby to be understood to be in need of continuing work and improvement.

Ultimately, the rabbis tell us, that is our job: *l'takken olam*, to fix up the world, to repair it, with the intention that our work will step by step advance the world to levels of greater completion, better functioning, perhaps even to the level of a dream vision, when there will be no more pain and no more suffering. This vision is certainly one of the ingredients of the ultimate human hope of where existence might lead to. In fact, the vision is really almost a condition of no longer being human, because at that point the very deficiencies, defects of our own beings experience lead us to imagine and dream about a form of existence in which none of these defects are present any longer.

So if this is true, theologically, as a general kind of understanding, then of course when we talk about my own suffering, or the suffering of any given person, it needs to be seen in the same context. An individual's suffering is no special kind of event. To put it differently, it is futile for me to search out why I am suffering, simply because suffering is part of the condition of creation. In fact, my own suffering becomes a little more tolerable when it is not seen as directed in some kind of cause-and-effect sequence to me personally. I reject the notion that illness or misfortune is direct evidence of God's displeasure with me. Of course, this implies that whatever wrongs I may be doing are not the cause of the afflictions I suffer, because it could be that I would never have in my own understanding done such wrong as to justify as a consequence the illness, or misfortune, or pain, or whatever it might be.

It is easy to understand our reliance on the old system of reward and punishment. It is the basic human experience of growing up, a setting where adults, especially parents, are doing the training and responding. So most believers who come out of the biblical background, whether Judaism, Christianity, or Islam, have had this idea implanted to the extent that most believers understand this to be the main relationship between God and humans. The name Islam itself means submission to God, carrying the immediate implication that there will be dire consequence if the submission is flawed in any way. Much the same is both implicit and explicit in the *mitzvah* system, the structure of divinely originating commandments.

What is true of Islam, whose very name has this notion at its root, is true of Judaism and Christianity. The understanding of ourselves as the children of a divine father or mother could be considered implicit in the whole notion of creation. When drawn to its ultimate consequence, however, this concept leaves us in an unavoidable role of total dependency. While this dependency is most obviously shown right now in Islam, it is easily traced in and found in both Judaism and Christianity. The need to replace the infantile dependency image of our religious life with an adult relational one will thus apply to all three of these religions.

It is the straightforward and almost incontrovertible consequence of this notion that if God is parent, then it is God's duty to respond. We assume that God would function in this way to protect us because that is how parents function, at least those parents who function according to the proper, normative way. Human experience clearly demonstrates the falsehood of this image and expectation. The evidence is overwhelming. Jewish history's testimonial of pain, persecution, expulsion, is overwhelming in casting radical doubt on the validity of the image and implied consequences of God as Parent. Most recently, in the Shoah, over and over again in the concentration and death camps, billions of prayers for relief, for rescue, for salvation, for life were uttered – and they went unanswered.

Once in a while it is said of someone recovering from a severe illness that God saved her or him. Then the question always is, Why did God intercede healingly for this person and not the tens of thousands of others who were in a similar condition and probably prayed just as fervently, or for whom prayers were said just with the same intent, and for whom there was no such response? All this is equally true for the reference to God as rescuer in accidents. The question always is why this person under these circumstances was spared, whereas innumerable others in like circumstances were not. The whole sequence of reward and punishment, of God interfering in a given instance of life, just simply does not add up as a tenable position and explanation.

This was one of the most important aspects of my new understanding of my relationship to God. It shattered the very strictly confining sequence of cause and effect. I came to understand that God is not the cause directly of anything that occurs in my life, notwithstanding the very existence of the world in which I live and the fact that I have life. These are totally unmerited gifts of which I am deeply conscious and which put me in the condition of the profoundest sense of gratitude, beyond the capacity to put it into words.

Personal suffering, then, is part of the totality of the perception of what my existence in this universe might mean and how I am led to understand it. Obviously at bottom, the mystery of the coming into being of this world, and subsequently of the opportunity for human life to develop, and then for my individual life to be part of this enormous, mysterious chain of events – all of these remain a given. But the mystery of creation does not lead to the assumption that I have so immediate a nexus with God that I can ascribe either good things or bad things to God's actions.

That is also why petitionary prayer is very difficult for me, and quite often at the verge of meaninglessness. I don't expect God to do anything for me beyond what I have already received, namely: the world itself, life, the capacity to function as a human being in the world, and other human beings with whom to live and relate. All of this is done in the unfolding of the creative moment, and therefore is not to be isolated into a specific kind of relationship between God and me, and between me and God.

I know that this is different from what many people, maybe even most people, feel, expect, and need. I can only say for myself that my main task, giving satisfaction and joy to God, who needs such reassurance because of His own tumultuous and painful existence in view of what humans are doing, is not only enough, it is very challenging and very fulfilling. I see myself as called to be so present to God that God could find in my presence, through all that life brings to me, reassurance that humans are not totally worthless, or worse yet, actually an obstacle to what God may have intended when He created.

My personal suffering is evidence of the possibility that I could understand what God may be suffering. Here I come back to this very haunting phrase, namely that we are made in the "image of God." In this context, it may mean that there is something in us that has the capacity of being sufficiently similar to what God might be so that whatever happens to us and whatever we are is somehow relatable in terms of a similarity, a comparison, maybe even approaching a kind of likeness to what the divine might be. The divine is undoubtably something significantly and radically other than what I am as a human, but according to that statement, a consequence of being human and our experiences as a human should allow us to know enough to be able to penetrate sufficiently far into the mystery of God so that we can fashion a meaningful existence for ourselves. Somehow, the result gives us the satisfaction, maybe even the assurance, that we might know what God expects of us in every aspect of our being and in every modality of our own existence – even in our suffering.

So first of all, illness, suffering, misfortune are not God's punishment. They are an inherent, inescapable component of being human, of being part of the created order. Second, to the extent that we are capable of doing so – and this becomes a highly personal matter – they are a test of how we can meet some of the worst setbacks and formidable hurdles that present themselves to us. I have the deepest empathy and even understanding for those who simply break under the most brutal tests of this sort and cannot find the power, the capacity, to transform what is so painful and hurtful into some affirmative response. Such a response is fully understandable, and at one point or another, that was also something that confronted me.

Nonetheless, my understanding of my function as a human in God's world is that I am to try to withstand these tests to the degree that I emerge from them, if not more whole than before, at least capable of functioning. Some of these assaults, as it were, actually produce new strength in the overcoming of them. In the small victories or even the larger victories that we score, there come not only new insights into ourselves and into the reality of which we are a part, but a new sense of our capacity, maybe even power, to deal with such setbacks, such challenges. How we respond to suffering, especially if it becomes known, can be a model for others, with the power to encourage them to call on their own reserves and on resources that otherwise they would not have had the knowledge or the will or the power to use.

It is easy to understand that there are boundary lines in our human capacity to manage these tests and therefore to emerge from them sufficiently whole to continue. It is easy to understand that personal pain and events can break a person, shatter a person. While some of us may have been fortunate enough that this has not happened to us, it should in no way blind us to seeing that this may well happen, and indeed has happened to others. Our deepest respect for their inability to overcome should be absolute, especially since there are those who enjoy inflicting pain, who know that such limits exist, and unfortunately are often successful in reaching and transgressing those limits to the point that they can destroy human beings at will. This is a unique part of the human scene. No other form of existence in the animal world or anyplace else has the capacity to abuse the sensitivity of the creaturely condition in this horrendous fashion.

Suffering is not simply a condition of being human. It is equally and inescapably also a condition both of the individual and therefore of whatever God may be. However God may relate to the totality of being, there is nothing that would be devoid of the presence of God, and therefore of the involvement of God even if a person breaks and is defeated. Part of the story of God's creating Adam tells us that if suffering happens to the individual, then there has got to be an event registered in the Mystery of God as well, whether affirmatively or negatively, whether in terms of the power to overcome and heal or the terrible experience of "shattering of the vessel." Individual suffering not only is not devoid of God, it is somehow another facet of the relationship to which there may be infinite facets.

I am always reminded of the Hasidic story of the devotee of a certain Rebbe who had been away from home to tend his Rebbe some distance from the little shtetl where his family lived. The man, husband and father, comes home unexpectedly to the elation and enthusiasm of the whole family. The next morning he is packing his *peckle* again. His wife challenges him and says "Man, you've just come back. Why are you preparing to leave again?"

He says, "Woman, you won't understand, but I've got to be at the Rebbe's house tomorrow to see how he ties his shoes."

"You want to see how the Rebbe ties his shoes?" His wife is near desperation.

He says, "Yes wife. You see, when the Rebbe ties his shoes, he binds the upper and lower worlds and advances the world toward *shalom*, toward its completeness."

And with that he left.

It is a brutal story in some ways, but what it really says is that there is not anything that is not inherently incapable of being related to and understood in terms of the presence of God. Of course, this is also true of a pebble or a blade of grass, one does not have to go to such magnificence in creation as a constellation. If one can immerse oneself in this understanding of the Mystery of God, there is literally nothing that is devoid of God's presence.

There is a prayer at the very beginning of the Siddur that acknowledges God as the fashioner of the physical body and of all of its multifaceted, almost infinite number of functions. It refers to the fact that all of the openings that should be open are open, all of the openings that should be closed are closed, all the veins and arteries function properly, and so on. This is a manner of acknowledging that there is the evidence of the omnipresence right in that circumscribed singularity that is called my body. This is a profound truth.

The mystics have very often understood how to redirect our thoughts and our understandings from the grand picture and from exquisite rational thought to the everyday, the mundane, and the immediate. Every religious system that has any persistent appeal enshrines this facet, generally termed mysticism, because it is simply a truth. This is why a theological understanding of God, a philosophical understanding of God goes just so far. Often it is a very beautiful and grand structure of reason, but few people live on that level all the time or even often. Maybe nobody. Life, real life, is always lived on different planes: eating food, getting up in the morning, meeting a friend, in suffering, in love, in searching, and in finding.

Again, I do not accept the notion that suffering is God's doing. Somebody happens to be in the wrong place at the wrong time, while somebody else happens to escape. Therefore God helped that one, but God did not help the other one, or God punished the one who perished?! The rejection of this understanding does not mean that there is not a divine presence, it is just that the divine presence is not active in the sense that it operates without me. If I find God where I can, then God is present in the sense that God becomes tangible, knowable, experiential. On the other hand, if I do not respond, it does not mean that God is not there. It is just that I have not found the capacity, or the understanding, or the grace, to see God at that point. Because finally, whether God is there or not depends on my perception, on my capacity and willingness to let the divine enter as a presence. The capacity to shut out is given along with the capacity to receive.

Chapter Six
Beyond Reward and Punishment

But how can a mortal be righteous before God?
(Job 9:2)

$\mathcal{B}$y rejecting the Mystery, the Source of values outside of ourselves, a person may take a position based on total human self-sufficiency, and that inescapably leads to a competition of power. The problem with making this choice is that if the question of morality is totally rooted and subsumed in the human sphere and condition, then ultimately it comes down to the question of who has the ultimate power to formulate the rules and who is to enforce them. Then the question of what it is to be good has no reference outside the human situation. Under those circumstances, for instance, the Nazis' contention that the Jews were like garbage to be burned up and removed from the earth for the well-being of the rest of the humanity was as "moral" as Himmler believed it to be, because there is no measure by which to gauge whether a given set of rules, values, is truer than others.

This leads me to posit that unless a moral system is anchored outside of the human condition, at least to the extent

that those who commit themselves to a given set of values accept them on the belief that they originate not totally within
themselves but in the encounter with a Being beyond them that
we call God, then there is really no valid system of morality
available. History is full of the most devastating consequences
resulting from that choice. Take the history of kings, of dictators, of despots like Hitler, Mussolini, and Stalin. Each of them
chose to set himself up as the final, indisputable source of good
and evil, and their lives ended in a disastrous way for them
and for countless millions of others. Certainly the aftermath
of Stalin's life, just to take one example with whom we are very
much familiar, would not encourage anybody to copy such an
utterly self-sufficient, self-enclosed "moral" authority.

Unfortunately, it is possible to find a given moral life that
can avoid the unfolding of negative consequences. Thus it is
possible to seduce oneself and other people into thinking that
they may be immune from any of the consequences inherent in
faulty morality. There is, as often, considerable delay in the consequences of given choices. Sometimes it can take generations
to realize the connection between a given act and the eventual
aftermath, and to trace and record it. But there are also plenty
of examples to show the more immediate consequences. Any
advantage gained through such a self-centered system is usually
temporary, operational only until somebody comes along who
has the bigger muscles or better equipment. Such success is subject to continuous combat and testing of the means and exercise
of power. It seems to be ultimately self-destructive, suicidal. In
the long run, any assertion of total human self-sufficiency is an
implicit challenge to someone else to become more powerful,
more effective. In reality it is a hidden death wish.

The main question, however, remains. Why act morally at
all? What is the motivation? The traditional standard answer
has been that it is advantageous, profitable, a guarantee against
painful, unwanted consequences. It is the avoidance of punish-

ment whether human or divine. It is the expectation of reward and/or the fear of retribution. The avoidance of divine punishment and the assumption of divine reward has historically been the most effective stimulus for "morality." And it makes little difference whether these fears and hopes are realized in this life or postponed to a "world to come." It is the latter construct that has proven to be the most accepted and successful in ensuring that God would always be right, and that we humans will be always wrong, sinful, and justly punished or perhaps rewarded.

Surely, this massive, well-constructed, and nearly universal understanding is no longer tenable after the Shoah. It collapses utterly in the face of the cruel murder of one and a half million children less than ten years of age for no other reason than their birth, their biology. Any attempt to justify this monstrosity by recourse to a system of reward and punishment by a "just" God is obscene. It flies in the face of ancient assertions by God's own prophets, for example by Ezekiel, that children no longer die for the sins of their parents.

If, then, reward and punishment are false reasons for adherence to a system of morality, what is tenable, what is the alternative? The struggle to find an effective, usable, genuine alternative is ancient. "Do not serve the Master in expectation of a reward, but serve the Master in anticipation of no reward" is taught in the Sayings of the Fathers. Do the right thing, the moral deed, because it is right, for its own sake! Serve the Covenant Partner because that is the covenant's purpose, its intent. Admittedly, this is difficult to achieve, difficult to teach and live, but it is the only possible alternative to the now-defunct reward-and-punishment motif.

The point is that committing oneself to the interactive grounding of a system of values in the assertion of the interaction of the divine mystery and the human mystery is life-affirming. Reliance on human self-sufficiency is simply an invitation for those who are more powerful to impose their will. Sooner or later there will be somebody more powerful, so the grounding of morality in the nonpunitive relation between humans and the divine provides a reliable, more compelling base.

I want to lead a life that is directed in such a way that it might help achieve some of what my understanding of our tradition tells me about God's intentions for human beings: care for the other, the needy, the helpless; avoidance of evil and violence; movement toward peace, toward *shalom*; towards justice; speaking up for those who need someone to speak up for them. All of these are part of what Jews have always understood to be major factors in the *mitzvah* system, as it came down to us through Torah and the prophetic tradition.

In this regard, however, there is a radical shift in the focus of the tradition. We are no longer performing *mitzvot* to be obedient, but rather to bring joy to the One whom we accept as the Source of the *mitzvot* as a constitutive fact of our Jewishness. So the motivation is different, and that is most significant. It makes possible an intimacy with the divine of a sort that obedience never did. It truly makes us "partners."

Since the Jewish Bible is so fundamental not only to Judaism, but also to Christianity, and so deeply influential for so much of what is in the Koran, the construction of obedience is more than basic. It has infiltrated Christian and Muslim thought to the point where it is their dominant idea. There is really no question that reward and punishment is the way that most believers who come out of the biblical background form their understanding of the basic relationship between God and humans.

Those of us who have taught the Bible and told its stories have paid far too little attention to what was happening within God. The key questions of the Torah texts should be: What does this text tell me about God? What does the story picture God to have done, thought, been, acted? Repeatedly, it is very clear that any attribution of omniscience to God is impossible, for God is pictured, directly or implicitly, as being surprised by human acts and thus often moved to anger, clear evidence of not knowing beforehand. At least, that is how the sacred text repeatedly depicts such moments. Moreover, it is clear that in the Torah the deity is not pictured as in total control. In fact, the deity is not in control nearly as much as later theological construction leads us to assume. That imagery and depiction of God is created with significant inferences about the nature of the divine, seen to be absolute, the King.

There needs to be, and hopefully someday there will be, a change in imagery and in perception, and, therefore, also in the understanding that comes from it. This change might be a way to break through barriers that have been erected between, and very often even against, other people's beliefs.

It is no secret that Jews are considered to be subject to punishment because they do not have the truth as others see it and have proclaimed it. We are called stubborn. We have at times been considered close to being infidels because we do not subscribe to key additions to the Jewish biblical and/or rabbinic views as they have been developed by Christianity and Islam. Our very deviation from the additions and persistent adherence to our own viewpoint has very often been a pretext for actions against us and the reality of our being different. Jews have been persecuted because Christians and Muslims have sometimes assumed that they are empowered, by what they believe God to be and how they think God acts, to judge on God's behalf, and then to become God's agents in the infliction of punishment on deviants.

Such a breakthrough in changing our understanding of our relationship with God would be of such profound persuasiveness that it would demolish some of the barriers that have been erected between belief systems. It would become a link between those of us who are struggling for a new understanding of what God might be and how we might relate to God and do God's work.

The kabbalists, the mystics, have intensified a related concept as one of the main keys toward the unlocking of whatever they sense needs to be discovered, or waits to be uncovered. *Kavana* is the intention to abandon the self-protected mode of being, to be willing to remove the protective armor in which we are so often encased either because of what we have experienced in our lives or because we were formed that way. The original meaning of *kavana* in Hebrew is "to direct oneself," an effort that cannot happen when you are loaded down with all kinds of preconditions. More effective penetration toward the Mystery only becomes possible when one divests oneself of all the shells and garments we use to keep ourselves protected, and thus come to the issue or to the moment really almost naked, certainly unprotected. This is what we must recapture, because this is what it means to be creature in the presence of the Creator.

There are several applications of *kavana*. One is toward human beings: to try to be nonjudgmental to begin with, and then to convey to people the willingness to be present unprotectedly – to take the chance even of being hurt. To me this is certainly what I consider to be the contribution I can make to a relationship, particularly when people are in pain, grief, and illness or in joy. To try to let others sense that I make no demands, certainly not for myself; rather to try to be there as totally as I can for the other. This seems to me to be a major contribution to the pastoral function of the religious ministry. All this does not mean that it would compel me to abandon my self, my identity.

That is what I want to be, and can be when I am at my best. Obviously I cannot fulfill myself all of the time. It is what time and time again I try to rally myself to be; because when we are not protected, there is a lot of potential for damage, for pain, for rejection, for all kinds of hurt. Our instinctual first reflex is to try to protect ourselves, not to be open, to be wary.

The hope is always that those with whom we would engage in this kind of unconditional relationship would be capable of a response of a similar nature, a similar quality. If this does not happen, then that effort is wasted and needs to be broken off. There is a level of trust that is indispensable in any interaction, but the level of trust we are talking about when the other is my alter ego, my counter-being, is a much higher level of trust, because we are in a way surrendering some of ourself to the other. Much depends on how we can learn to perceive one another's depth and capacities.

What is being discussed here is not terribly new. Surely the history of human beings with each other is clear evidence that this kind of relationship has not yet worked, or maybe has not been tried sufficiently. There is a reason why it has not been attempted more, and that is that there have been so many failures, and so much hurt. Therefore, the effort to enter into this kind of relationship and live a life guided by this principle is quite often either abandoned or produces so much negative fallout that we and others shy away from it. Nevertheless, despite the risk, this idea cannot be abandoned, because it still is the only way.

I find, on the whole, that when others sense this kind of readiness to be in an open relationship, few take unfair advantage of it. Somehow or other, quite the opposite happens. The others discover in themselves a capacity for a similar openness, and moments spring up between people that are totally remarkable. Good teaching is like this, as well as relationships with those whom one loves.

When I speak to young couples who come to me before marriage, I make the point that marriage is ultimately an exercise in mutual opening of oneself to the other. It is, at bottom, a matter of belief in the other, trust in the other. To speak of a marriage as a 50/50 proposition is a mistake. A marriage is 100 percent and 100 percent, because if one partner holds back, then the other is undoubtedly likely to respond in a similar fashion. Each one needs to be out there totally, and if one of the partners is not capable of that openness, then something is lacking, something fundamental is being diminished.

This also applies to relationships with children, who sooner or later, and probably very early on, can sense the safety and bliss of being taken totally seriously and accepted as what they are at that moment. This does not mean that children do not need to be shaped and formed, but rather that they can sense a basic mutuality in their upbringing.

Experience tells me that most people either have a fear of revealing what they want to express or ask, or do not know what they are really about. It is a kind of self-camouflaging or even self-deception to some extent. Over and over again I try to get fairly quickly to what I sense to be the real issue, because my experience is that most people are either self-protective and shy away from touching what really bothers them, or they are genuinely unaware of what it is. If, after a little while in listening to the person, I can sense it and then penetrate to the underlying cause or layer, then all of sudden, matters that sometimes neither the person nor I expected, get opened up and sometimes even clarified.

This immediately translates to a relationship to God. I attempt it for myself. It is my total attempt to be there for God. Whatever God may be or how God would receive it or respond to it or know about it, I really do not care. It is my gift, my unconditional gift: my gift in response to, among other things, the very fact that there is a world in which to live. As we begin to learn more and more about what kind of a miracle each of us is, it is clear that our bodies, our lives are a total gift. As a result, I am so overwhelmed by what has been given to me that whatever little I do is not enough. I am in a total posture of gratitude. To use Abraham Heschel's most famous, felicitous phrase, I am filled by "radical amazement."

In fact, the scales are all skewed in favor of the Donor, not in favor of whatever I return as a result of my discovery that so much is given to me. I have no difficulty with prayer. It is, to me, my return to the Donor. It is my awareness of my need to say over and over again that I understand how much has been given to me without any merit, without any dessert, without my having worked for it. It is overwhelming. I am in debt all the time. A perhaps unexpected consequence of such an understanding of my identity and relation to God is that I need no further contact, encounter, revelation. Enough, overwhelmingly enough, has already been given me. Hence the traditional Jewish assertion that God no longer "speaks" to us, the prophet Malachi having been the last such communicant, is easily acceptable, though stunning.

There are major differences in this regard between Christianity and Judaism. In Christianity, the possibility of God's interaction by direct word or direct appearance is not only desirable, but considered to be factual and valid. God interacts, and people are visited by God, hear voices, or have personal revelations of God. Judaism is satisfied that we have "heard" enough of what God wants. The point now is the doing of it.

There is another problem. That haunting phrase in Genesis that humans are made in the image of God inevitably leads some of us to project into divinity whatever humanity is. This is the great insight of idolatry. The notion that one's gods are somehow elongated beyond our own humanity and hence less limited than human beings is persuasive. Gods can live a lot longer than people, are mostly untouched by death, even though in most mythologies the gods finally also die. And the gods often are believed to be able to do things that humans cannot. They can journey afar; are less rooted to time and space than we are, and so on.

The self-perception of being human leads to this imagery, this perceiving of the divine in a way that is devoid of all that inflicts limitations on the human, especially death and inescapable rootedness in earth. Paradoxically, the identity of characteristics of the human with the divine can also lead to the exact opposite, namely the abolition of the human, its total merger into the divine. Sometimes this leads to the abolition of the self. The self in this perception is seen as the great wall that hinders us from becoming what we ought to be. Even the attempt to empty oneself can be understood as desirable because sometimes the limitation of the self becomes overwhelming, becomes an obstacle.

There are those who think that in meditation they can escape this limitedness. I frankly do not think it works. The biblical story of creation tells it differently. Adam and Eve are selves, selves with free will. They are counter-players of God. They are portrayed as individual selves in relation and opposition to the self of God. We are all irreducible selves. Ultimately, this is a limitation and a blessing which we simply need to accept.

Even an individual life requires such definitional limits, and once there is community, there must be discipline, order, rules. There cannot be community randomly. The Torah texts indicate that we are to live with each other, and the moment we intend community, then justice is indispensable. A single person, a hermit, a monastic, possibly could exist by himself or herself in total self-control and self-enclosure. However, the moment we start living with others, a whole set of interactions, and it can be a vast set, becomes necessary. These are the threads out of which the web of justice is spun. So justice becomes inescapable and fundamental.

Here again we have a typically Jewish notion that life is to be lived in community, with the other. I think it is fair to say that I can only become myself totally, or even sufficiently, only in relation to the other. It is the other who really helps shape me into the human being I could and ought to be. Without the other I am struggling all by myself, or in fact being seduced into satisfaction with the unfolding of my own self, when in reality it is only possible and necessary in relation to another. So the other, that is, other human beings, is the absolutely necessary and unavoidable framework and setting in which I become who I might be.

But then even that is not enough, because it is too general. It has to be broken down into specifics. How do we do this? How do we advance, guard, nurture life? What is justice? And how is justice administered? To whom? By whom? What are its categories, boundaries, definitions? The same is true with peace, which as a slogan is quite formless. But once we really ask ourselves what it takes to work toward peace, let alone achieve it, then so many complexities and subtleties begin to surface that need to be examined and then implemented that it becomes very clear that merely stating the desire for peace is good, but is totally insufficient.

These categories – peace, justice, the advancement and nurturing of life – need to be accepted as God's specific intention for the human. This is exactly the purpose for which human beings are differentiated from the rest of the created order. The rest of the created order does not have any similar intention or purpose in the pursuit of the ideals and visions that we humans are obviously capable of shaping for ourselves, and of finding in the texts our ancestors created and put before us as guidance and as the norm.

All morality is between humans, though derivatively we have moral obligations to animals and the earth as well. If someone becomes an anchorite or retreats into a Himalayan cave, then one could say, from a Jewish point of view, that he or she is a person who is thereby expressing an ultimate despair and denial of the human situation. Therefore, such persons are not the measurement of what humans could and need to do when they try to live with each other and thereby, by that attempt, make at least a principled affirmation of the possibility of human interaction on a level conducive to ultimate values.

Ultimately one has to live with oneself. Whatever each of us has really tried to do with our own whole being has to be enough. And there must be and will be others also trying similarly. It does not all depend on one person. It cannot. Each of us must find others, possibly even inspire and arouse others to do whatever they can do. The whole process is totally dependent on incremental progress. It is not a revolution. It is by and by, slow and slow, drop by drop, stone by stone, act by act.

Of course there is also the consideration that the human race is still in its diaper stage. Archaeologists have just discovered a skull that could possibly push back the date of the earliest immediate ancestors to *Homo sapiens* by seven million years. Nevertheless, compared to the alleged age of the earth, not to speak of the universe, we humans are still not even toddlers. We are still unable to walk. We use less than 20 percent of our mental capacity. The hope is that as we grow up as a human race, as a phenomenon, that step by step, or sometimes maybe by a great leap forward, we will learn how to be human in a way that we have not yet even the imagination to dream about.

There is no question that, comparatively speaking, we are so new as humans that there are still many basic original ingredients in us that need to be overcome, redirected, and reshaped. Violence is simply part of our human condition at this point, and no one knows of any way to overcome it immediately or even significantly. But it is also clear that if this is the end of our unfolding, then we have not become what we potentially might become, what we might imagine and believe God intends us to become and eventually to be. Optimism in this regard can be based on the fact that when a child is born there is no way of predicting what the child might become with nurture, love, the opportunity to grow. We are in the very earliest stages of being human. After all, the dinosaurs were around for 300 million years before they became extinct, and we have been around for only a tiny fraction of their existence. We are newcomers, a new experiment in life.

Hopefully, we will have hundreds and hundreds of millions of years to keep going and to build better and better levels of being, of life, insight, justice, peace. Some progress has already been made in some aspects, at least by some. But we must not become impatient with the whole human endeavor, and that is an affliction from which both Judaism and Christianity suffer as a result of their messianic vision and belief. In the messianic belief, there is an urgency and a pressure for immediate and early ultimate completion, and that ultimate completion does not mean hundreds of millions of years away to the vast majority of the believers in these two religious systems. Rather it is projected, anticipated, hoped for to be more immediate, say, a few hundred years or at most a few thousand years from now.

Why not hope that the human enterprise, the experiment called *Homo sapiens*, would go on for a billion years, or even longer, to the time when this earth will disintegrate into a burned cinder, leading to the export of humanness into other forms of existence in other parts of the cosmos? What we have done as humans, our being able to think, imagine, create, all of this is just simply too precious, as over against a wolf, say, or even a dolphin, to be totally lost. The incremental advance that we represent over the rest of the created order, somehow or other ought to find a chance to achieve its optimum. And if that is not possible on earth, maybe there should be enough imagination to think of it as carried forward in other places in the cosmos by our own descendants. After all, at one time we seem to have lived as aquatic creatures. In fact, we still do for the first nine months, and then we learn how to breathe oxygen. Maybe we will learn again how to live without oxygen if necessary, to exist on other chemicals, to develop a very different form of life, a vast new step in evolution on a cosmic scale, but one that will still somehow retain all the possibilities and glories of being human to the extent that we now know or recognize it or can discern it.

To be truly human is not to give up or yearn for an early eschaton, an early end-time. To be truly human means to be open to possibilities undreamed of hitherto, to dream of time and time to come of as yet unknowable possibilities. To be truly human means to be of hope unlimited.

Chapter Seven
Reinterpreting Covenant

I will take you to me for a people, and I will be to you a God.

(Exodus 6:7)

*B*ecause the covenant remains the single most important characteristic of Judaism, we should look again at the Torah texts concerning its nature. The Torah says, "Noah was considered to be righteous in his generation" (Genesis 6:9). The rabbinic interpretation of this evaluation of Noah has always been that it can be read in two ways. The first reading is that the whole generation was so bad that even though Noah was not much, compared to the rest he stood out. Or it could be said, and this is great praise of Noah, that while everybody else had become corrupt, Noah had stuck to his own ideals. Therefore Noah is an extraordinary example of goodness and virtue. Thus the rabbis have always understood Noah as a kind of in-between figure, difficult to judge as an example of the prototypical human.

And as for the results, the story of Noah's descendants was no real encouragement to think that human beings had changed substantially. So God needed a new idea, a fresh start, an experiment with a different relationship between the divine and the human.

God needed Abraham. God needed to find someone on whom God could rely, someone who would be a suitable partner for whatever God had intended humans to be. So God sends out the question: "Who will be for me? Who will listen to me? Who is willing without condition to follow me?" God needed Abraham because, according to the Torah, creation had not gone the way God expected.

From God's contact with Noah, it is clear that God has been looking for someone other than those failed experiments called human with which he has had such bad experiences, ultimately even leading to a total breakdown of divine/human relations. And so, after the flood, God begins to seek and needs to find someone who will be willing to relate to God in a new way, someone who will entrust himself or herself to God's guidance. God was really looking for someone with whom he could start a wholly new experience called covenant, a new relationship where there could be mutuality, reciprocal trust. God sends out the question; Abraham answers.

Why Abraham? It is a puzzle. What made him different from the millions of others that God may have tested, constantly probing with the questions: "Who will go for me? Who will be with me? Who will be willing to leave behind all that he was, or imagined himself to be, and come to a truly unknown place?" Only Abraham answers. And this is so radical a departure from anything God had apparently experienced before in any relationship or encounter with any human that Abraham's response is what makes him the first Jew.

Clearly Abraham was able to see beyond the very primitive, pagan religion of his fathers. The rabbis were intrigued by this, and the Midrash tells the story that Abraham's father was a manufacturer of idols. One day his father had to go on a trip and put Abraham in charge of the inventory. While he is gone, Abraham smashes all of the idols except the tallest one. After he finishes the destruction, Abraham puts a stick into the last idol's hand. When his father comes back, he is absolutely aghast at the destruction of his whole collection, his whole wealth, and he questions Abraham, "What happened here?" Abraham responds, "Well, the big idol got angry and smashed all the others to bits." Abraham's father says, "Fool, he can't do that!" And Abraham replies, "And this is the god you worship?"

So the rabbis, in a semi-jocular fashion, indicate their belief that Abraham somehow had an understanding of what deity should be and what the flaws of idolatry were. They further say that before he responded to God, he tested natural phenomena to determine which was the most powerful. Was it finally the moon? The sun? But even the sun went down, and so Abraham believed that there must be something beyond these natural sources of power. These stories try to resolve the question of what made Abraham different, willing to accept without hesitation the invitation to move out that was issued by the unseeable God.

And God says to Abraham, "Go forth from your land, from your birthplace, from your father's house to the land that I will show you." In a way, these three – land, birthplace, and father's house – can be seen as one roadblock after the other to choosing God. Traditional interpreters detected in this progression the remnants of a dialogue between God and Abraham. They suggest that Abraham asks if he has heard correctly each time, "Leave my culture, my country, my family, leave my place in the world?" Each time, the response is the command in his ear, "Move out." According to the Scriptures, Abraham responds totally. He doesn't even ask where he is going or what the purpose is. Instead, at this point he entrusts himself without limitation to that unknown divine presence. It is a pure act of the profoundest trust that Abraham offers God. Abraham, who is free, uses his freedom not to challenge, not to disobey or to distance himself. Instead, Abraham freely entrusts himself to a hitherto unknown God in a gesture so significant and revolutionary that God, in turn, binds the divine to Abraham and his descendants forever. The moment of Abraham's unconditional response to the call of God is so extraordinary, and its power so immense, that it has lasted until this day, over thousands of years, and will last as long as there are Jews and other humans who listen to this story.

It is a radical departure from the relationship God had with Adam, embodied in the prohibitions in the garden. Now, in contrast, there is a promise, a land not known to Abraham, and a vague destiny to become a blessing for all humankind. This is also a totally different covenant than the one God made with Noah after the flood. That covenant was a one-sided undertaking to reassure a frightened, traumatized Noah that God would not again attempt to destroy His creation. There was no implication of or demand for any reciprocity by Noah. It is different with Abraham. God is now dealing with a person who voluntarily entrusts himself, his future, his entire destiny to God without so much as a question about details. It is unprecedented; it opens up an entirely new kind of relationship between God and a human being.

God approaches Abraham in a different manner than had been the case with Adam and his successors. God offers, and Abraham accepts, to be covenanted to each other. The text implies that God has "learned" something, that God understands human beings differently now, that God is testing a new mode of relation. Abraham is the first human in this kind of relationship, and for this reason he cannot function optimally as yet. He does not totally understand what is expected of him. So God tests him repeatedly. Abraham may fail. He may prove to be just an ordinary being, as all his predecessors.

Abraham may also fail because ultimately the covenant is

a very difficult assignment. For those who take it seriously, it is an almost impossible task. To be so intimately linked with God for a purpose is a burden. It is the opposite of chosenness, which is a word that always implies preference. The opposite is true. A destiny has been imposed, a people have been selected out for no other reason except that Abraham apparently had sufficient capability of responding to God, so that God apparently said at last, "I'll try it with him and his descendants. There may be enough here on which to rely, to depend."

As an enticement for Abraham to consider God's invitation, God promises to make of Abraham a great nation. But it can also be looked at the other way around. Abraham's response surprises God, and it pleases God to the point where God progressively raises the stakes of the relationship. In fact, one can read the whole Abraham episode as joy on the part of God at having found somebody who is willing to become God's partner, and maybe even capable of succeeding in this role.

And then comes this utterly delicious but very significant story about Abraham standing up to God and arguing with him over Sodom and Gomorrah. God must have had a wonderful experience. God must have been pleased to have found somebody who not only takes God seriously, but who is also willing to stand up to God. One of the phrases that Abraham uses is, "Should the judge of the whole world not do justice?" (Genesis 18:25). This is a bold, unprecedented act, a radical, cheeky challenge to what supposedly is the divine. No one before had felt emboldened enough to directly question God's intentions. Abraham had the audacity and courage to confront God from a human point of view. Daringly, he sought to bargain with God over the fate of two cities whose evil had, in God's judgment, rightly doomed them to destruction. "What if there should be fifty innocent within the city; will you sweep away the innocent with the guilty?" (Genesis 18:24–25). The discussion ends when Abraham reaches the number of ten possible innocents to be found there, and God breaks off this astounding encounter by leaving.

It is always very dangerous to try to figure out God's mind Nevertheless, a question is raised by this story. Would God rather have someone who grovels and submits, and is always trying to be totally obedient and nonrecalcitrant, or would God want somebody who would stand up and challenge God, and with whom God could really enter into a dialogic relationship? Abraham's unconditional willingness to trust himself to this newly appearing God may have given God an opportunity to experiment with what was perhaps the ultimate that God could expect from a human.

So God tests Abraham again and again, ultimately commanding Abraham to offer up his son Isaac as a sacrifice. Why was this necessary? If God had tested Abraham in Ur of the Chaldees and found him responsive, one might assume that the same God calling again and commanding another impossible act from this new covenantal partner would find him similarly willing. Does Torah want to suggest that God was unsure of Abraham's reaction? Is not God supposed to be omniscient, truly all-knowing, and therefore also able to know Abraham's reply before he gives it? Is God not supposed to be omnipotent, able if desired, to force Abraham's hand?

Even if God knows all, could God be unable to compel compliance? God may have total awareness, although from a human point of view, such awareness is not only never attainable, it is virtually beyond our imagination. We really cannot understand the true depths of that statement. Surely Abraham did not know whether God had fore-knowledge of his response to the divine command. Torah's assertion "and God tested Abraham" (Genesis 22:1) is certainly true for Abraham, but in a very significant way, was it also not true for God?

We experience ourselves as endowed with freedom of will. We know ourselves capable of following God's command and expectations, or disobeying and thus disappointing them. We know ourselves to be, in a measure, free even from God, precisely from God. Why else would there be commandments to do and not do if we were not free and God did not want us to be free? This profound basic fact was established at the very beginning. It was established with Adam and Eve, who promptly used their innate, distinctive, and unique capacity of freedom, so totally different from the condition of all other creatures, to disobey God.

To put it differently, God took the risk in creating Adam that there would now be a creature who willfully, freely, could choose to be with God, against God, or indifferent to God. God did not know Adam's response to the prohibition against eating of the tree of knowledge of good and evil, or else why get so angry as to expel him and Eve from *Gan Eden*? And neither does God know how Abraham will react to the demand to offer up his son Isaac.

The test of Abraham, then, is real. It is not a pretense or, even worse, a cruel game played. God really cannot know what Abraham will do. God can foresee all the many options resulting from this ultimate test, the commandment to offer up Isaac, but God cannot know which of these Abraham will choose. It is a real test.

We still need to ask why the test was necessary. What did God need to know about Abraham that made it necessary to test him so radically, so painfully? Had not Abraham already proven himself to be a reliable covenant partner? Could God not trust him to have the qualities that would make him the root of the people who would become the people of the covenant? Apparently not. Perhaps God had detected a flaw in Abraham that drove God to the ultimate test.

The chapter describing the final testing of Abraham begins, "And it happened after these matters" (Genesis 22:1). Traditionally, these introductory words portend weighty, often painful events to come. By referring to something in the past, the words intend to prepare us for dire consequences. What were "these matters"? The text clearly refers to a significant episode in the relationship between Abraham and Sarah.

So far it has been a most strange relationship. Twice Abraham pawned off Sarah as his sister to save his own skin. First she was taken into the Pharaoh's harem, and then into Abimelech's palace. For what reason? Because she is a beautiful woman who is sexually desirable and, therefore, would be forced into the household of the ruler at the cost of the husband's life. This deception happened twice. It is understandable that after these incidents that Abraham and Sarah may not have had the best of relationships. She may have understood and apparently agreed to the need for the deception, but she could not help being wounded by it. Sarah's barrenness may well have been prolonged by her anger and resentment at being humiliated and turned into a sex object by the man who, as her husband, was supposed to defend and save her from harm. Perhaps her continued inability to conceive was her unconscious response to what she had to understand as a shameful betrayal and humiliation. We know that conception may well depend on proper hormonal levels, and that trust and affection can play a role in the quality of those levels.

Finally, unable to conceive, and eager to ameliorate what her contemporary culture always understood as a defect, Sarah offers Abraham her handmaid Hagar as a sex partner. Hagar promptly proves Abraham's virility by providing him a son, his firstborn, Ishmael, whose name means "God hears." Ishmael thus is presumed to be the legitimate heir, and Abraham's self-esteem was secured. Sarah's was not. On the contrary, Hagar's continuous presence was a constant unbearable reminder of her own lack of ability to conceive. It remained so even after Sarah's own child was born, a child, we are told, who was the result of divine annunciation.

Divine annunciations invite skepticism. For example, Samson is born nine months after his mother goes out into the field alone and returns saying that there she encountered a man who told her that she would have a son. Here we have three strangers who arrive one day and receive a meal and hospitality from Abraham under a shady tree. Sarah remains alone in the tent. After spending the day together, one of them says to Abraham that in nine months Sarah will have a child. And Sarah, who is listening, "laughs." Now the Hebrew word for "laugh" also means "have sexual dalliance." There is no other word. So when Sarah "laughs," is this just a euphemistic translation of the Hebrew? Does the story really say that she had an erotic event? Isaac's name in Hebrew has the same root, the same verb, "to laugh" or "to have sexual dalliance." There is a question then: Did Abraham name him as an offspring of an illicit relationship? Was he really Abraham's son? Did Abraham have any doubts about this? For surely, even if *Yitzhak*, Isaac, does in fact mean "He will laugh," it is a most curious and unusual name.

On the other hand, there is no question about the legitimacy and parentage of Ishmael. Upset and jealous, Sarah demands that Abraham send him and Hagar away. Abraham is so deeply upset by this request of Sarah's, which touches the very nerve of his own selfhood, and is, therefore, a serious challenge to his being, that he consults God as to what he should do. God replies, "Do as Sarah requests" (Genesis 21:22). And what happens? Abraham meekly collapses into obedience and drives Hagar and Ishmael into the desert, a virtual death sentence, and in fact the text tells that it takes a miracle to save the two. Abraham yields despite the fact that Ishmael is his firstborn and Hagar the woman who authenticated his manhood. We may assume that Abraham did so most unwillingly and in great pain. So why did he do it? Why did he not assert himself? Why did he not challenge both Sarah's right to request this removal and God's advice to listen to her? After all, once before he had questioned God's intentions, challenging God's plan in the notorious case of Sodom and Gomorrah.

If Abraham had been moved to confront God over Sodom and Gomorrah, and to challenge God's wisdom in executing their destruction, one would be right to assume that he would make a similar response when confronted with Sarah's bitter demand. After all, the people of Sodom and Gomorrah were strangers to him; here the issue is his own son and substitute wife. Did God expect Abraham to stand up and refuse to send them away? Why did he not question God's justice in this case as he had so boldly earlier, "shall not the Judge of all the earth deal justly?" (Genesis 18:25). The text leads one to conclude that Abraham simply gave in.

Was God disappointed by Abraham's response? Was God astounded to encounter no resistance in such a personal, flagrantly unjust event? It is plausible to conclude that God may now have been doubtful, disappointed, surprised by the action of the man whose earlier defense of justice may have pleased and reassured God that Abraham was the right person to be the covenant partner?

So, it was "after these matters" that God tested Abraham once more to see if he was indeed the human being God was searching to be the new covenantal other. God needed to test Abraham to make sure that he was fit for his ultimate destiny.

But it is also true that this was a two-way test, that Abraham, in truth, was testing God. What God needed was a probing act, the offering up of Isaac. What Abraham needed was to ascertain what God really wanted from him and for him, whether he had understood his relationship with God properly, and whether God's promises were true, that Isaac would be his successor and heir.

Abraham is stirred out of a deep sleep by God. "Take now your son, your only one, the one you love, Isaac" (Genesis 22:2). Traditional interpreters take this curious sequence and read into it the astonished retreat by Abraham, who did not want it to be true that God was ordering him to offer up the only son of himself and Sarah. Because it goes "take now your son," the Midrash reports Abraham objecting, "I have two sons." "Your only one." The Midrash has Abraham reply: "Each is the only one of his mother." "The one you love." "I love both of them." "Isaac." Now he was caught. It was as he may have feared all along: Isaac was God's intended victim.

Abraham's confusion is palpable. But his argument is rather weak, and it is immediately overrun, overruled, overwhelmed. Again, he goes along with the request. Was this God's revenge for his having expelled Ishmael without resisting? Was God now taking the remaining son from him in punishment for not having vigorously protected his firstborn? How could he understand and trust this God who seemed to have encouraged him to give in to Sarah's caprice and now was inflicting a final wound on him? What had God meant when earlier the promise had been given that Isaac was to become his heir, his and Sarah's future life, their continuity? He had entrusted himself and his destiny to this God in Ur. He had believed God about the covenant, about the possession of this new land, about becoming a mighty nation. But all of this now depended on Isaac's life, and now the very same God who had made all these earlier solemn promises was asking for the sacrificial death of Isaac! He really could not comprehend any of this and was overwhelmed by the ultimacy of the catastrophe that loomed before him. Thoroughly confused, he needed to probe God's will and intent. He, Abraham, had to test God.

But another question remains. Perhaps Abraham was willing to offer up Isaac because he was unsure whether Isaac was his son. Maybe he was resentful of Isaac for being the reason he had to send Ishmael away. In any event, Abraham seems only momentarily to have engaged in any kind of resistance or even expressing any doubt at this monstrous demand. The

Midrash says that Satan whispers into his ear, "Don't do it. Don't listen. It wasn't really God speaking." But Abraham persists nonetheless.

When God spoke to Abraham, Abraham answered, "*Hineni.*" "Here I am." Having said "Here I am," Abraham had committed himself, had placed himself at God's disposal no matter how startled and initially tentative his response may have been.

Abraham says "*Hineni*" a second time when Isaac breaks what must have been an unbearably silent journey and addresses him as his father. In the three days since they set out together on this journey, there had been nothing but silence between them. This silence was the inescapable reflection of Abraham's unease, his continuous struggle with whether or not he was doing the right thing, whether he should really go ahead with God's command or turn around and refuse to comply. This *hineni* is measurably different from the first. It is meant to reassure his son, to show Abraham's readiness to acknowledge Isaac's presence, to give him to understand that he senses his son's perturbed state of soul. The silence, after all, must have hung heavily between them, probably unusual and ominous. Abraham may even have been relieved that Isaac had addressed him, though his brief reply did little to reassure Isaac, and, on the contrary, may have reinforced his sense of foreboding. But, again, he was not evading, not hiding. He was there; "*Hineni*, here I am."

There was to be a third *hineni*. When Abraham and Isaac arrive at the place of sacrifice, "He stretched out his hand, took the knife to slay his son, and the angel of God called out to him: Do not stretch out your hand against the lad and do him no harm." Abraham answered, "*Hineni*" (Genesis 22:11). Only this *hineni* was one of profoundest relief at this reprieve.

We need to look closely at this story, not only at the rabbis' questioning of Abraham's resolve to go along, but also at the clear sense of the Torah and the rabbis that Isaac is not a child. Isaac is a full-grown young man, perhaps even in his thirties, and certainly he is not unaware of what is happening. The questions he asks indicates there is something going on that does not make sense to him. First of all, the walking three days in silence with each other, except for an occasional question by Isaac, must have been unusual. Second, they are going to make an offering, and there is nothing to indicate what the substance of the offering is to be. Surely it must have occurred to Isaac, "It is me?" Abraham's terse reply, "God will furnish the lamb for the sacrifice," could not have reassured him. On the contrary, it would have increased his unease, his awareness that things did not add up.

Therefore, when Abraham and Isaac get to the point of making the offering, there are complications in the story. One of them is that Abraham is an old man. If he was one hundred years old when Isaac was born, and now Isaac is in his thirties, one must ask how an old man could overwhelm and bind a strong young man in his prime. How could an unwilling, resisting Isaac be bound and placed on the altar? So it is quite clear that Isaac must have collaborated in his being sacrificed. Why?

Is it the son's final gift to his father? Isaac apparently understands that his father is doing this, not out of spite or whim, but because God had commanded him to do so. Isaac really is Abraham's "son," and is willing to let his father live up to and act out his understanding of an obligation imposed on him by his having entered into the covenant with God. Isaac was willing to confirm and establish Abraham in this unprecedented role and identity. Without Isaac's tacit complicity, Abraham could never have been in a position to fulfill God's command to offer up Isaac. So great was Isaac's love for his father, and so great his grasp of the strange bond between Abraham and God, that the son is willing to let the father square himself with his God even if it is at the cost of his own life. There is something in Isaac here that is utterly, astonishingly admirable.

If there were any doubt that the Torah implies that God needed to test Abraham because He could not foretell his compliance, the text settles the matter: "Now I know that you would not withhold your son, your only one, from Me" (Genesis 22:12). *Now* God knew, not before. *Now* God could be sure, but not before the test. God had to learn, and had learned, a reassuring fact and truth.

And Abraham had also learned something. He now knew that the earlier promise concerning Isaac was true, reliable, firm. There was to be continuity and future. Set on bringing an offering to God, Abraham found a goat conveniently caught in a thicket to serve as a substitute for his son. It is the conclusion, the completion of a sequence that until the last moments seemed headed toward catastrophe. This closes the incredible, pain-laden episode.

Or perhaps it does not. The Torah states, "And Abraham returned with his two servants to Beersheva. And Abraham dwelled in Beersheva" (Genesis 22:12). There are at least two remarkable omissions here. The returning party consisted of three persons, Abraham and two servants. Conspicuous by his absence is Isaac. A daring medieval commentator explained his absence by suggesting that God's angel came too late, that Abraham had gone through with the sacrifice and had slain Isaac, and a miracle of resurrection was later needed in order to lead smoothly into the chapters following this story that describe Isaac's life and fortunes. This fanciful alternative may well have been influenced by Christianity. More traditionally, the Midrash says that Isaac went to study Torah with his ancestor Enoch, who had established a yeshiva. After all, where would a nice Jewish boy go when he is seen as absent from his father's house? Obviously, the story is just a way of trying to explain away the silence concerning Isaac's absence from the return.

Or one could come to the simple conclusion that Isaac no longer wanted to have anything to do with Abraham. Isaac's absence from the text may be implicit evidence of a break between son and father that was never to be healed. Nothing in the Torah reports that Isaac ever sees his father alive again. For instance, there is no mention of Abraham when Isaac marries Rebekah. Even though it was Abraham who sent his trusted servant to find a wife for his son, significantly, Isaac takes his wife to his mother's tent. That is fascinating in itself. In other words, Isaac is really in his mother's ambience. There is no mention of a wedding, anything to signify the arrival into the clan of the wife of the heir. So there appears to be a total rupture of relations with the still-functioning head of the clan, Abraham.

Isaac apparently bore the stigma of his father's near-sacrifice of him throughout his entire life. This is attested to by his generally passive demeanor and the fact that he is the one patriarch who is more victim than actor, more recipient of his fate than active producer or participant in it. In a way, then, he may never have recovered from being bound. Apparently his spirit was broken. The event on Mount Moriah left an indelible, irreparable mark.

The other equally conspicuous absent person is, of course, Sarah herself. Not only is there not a word of her being notified, let alone consulted, when Abraham took her son away, but also there is no word about her when Abraham returns to Beersheva. The next time Sarah's name appears in the text is after her death. Apparently, it was told to Abraham that "Sarah had died" (Genesis 23:2). And where had she died? In Hebron! Apparently, Sarah is gone when Abraham returns to Beersheva. This incident, the binding of Isaac, shatters Abraham's life irreparably. Apparently he is left without son or wife. Isaac takes Rebekah to his mother's tent, which was still standing even though she is gone. At Abraham's death, Isaac and Ishmael come to bury him, apparently reconciled over their father's grave. Abraham is buried with Sarah, thus reunited in death, but immediately after the binding, he is left solitary.

There is still one other possible sequel to the story of the Binding of Isaac. In this reading, Abraham fails the test. Why did he yield to God when he sent Ishmael away and was apparently willing to sacrifice Isaac? Perhaps God wanted Abraham to stand up and challenge the divine will, as he did at Sodom and Gomorrah.

Is this the reward for submitting oneself to God's test and apparently passing it successfully? Did the father of the covenantal people, himself a covenant partner of the covenantal Lord, deserve such a fate? Painful questions these, leading to the query whether the covenant is a prize or a burden, a blessing or a destiny to be borne stoically. Probably both are true, and at the same time. Covenant is a gift, but also an obligation. It is an act of grace by a loving God, but also a task difficult if not impossible to carry out adequately. It is a boon, but also a fateful burden. Abraham began to understand all this, although his biological and spiritual descendants have often forgotten the lesson. To be God's people is at least as much an impossible task as it is the blessed evidence of God's grace and love.

Abraham was the first in the tradition, first in understanding the inevitable ambivalence of knowing God and becoming God's covenantal partner. His acceptance of God's promise is ours, but so is his pain and woundedness. Abraham experienced and came to understand that God is not an easy partner, and that it is not easy to enter into partnership with God. On the other hand, Abraham learned and teaches us that the only worthwhile life is achieved through bonding with God. Isaac lived, and handed on the painfully gained, ever enlarging insight into that bond out of which flowed and continues to flow the impulses of justice and love, visions of healing and peace, that are the heart of so much Jewish and human striving and hope.

It is through this utterly novel manner of accepting God that Abraham becomes the ancestor of the Jewish people. It is in this act of trust that he becomes the root out of which all else will grow. There are renewals of the covenantal bond, first with Abraham himself, then with his son Isaac, and with his grandson Jacob. And, most significantly, an entry into covenantal bonding with the entire community at Mount Sinai. They, the now numerous descendants of the first covenantal Jew, are being invited by God to enter into a communally covenanted relation. No longer is it just individuals in this new relationship. Now it is the entire community freed from Egyptian slavery that freely accepts the divine invitation. "I will take you to me for a people, and I will be to you a God" (Exodus 6:7). This is the culmination of the new way by which God seeks to test the readiness of human beings to be God's partners and not antagonists, to be God's helpers in the promotion of the good impulses of the original creation and not God's adversaries.

This is not an elevation to a superior plane of favor and destiny. It is conceived as a collaboration on the part of the Jewish people with a God who desperately needs a new way of using human beings to fit into the original purpose of creation. The people respond to this challenge, *"Na'aseh v'nishma"* (Exodus 24:7), "We shall do it and hear." In other words, we will do it unconditionally, and only then will we hear. This incredible answer of the people at the foot of Mount Sinai fulfills a yearning and need in God to find willing human partners to help unfold and promote an incomplete creation. It is also a radical commitment by the people to an unknown and unknowable future. And while it is abundantly clear that this newly found human partner, the Jewish people, will not and perhaps cannot ever fully live up to the inherent and explicit consequences and demands of the covenant, the relationship has endured to the present day.

And yet, the way the story of the Exodus is told has a major puzzle in it. The Torah text actually says that God remembers the pain of the slavery of our ancestors. So why did it take so long? Why was it necessary, by the adjusted reckoning of time, that some two hundred years of slavery had to be endured? Twenty years of slavery was not enough? Fifty years of slavery was not enough? Why did the people have to be put through this prolonged and devastating experience?

There is another fundamental question. The story of the golden calf is the story of the quintessential sin of the people. According to the text, the creation of the golden calf happened after the people became desperate and panicked because both God and Moses had disappeared. Here was a people, newly freed from slavery, unaccustomed to the desert, who are left leaderless for a long time. Finally, after "forty days," this leads to a tremendous upheaval, which then in turn leads to awful consequences. The people seek reassurance by returning to what they may have been doing in Egypt all along, namely the worship of an idol. Could not God have foreseen this? Should not God have known that when God kept Moses for "forty days and forty nights," as the story tells it, something like this was bound to happen? Why did God not send Moses down after eight days? Why wait forty days and then punish, and punish draconically, severely?

The way the story is told asks us to pay attention to what was happening within God. As with the stories in Genesis, the key question with Torah texts of this kind concerns what they tell about God. What does the story picture God to have done, thought, been, acted? And over and over again, one perception is very clear. Any attribution of omniscience to God is impossible unless God is depicted as monstrous, unless God is depicted as being willing to play a cruel game with the most hurtful outcomes and results for the people. In the Torah, the deity is not pictured as being in total control. In fact, the deity is not in control nearly as much as later theological construction would indicate. In these two instances alone, surely the whole notion of omniscience is not just of radical concern, it is completely contradicted.

Central to the identity of the people and to its faith commitment is the Jewish people's understanding of their covenant with God. Initiated with the first Jew, Abraham, and then with the other patriarchs, the covenant was concluded with the entire people in the epochal theophany at Mount Sinai. Judaism's greatest teacher and leader, Moses, guided the people and taught and interpreted God's will to them. Torah is the written enshrinement of the teachings, commandments, and history of the ancient Jewish people and now, as it has always been, is at the center of the community and is its lifeblood.

The covenant, at bottom, is the understanding of an unbreakable bond between God and people, and the mutual commitments and expectations that flow from it. The key to all of it is reciprocity, mutuality. God and people are interactively related to each other, mutually dependent on one another. In the dynamic interplay between the "partners" lies the secret to clearly understanding the roles of each partner, as well as the expectations and disappointments unavoidably built into such a dialogic bond. The Jews need for their very survival various forms of belief in God and the commitment to discover and live by their diverse interpretations of God's will and demands upon them. And God? God needs the Jews to witness to the fundamental truths they have learned about the infinite mystery of the divine, and to the moral imperative and ritual norms springing from this compelling, everlasting search for meaning and fulfillment.

God is the God of the Jewish covenant community, but also and equally of all the world. The Jewish people are called to be witnesses to their God by their lives. The specific understanding and revelation of God to them is not only for their own use and exaltation, but ultimately for all humanity. It is humans, as far as we know, who alone know God, probe God's mystery, and seek to live by insight into it. The way to God is only by way of humans. Not only are we bound to God, but God inescapably needs humanity.

At first blush, Scripture seems to exalt God to dimensions where God becomes impervious, all-powerful, all-knowing. This is, however, not the prevailing insight into the divine found in the Scriptures. Humans arouse God to anger, are clearly depicted as inflicting pain on God, causing God to suffer. The stories of Adam and Eve, the murder of Abel, the Tower of Babel, and many others depict God as painfully surprised by human acts. Over and over again, we find that biblical texts lead us to understand in particular that God suffers.

For some Jews, this sounds too Christian. It is important to remember that Christianity came out of Judaism, and that the suffering "son" is a Jewish understanding, as, for example, Isaac's three-day journey and binding.

The classic covenant text in Torah is "I will take you to me for a people, and I will be to you a God" (Genesis 6:7). Right from the very beginning, this needs to be read and heard as a mutually binding relationship. Then, much later a talmudic interpretation spins it to read: "*If* you are my witnesses, then I will be your God." This is connected to the passage from Isaiah: "You are my witnesses, and I am Adonai" (Isaiah 43:12). One interpreter reads it: "As long as you are my witnesses, so to speak, I will be God." These nuanced interpretations indicate that the relationship is mutually dependent; it is not only humans who depend on the divine. In a very strange way, the divine depends on the human.

Chapter Eight
Creating *Tikkun Olam*

Then I heard the voice of the Lord saying, "Whom shall I send? And who will go for us?" And I said, "Here am I. Send me!"

(Isaiah 6:7)

*W*hen I was an active rabbi, I never went to bed having the sense that I had accomplished everything I needed to do that day. There were always additional tasks, sometimes more, sometimes fewer, that I knew I needed to do but could not, simply because I was only one person and only had so much time, so much will, so much energy to give. Each of us, in our very circumscribed understandings of who we are and what we can do, each of us is continuously confronted by our inability to do even a minor fraction of what we perceive needs to be done. Time and again, therefore, we are subject to despair and even to paralysis because the need becomes so overwhelming that we are literally willing to throw in the sponge and say: "This cannot be fixed. It is beyond me. No matter what I do, it is not enough."

Being active in local, national, and international organizations is, in part, a way to combat that despair, to overcome it by associating with bright, competent, goal-oriented people with a vision for the well-being of humanity and the earth, and with the will to work on such goals and issues. I am currently only active in a few of the organizations to which I used to belong. One is the Parliament of World Religions. I have been on the program committee for several terms, since 1988. I also still serve on the board of directors of the Millennium Institute, where I serve with fascinating people with whom I otherwise would not have come in contact. My role on the board was jokingly described to me as "moral irritant." In truth, the opportunities for that kind of expression are rare, which is an indication of the quality of the leadership and the stature of the other participants.

It is this tension between the overwhelming need and our ability to address the need, this paradox, that is really at the heart of our humanness. It is only under these circumstances that we can even venture into becoming a partner of God. First, we must realize that we are not God, and second, that God apparently assigned this task through Adam to all humans. We are given this assignment for reasons springing inescapably from our understanding that creation cannot be perfect – it would, perhaps, *be* God otherwise. The dilemma is this: even as, or precisely because, we know that each of us has to do something, yet we know we cannot do it all. Even what we can do we often cannot do well enough or sufficiently. In order to keep from judging ourselves as failures, the result of which would induce a paralyzing despair, we need to understand that we have no right to quit. This is a very hard wisdom to come by, because it is very easy to despair and to simply give up, to surrender to whatever other ways there are of being in the world.

What do we do in the face of this new understanding of our potential and the overpowering realistic need? We can take refuge in the saying from Pirke Avot that has virtually become the motto for my life: "It is not up to you to complete the work, but neither are you free to desist from it."

The ultimate definition of the human identity as understood by Judaism is to become God's helper in the fixing up, the repairing, the gradual unfolding toward a higher level of perfection of the created order. This leads to the other major component of Jewish identity, and that is hope. Because in a way, if reaching toward greater perfection is our assignment, then there is a powerful implicit promise that it is possible to achieve it, and that is the basis of hope. The ultimate trust in God is to trust that this unfolding, this fulfillment of the human identity is possible. Therefore, any of the defeats we suffer, any of the many mistakes we make, are not the ultimate. Rather, they are just the inevitable price we pay for not being God, but instead are human, with all of our virtues, and also our limitations. With all of this having been said, *tikkun olam* is a statement of the ultimately possible, the ultimately necessary, and therefore, of the drive toward the end that needs to be found and released in the human enterprise, step by step.

In other words, we are beings with multiple levels. If we know that one of our possibilities, perhaps our ultimate possibility, is to be linked to that Mystery which can be sensed in everything and that is all-pervasive and omnipresent, then the potential consequences for each of us are enormous, exceedingly vivifying, exciting, and energizing. On the other hand, once we understand ourselves not to be eternally dependent upon a powerful and ever-functioning, saving, rewarding God, once we see ourselves as engaged on God's behalf, a God who has assigned these tasks totally to us as humans, then we are threatened by being overwhelmed by what is simply a huge of amount of injustice, of evil, of lack of completion. Often we experience an accumulation of grievance, suffering, and evil that is well-nigh overpowering.

What we can learn from Martin Buber, and what needs to be attempted, is to live in unconditional openness and a total willingness to take the risk of vulnerability. One should not approach life, or whatever God may be, with preconditions and preset expectations, or with defensiveness and self-protection. Unconditional openness is the ultimate stance for the experience of *emuna,* trusting faith. It is to be vulnerably present to the Mystery.

This vulnerability has two immediate applications. The first is toward human beings, and that is to try to be as nonjudgmental as possible to begin with, and then to convey to people our willingness to be present without protection and, therefore, to take the chance of being hurt. This is the contribution we can make to a relationship, particularly when people are in pain, experiencing grief, illness, joy, or whatever. We need to try to let others sense that there are no demands, no preset conditions, certainly not made by ourselves. *We need to be there as totally as we can for the other.*

Then this vulnerable stance immediately translates to a relationship to God, however we speak of God. How God receives it, responds to it, or knows about it is not important. What is important is the total willingness to be there as a gift from the human to the divine.

One could trace such developments as evidence of growth within the believing community as it becomes acquainted with God and increasingly understands itself to not be totally dependent on God, but instead encouraged, called on, challenged, to assume, as part of the relationship, greater and greater responsibility. As the Shoah demonstrates to me, if God is not capable of interfering in such a way that evil is averted, then it becomes very clear that what God demands of us now is to be God's instrument, God's "other," God's partner. Most likely this has always been true, although it became hidden and overlaid by the servant and dependency model and belief.

My ultimate understanding is that *hineni*, "Here I am," is what God wants of each of us, maybe even what God *needs* of us. Since the Shoah, it seems likely that what God wants of us and needs of us are the same. God's self-induced reduction of power and, concomitantly, God's suffering have become overwhelmingly evident. This suffering induces a desire to somehow have God be reassured that we are here, and perhaps to even find some joy in our unconditional response. What God needs is my *hineni*, my presence.

Hineni can have many nuances. As we know from the story of the binding of Isaac by Abraham, there are three. First, when God calls Abraham in the middle of the night, he answers "*Hineni* – here I am." And again, when Abraham replies to Isaac on the journey taking Isaac up to be sacrificed, Abraham answers, "*Hineni*." Finally, at the moment when Abraham would have slain Isaac, the angel stops him, and Abraham says, "*Hineni*." Samuel likewise responds to God saying, "*Hineni*, here I am." Each of these takes place in a different setting and has a profoundly different meaning. Always, however, the response indicates a readiness to respond, a willing vulnerability, an unconditional acceptance.

I have already been given much more than I ever knew I would receive and certainly did nothing to deserve: my very life; the universe in which I meet God as Creator and other human beings; the whole, virtually infinite list of gifts of which I am conscious. Being the recipient of so much forces me into a basic stance of not only being willing, but also feeling an irresistible total need, to give something back. *Hineni* represents my gratitude, my willingness to do, my awareness of being graced.

When I am at my best – and none of us can achieve all that we desire of ourselves all of the time – the way I want to relate to the world and to God is represented by *hineni*. Time and time again, I try to rally myself to achieve this goal because this open stance, this vulnerability has a lot of potential for damage, for

pain, for rejection. One is not protected. Our instinctive first reflex is to try to protect ourselves, to not be so open, to always be
a bit wary and careful. I have found, however, that when others
sense such readiness to be there, few take advantage. Somehow
or other, quite the opposite happens. They discover in themselves a capacity of a like nature, and remarkable moments of
mutual presence and trust spring up between people.

There is nothing sacrificial in this way of relating to the
world and to God. It is a willingness to share whatever very
deeply engages me, or makes me who I am, with the other. The
paradox is that this openness and vulnerability enlarges and
deepens us, so that there is actually joy and a sense of being
fulfilled and restored.

To be a person of *emuna* requires this openness, this awareness, this intentionality. The kabbalists, the mystics have taken
the concept of *kavana* as one of the main keys toward unlocking whatever they want to discover, or what they sense needs
to be discovered, or waits to be uncovered in themselves. Intentionality is the willingness to remove the protective armor
in which we are so often encased, either because of what we
have experienced or because it is in our nature. *Kavana* is the
intention to abandon that mode of being. This self-direction
cannot happen when we are loaded down with all kinds of preconditions, but only becomes possible when we divest ourselves
of all the "shells," or "garments," and come to the issue or the
moment almost naked, unprotected. This is what it means to
be a creature in the presence of the Creator.

The question of why God created anything at all is one of
the key puzzles with which anyone who thinks about creation
in any depth is likely to wrestle. One possible answer is that
God created in anticipation of what would arise as sequel to
the act of creation, namely the human being. God was perhaps
expecting a partner, a respondent, an other, who could be a
joy to the Creator, who could provide an additional capacity

for fulfillment, an enrichment. Creation could then really be considered an act of loving anticipation of God's own growth or fulfillment. To put it in a different way, we can imagine, because all of this is our fantasy, God being all alone before creation. From our human point of view, we can then conjecture that after untold eons of such solitude, God became slightly dissatisfied, perhaps eager to try a different kind or form of being. Certainly God was willing to enter into the risk of the other, because the other is always a risk, and immediately of necessity incomplete and therefore possibly flawed, and if in fact it is our task to help complete, or at least advance, the nature of the created order, then this is the elevation of our role to a level that is other than parent/child. A child is never called upon to take such responsibility while still seen as a child. If we are no longer the dependent child, but are instead elevated somehow into a relationship that is closer to being a partnership, then our status and relationship to the Partner is no longer described by parent-child imagery. A new relationship requires a new kind of language.

Even in our modern practices now in rearing children, we have come to levels of understanding in which children are being drawn increasingly into decision-making processes, and become not just the created dependents of the creator parents, but are taken in as part of the family community. Depending on what the decisions have to be and how they are arrived at, children are increasingly given a much greater share of responsibility. Responsibility is an important word in this context, because it comes from responding to other people, to specific tasks, even to an idea. This modern progress is a very wholesome development, and if it is possible in family life, in child-rearing, then it ought not to be so difficult to also envision it in our relationship to God.

With this new language and imagery, the impact of the Shoah begins to center not only on the terrible loss and catastrophe that befell the Jewish community and the unstoppable pain of that loss and breakdown, but also on the question: What did it do to God? What about God? With this expansion of focus, our whole understanding and therefore also our relationship to God must undergo a major change.

With regard to the *mitzvot* system, the fact that God could not stop the Shoah and could not respond to the billions of prayers uttered for relief, indicates that one of the images of God that needs to be incorporated into the lives of the faithful is of a God who at bottom is not powerful, but needy. We need to understand a God whose main relation to us is not that of the superior, with limitless power, ruling and reigning and demanding, but rather a God who is currently in terrible need of reassurance. Horrible things have happened in God's world that God apparently did not anticipate, did not stop – because God could not. Therefore, God must be in excruciating, maybe unstoppable pain. Pain exists not just for the humans on whom it has been afflicted, but possibly also for God.

Just as it is certainly a *mitzvah* for us to try to do whatever we can to soften pain and bring help to fellow humans who are in need and who cry out, it appears that this is what God also needs. In other words, God does not need the individual as an obedient servant so much as a helper, as a comforter. The question we need to each ask is: How can I bring comfort to God?

The answer, in a most profound sense, is simply by letting God know that we are here, and here for God. That we are here for *God alone* may be a reassurance to God, because there are many who are no longer for God, never have been for God, or are not for God in any way that would make a difference.

To be for God in a way that makes a difference is to lead a life that is directed to achieve some of what Jewish tradition tells us are God's intentions for human beings. These intentions include caring for the other; avoiding evil and violence; working toward peace, toward *shalom*; helping the needy, the helpless;

speaking up for those who need someone to speak up for them. "Justice, justice you shall pursue" (Deuteronomy 16:20). All of these are part of what our ancestors understood all along to be one of the major foci in the *mitzvah* system, certainly as it has come down to us through the prophetic tradition.

In this regard, a slight shift in focus is called for, but an important one. We are not performing *mitzvot* to be obedient, we are performing the *mitzvot* in an to attempt to bring joy to the One whom we accept as the source of the *mitzvot*, and as a constitutive fact of our Jewish and human identity. So the motivation is different, and this change in focus makes possible a degree of intimacy with the divine that obedience never did or could.

We return again to that haunting phrase in the Torah about our being made in the image of God. It is best understood as a probing of the mystery that bonding is possible, a relationship possible between God and the human that we do not have with a tree or an animal, or even with another human, even though those relationships are often very close and similar. Bonding and relationship are strange terms to use in this context. But all of our language, including the theological, comes from our human experience. We have nothing else. Language is rich, subtle, and highly useful, but it also limits what we as human beings can experience and say. So whatever God is, we express it in those terms that are our only avenue of expression, in human language. Of course, the Talmud insists on this anyway. It says repeatedly: "The Torah speaks human language."

The "Ground of all Being," Tillich's phrase, out of which everything that can be experienced and understood has somehow sprung, is just a phrase that is trying to paint a picture of the Mystery we must confront. In this early stage of the human journey, words are certainly the best tool we have in our human armamentarium with which to express ourselves. Human language can be very subtle and nuanced; however, each word also can, and needs to, carry the load of definitional precision. Hence, words are inherently incapable of conveying what may really be ultimately unspeakable, ineffable.

Thus, sooner or later, it becomes clear that the only way to confront that which cannot be spoken is by saying "Mystery." Mystery is the term to which we are virtually compelled to resort because we are confronted by the immensity of what is not only the unknown, but is mostly unknowable from a human point of view. It is just there and cannot be bound in the shackles of language. The moment we try to choose words, and all words define, we are attempting to constrain, set limits to the Mystery. We try to use words to deal with the ultimately wordless, unwordable, that which is beyond the capacity of a human to imprison in words, because if we could find the right words, then we would be the ones in charge. We are then defining the Mystery, giving it outline, and precision. Inherently this is not what one can do with God. All our words concerning God are, at best, hints, allusions, approximations.

It is also clear that we are not a community of the silent. Quite the contrary, we are very verbal. We talk a lot, we think a lot. Thought, too, is in terms of definition because thought also uses words, and whether they are spoken or soundless does not really matter. And we write. We were the first civilization to center around books. Our sacred texts, even if originally oral, were eventually written down. In this for us they became the very foundation of our belief system, of our traditions.

The very fact of being an individual is a definitive term, which tells that we are so tall, so heavy, so old, and so on, inescapably sets up a framework of limitation. It is quite clear that each of us has a framework we have been given, but we need to understand that even though this is what we have been given, it is not our totality. We each have the capacity to transcend ourselves and the given limitations, if only to a point. Our transcendence is couched in language, speech, and thought.

The notion of the self as a great wall, an entrapment that hinders us from becoming who we ought to be, and therefore that the self should be abolished, does not fit into the biblical understanding of the relationship of Creator to creature and of being the creature of a Creator. This perception does not mean a total and utter dependence; it means relatedness. Though we are created, it is precisely because we are created that we have final meaning, an irreducible presence while alive. Ultimately, these our limitations are simply something we need to accept and bear.

Some people understandably think that in meditation they can escape this limitedness. Sometimes the limitation of the self becomes overwhelming, and there is the drive, the desire, the attempt to empty oneself. However, each of us is a self, and each of us needs to remain a self. The statement that humans are made in the image of God may lead some to project onto divinity whatever humanity is, but it is improper and excessive to assume God to be a self in the same way we humans are. The biblical "likeness" is a metaphor, a hint that the divine Mystery and the mystery inherent in being human are capable of relation.

With the appearance of Adam a radical shift occurs. God now hands over creation, the created order, to Adam and his descendants. God was in total unchallenged control in Paradise, *Gan Eden*. None of the nonhuman and prehuman elements of creation gave God any trouble. But Adam and Eve immediately cause fundamental trouble, so much so that God expels them from Paradise. Now that *Gan Eden* no longer exists, because it disappeared after the expulsion, the world is in our hands. We have a choice; we can either be God's opponent and ruin it, foul it, even destroy it. Or we can become God's partners, God's agents, in what is, according to Jewish tradition, the *tikkun olam*, the gradual fixing up of the world, the created order, which is not perfect, not flawless to begin with. The flawlessness of *Gan*

Eden is gone irretrievably. It is replaced by the covenant. The mythic construct of a perfect *Gan Eden*, Paradise, in itself an image of unrealizable perfection, gives way because of Adam and Eve to the recognition of a world in need of work, of improving, of perhaps striving toward a discovery of such perfection as has never existed in reality. Fantasy is replaced by the obligation and opportunities of covenant.

The goal of the covenant has always been *tikkun olam*, fixing up of the world, except that it must also be said that the notion of humankind's involvement in this assignment, and to an extent even our understanding of our ultimate destiny, is not explicit in the biblical working out of the implications of our covenantal understandings and relationships. *Tikkun olam* as a concept is not stated that way in biblical texts; it is a rabbinic discovery and understanding

In light of the Shoah, the question of the covenant's meaning and continued validity shifts noticeably, if not radically. It is no longer God who is expected, and has been assumed, to shoulder the responsibility for the maintenance and perdurance of this divinely instituted experiment of a different relationship between the human and the divine. It is now ours. We, the human partners in the covenantal relation, now understand the necessity to become the guarantors, the maintainers of this unique bond unless we are prepared to declare the covenant at an end, to write *finis* to the experience of the first three thousand or more years which has given us a unique sense of our place in the world. Unless we say to God that this experiment, begun so magnificently with Abraham, is a failure and therefore doomed, then we need to rescue it, breathe new life into it by added care and devotion. Above all, we need now to reassure God that creation is still valid, that God's intention to fashion a cosmos in which we have a meaningful place and an assignment to help move the creation toward *shalom*, wholeness, still holds. In a strange yet stunning fashion, we now know what was perhaps always implicit but has become glaringly explicit, that God depends on us, needs us, simultaneously with and comparably to our need of God.

That this was the meaning of the life of the covenant from its beginning we understand more fully now, and so it is to this day. By being God's indispensable partners and helpers in *tikkun olam* – in the ever necessary, incessant, and still far from complete repair and advancement of the created world, in the forging of such relations and bonds with earth and, above all else, with human beings of every kind, of every place – we will help advance life to come ever closer to the visionary dream goal of *shalom*.

Chapter Nine
Does God Still Speak?

Call to me and I will answer you; I will tell you things
great beyond the reach of your knowledge.

(Jeremiah 33:3)

In Christianity it is assumed that anyone can have direct contact with the divine, and individuals often claim it. Not only
Joan of Arc, but many hundreds of thousands, even millions
of people, some of them living right now, claim to have had
direct communication from God. When I was organizing the
camp in Oconomowoc for our Reform Jewish movement, I
needed a cook. I contacted the woman who had cooked for
the former owner of the camp. She told me that, having heard
that the camp was being sold, she had agreed to cook for her
Baptist community, which had a camp in Minnesota. She was
very regretful, but she could not help me. Three or four days
later, I got a phone call. It was the same woman. "Rabbi," she
said, "I prayed, and God told me that I should cook for you.
So I told the Baptists I wasn't coming, and I'm coming to cook
for you this summer."

Well, it happened to be a solution to a major problem I

had, and I was very grateful. But the notion that this woman really believed that God had given her a direct command, as it were, and not just a hint, has always been puzzling to me, to say the least.

Incidentally, she knew her Bible as none of us did. Whenever we needed a quotation we would go into the kitchen and ask Emily. She had a Bible on top of the stove, and she would take it down and within moments would find the passage we were struggling to identify.

But this kind of divine communication is not a Jewish concept. Jews do not have individual covenants. Since Sinai, I have had a covenantal relationship with God as a result of my being part of the covenantal community. That community is not faceless, it is not a blob, it is made up of individuals, but the individual gets his or her standing, character, identity from within the community. From the traditional Jewish point of view, God has ceased communicating directly. The rabbinic movement, the Pharisaic movement, established and defended the assumption that whatever the oral tradition was, it came from the same time, event, and source as the written, namely Sinai. With that fictive assumption, it established the rabbis' authenticity and their claim to authority. The rabbis successfully implanted this assumption in the Jewish tradition and the lifestyle of the Jewish people. The whole methodology which they developed – the minute inquiry into the meaning of words, the freedom, deriving from this methodology, to expand and investigate every sense of those words, even with conflicting opinions – is the hallmark of the rabbinic movement.

The rabbis made a categorical declaration that the prophet Malachi was the last authentic communicant with God. He is considered to have been the last *navi*, the last authenticated spokesperson whom God authorized to speak on God's behalf. The midrashic story of the total rejection of the voice from heaven asserts that such revelation is no longer acceptable. The first-century story concerns a controversy between four rabbis who split three to one on an issue of ritual. Rabbi Eliezer, who was always considered to be the most renowned and highly regarded decisor, gives one opinion. The other three oppose it. A series of miracles support the position taken by Rabbi Eliezer, but the other three rabbis deny any validity to miraculous intercession or interference. Finally, in despair, Rabbi Eliezer says, "Then let a voice from heaven decide the issue." And sure enough, a voice from heaven is heard, saying, "Yes, Rabbi Eliezer is right." Whereupon the spokesman of the three in opposition jumps up and shakes his finger and says, "We do not listen to voices from heaven any more."

And there is a sequel to the story. After the decision is made, one of the three in the majority goes to the market and meets the prophet Elijah, who, it seems, is always around, and asks him, "Were you with God when we had this quarrel?"

Elijah says, "Sure."

"So what did God say?"

Elijah answers, "God laughed and said, 'My children have won a victory over me. My children have defeated me.'"

The story clearly illustrates the position that Torah has now been given to us humans, wherefore we no longer listen to voices from heaven. In the postscript, the further assertion is made that God rejoiced over this rejection of interference in the human dispute by heavenly agency, declaring, "My children have won a victory over me."

For anybody to have the gall to say anything like this is close to blasphemy. And for it then to become part of the body of rabbinic tradition is just extraordinary. So there is perhaps inherent in the Jewish tradition an aversion to the claim that one has such a relationship to God, that one can thereby be different from others, more authentic.

Now, on the other hand, one of our greatest codifiers and legislative giants was Rabbi Yosef Caro, who in the sixteenth century wrote the famous *Shulchan Arukh*, which is the most accessible and popularly used code of Jewish law, practice, and life. Rabbi Caro said that very often a "voice" came to him at night and told him the solution to difficult legal problems, so that he would know the next day how to make the decision. As a member of the mystical kabbalist movement, Rabbi Caro claimed that his nightly visitor was a *maggid* – a "teller" of the resolution of legal knotty problems. All of which indicates that there is really no struggle here, no ultimate distinction between mystery and rationality.

The struggle to understand God as Revealer is inescapable. The general assertion within a traditional framework is that if there is no possibility of any communication between the mystery of God and the mystery of the human, then there is really no basis for what, at least traditionally, is understood to be the sacred or the religious. The possibility and the actuality of contact between the divine and the human need not merely to be posited, but also to be believed in order to form the ultimate basis for the construction of a religious system. The only question is how we express this notion, how we articulate this idea, what word imagery we use. Tradition has always been careful when someone claims to have had a personal encounter or experience of the divine that resulted from something that could rightly be called revelation. Yet we as believers need to be prepared to assert the possibility and actuality of such an event, in order to form the bedrock of our religious affirmations.

The main question concerns what form such an encounter might take. Tradition has always insisted that God "speaks," that there is a verbal content that is recoverable in such encounters between God and the human. This claim raises a real question. Surely language, at least to the extent that we now understand anything about it, seems to be the crowning achievement of the human species. The subtlety and nuances of our capacity to express ourselves verbally so far exceeds anything we have discovered up to now in the rest of nature that one can state without serious challenge that language is the supreme achievement, perhaps even the basic identifying aspect, of being human. Does this awareness lead necessarily to the expansion of the evaluation of language into the realm of the divine?

Obviously in traditional religious formulations it has. Because we have found our capacity at wording to be such an extraordinary talent and gift, it was unavoidable and natural that we would introject a like capacity into the deity. Most of our images of God are, of necessity, inescapably linked to our own humanness. Torah is full of expressions that use anthropomorphisms in speaking about God. Thus our capacity to speak is introjected into the very nature of the divine.

However, we cannot exceed ourselves. We cannot speak God. If God, in fact, has the capacity of communicable sounds comparable to our own language, then the only way in which such sounds can be grasped by us and understood by us is in human terms. Hence quite consistently, the traditional assumption in Torah is that God speaks Hebrew. In fact, according to the Midrash, God used the letters of the Hebrew alphabet as the constructive elements of creation. So when Torah says God speaks, and such-and-such happens, we are encouraged to understand that it is words cast from Hebrew letters that are the divine creative and commanding instrumentality. This is charming and also, at the very same time, profound, because it underscores the extraordinary level of appreciation of the fact that we can speak, that we are endowed with the capacity of language.

Does God speak as we do? Is there a *verbum divinum*? If that is the case, then those who claim that the sacred texts are the absolute truth because they are in fact the utterance of the deity cannot be challenged. So much of traditional religion has not only made that assertion, but has also propounded and defended it with such vigor, that those who would not accept it

have often either been declared heretical or have found themselves without any possibility of retaining a foothold within
the traditional framework for the formulation of their own
beliefs. Therefore, it is necessary to establish an image and understanding of revelation that, while it preserves the human gift
of speaking, does not inject actual "wording" into the part of
the revelatory act that begins with God. The possibility which
needs to be explored and asserted is that the very experience of
the divine, in itself wordless, impels the human participant in
the encounter to express it, articulate it, put it into words.

To put it differently, the assumption is that God does not
encounter a given human being merely as a private experience.
The human partner is not a privileged individual to be satisfied
and fulfilled by such an encounter as the end and purpose of
such an experience. According to Jewish tradition, God only
"speaks" for a purpose beyond the individual. The individual
becomes a *navi*, a spokesperson for the divine, a public witness
to the divine and its intention, as expressed by the human partner. The encounter itself is wordless. To put the record of such
an encounter in communicable form is the human partner's
necessary and unavoidable task. Words of revelatory events
are the human product of the event. The record of the event,
its communicable content, is always a result of the capacity
of the human partner to the revelatory event to transmit it in
human language.

This leads quite naturally to different revelatory contents
because individual human partners, of necessity, differ from
each other and articulate their understandings of the divine
encounter in their own specific ways. None of them can do it
any differently. An Isaiah cannot speak Micah, and a Habakkuk
cannot speak Ezekiel. And a Jewish participant in a revelatory
event cannot speak Buddha or Jesus or Muhammad, or whoever
else is recognized and accepted as a credible partner in, and
recipient of, similar divine revelatory encounters. What this

means is that there is very little profit in trying to compare the contents of revelations with each other in an evaluative fashion. Judgments about the validity of revelations are futile because the human partner, of necessity, speaks out of his or her own givenness. It is the human capacity to articulate, as guided and shaped by age, education, culture, condition of mind and soul, historical setting, and so on, that governs the actual communicable content of these unique events. It is therefore possible that a *navi*, a spokesperson for God, will at a young age communicate the message in a different way than if such an event occurs at a later time. A human partner in such an event in a state of elation will grasp it differently and therefore articulate it differently than when the human partner is saddened or depressed, threatened or shocked.

The question arises: Who has the initiative? We need to understand that one cannot intend oneself to become a partner in a potential encounter of the divine. Or to put it even more forcibly, one cannot compel the divine to pick this or that person as the best, most reliable, or even the most available recipient of the encounter. The initiative has to remain in the mystery of the Godhead. Immediately then, and without possibility of evasion, this not only leaves the initiative totally to God, but whoever we then experience as the chosen one to whom the mystery of God reveals itself, is identified and authenticated thereby. We have only one choice, to accept or reject. This is a risk which cannot be avoided.

There is a another fundamental issue. Those who believe in the existence and power of the sacred would at the very same time also be under a compulsion to be open to the consequences of such acceptance, such belief. To put it differently, if one were to deny categorically that the mystery of God has the ability to communicate to the mystery of the human, then the whole question dissolves. But to believers, it is virtually impossible to have a consistent and firm enough base for the construction of their own system of belief and life without the theoretical possibility, and therefore also the actuality, of contact between the two mysteries.

What I am talking about has tinges of mystical vocabulary and is a reflection on the experience of mystics striving for an understanding of themselves and of God. However, there is a major distinction between Judaism and certain other mystical teachings that needs to be made clear. Judaism stands in contrast to perceptions in which the final, most highly desirable achievement of the human is to lose himself/herself totally in God, to be abolished as a self, to merge in the *unio mystica* to a point where the self becomes indistinguishable and no longer is identifiable as separate from God. In Judaism, just the opposite is true. On the whole, in Jewish mysticism the individual is maintained, in fact affirmed, because the self always remains the "other" – even to God, precisely to God. And the ultimately dialogic, relational understanding of the human's presence with God, our searching for God, is maintained, is basic. This is especially true as a consequence of the idea that we are made in the image of God. This idea leads to an affirmation that human selfhood is part of God's intention, is complementary to God and separately identifiable, and therefore that humans retain an unimpaired relationship with the divine self.

In Jewish mystical literature, there may be here or there, under the influence of the commonality of mystic strivings and understandings in other communities, some occasional reference to the union with the divine. But basically, there is an assertion that the self is maintained in its integrity. In Hasidism, the pertinent term is *devekut*, which means "clinging." But clinging is something other than union, other than merger or absorption. Clinging means inseparably close embrace or contact, each with the other. This term means precisely that the human remains intact, is not absorbed, is not abolished in a final moment of ecstasy.

Even the word "ecstasy" is troubling in this regard. Ecstasy really means to take a stand outside of oneself, which could be interpreted, without too much fantasy, as leaving the self behind in the moment of elation, of a transformation of being such that one really is no longer the self, but is now "ecstatic," taking one's stand, experiencing oneself, beyond one's own natural self. Very curiously, researchers claim that out-of-body experiences may be due to some fault in the wiring of the brain, and that reports of such experiences, in other words, are not imaginary in the sense that they are fictitious. Some people really can experience seeing themselves, for instance, on the operating table in a surgical procedure. The current finding, although no one knows how long it will be accepted, is that the experience is a misfiring in the brain. So perhaps the whole notion of mystical ecstasy has a similar explanation for an experience that some people may really undergo. Therefore, one should not necessarily suspect the mystics of fabricating such reports and experiences. It could really be that in terms of brain function, they are anatomically both capable of and actually led into the experience of an extraordinary state of being.

Nonetheless, my perception of the human personality is that there is never a moment when the self is considered to be in need of abandonment, because implicit in any of the teachings of the absorption of the human into the divine is a value judgment that ultimately the human self is neither worthy of nor capable of entering into solitary close relations with the divine. Quite the opposite is true of Jewish mysticism, of the Jewish understanding of the divine-human relation. The human unfolds, maybe beyond anything anyone had ever expected or hoped for, in whatever great moments of encounter or sense of the Presence those moments may furnish. The human comes out of those extraordinary events more fully human, more truly human, more capable of unfolding and using gifts that have been there all the time, but that up to that point may have been unknown, unsuspected, or not used fully, sufficiently. This is an important distinction, and no mystical system other than the Jewish one seems to make this claim.

This is perhaps the starkest kind of theological position about, first, the lack of need for further direct revelation in the same fashion as occurred long ago. Therefore, second, there is an implicit and explicit assertion that Torah, once given, suffices. What all of this indicates is that the whole problem of how the mystery of God can be perceived, understood, and spoken of by humans is highlighted mercilessly. We are continuously confronted with the necessity of choosing, deciding whether those whom tradition has accepted as true *nevi'im*, true spokespersons of God, are in fact to be so considered, or whether all of this is purely imaginary, reflective of the human struggle and need to try to anchor our values and understandings of truth in that bedrock Other, which then can put it beyond human reach and therefore doubt.

To me revelation is not a spelled-out event of this kind. By revelation I mean that there are humans to whom it is given, possibly even to this day, to experience something, to grasp something, to be vouchsafed new insight that we would call revelation by a Being outside of them. The good word here is "encounter," because it is so indefinite, so imprecise. It denotes a reciprocal process. It is one of the instances in which God is totally dependent on the human. To use a different simile, God is the sender, but unless there is a receiver nothing happens. No revelation occurs.

Moses is one example of a revelatory text issuing from such an encounter. Jewish tradition insists that the relationship of Moses with God was unique, unrepeated, and unrepeatable. All the other prophets had visions or dreams. In such visions or dreams, the prophet is passive. As some of the prophets described it, they are seized, overwhelmed, captured by the divine, compelled by the divine to speak. The implications of this reception of direct communication by the divine to the human require the human to be passive at first. Obviously, the initiative is with God. God chooses the time, the person, the circumstance. This is clearly part of the understanding of prophecy in the Jewish tradition. One cannot train oneself or prepare oneself to be a prophet, nor initiate the contact. In prophecy, the total initiative rests with God. But the human has to be capable, even willing to share such an event, to participate in it; for without the human partner, God is truly "the voice crying in the wilderness" where there is no human presence. All of these conditions are applicable to Moses according to the text of Torah. There, again and again, Moses inquires, initiates the encounter. This is so remarkable and unique that in his eulogy it is said of Moses that "God knew him face to face" (Deuteronomy 34:10). This was unprecedented and never repeated again in all of Jewish history and life.

Apart from the prophetic experience in Jewish tradition, there is a continuous thrust toward the active involvement of the covenantal partner in the covenantal obligation. This means that radical passivity is contrary to this understanding. The Jew needs to be actively involved in searching for answers, in probing the mystery, in looking for whatever truth can be found in the sacred texts, or in whatever other materials and traditional sayings and deliberations are available and useful. Therefore, the failure of the Jew to engage in study, to engage in continued immersion in sacred texts, is inherently contradictory to the understanding that God needs not to become active in communicating all over again. It is now necessary for us to probe, to search, to investigate, and ultimately, basically then, to *do*. It is, as Buber would have it, that reality is a question to which we are bidden to give an answer, to respond.

Furthermore, the validity of the revelation to the prophets has to be judged against the revelation at Sinai. It is traditionally assumed that none of the prophets taught anything that was not already been given, either explicitly or implicitly, in the Sinai event. Therefore, Jewish tradition takes the position that in a proper covenantal life, the Jew has no need for additional or new instructions. We know full well what is expected of us, how we are to live, how we are to behave, what kinds of human beings we are intended to be, in order thereby to reflect our covenantal relation with the Creator, and to fulfill its intentions.

What is necessary is for us to wake up to our responsibilities. The word "responsibility" should be heard as the answer we give to something that may have long been known and taught. The failure in our world is not the absence of God or a lack of communication by God; rather the failure is our own unreadiness, lack of capacity, and lack of the will to do what we all know we are "commanded" to do, are meant to do. We can even go further and say, what we all know we *need* to do.

This leads to the justification of Jewish tradition that says there is no more need for further disclosures. One can even put, as tradition has, an arbitrary end to such communication between the divine and the human as is implied in the statement that the prophet Malachi was the last instance of God's communication to Jews.

The lack of further communication does not lead to the exclusion of God from history. It does not mean that history is only between humans, although it is clear that the responsibility for the human sphere was turned over to us when God gave the first commandment to Adam. That action made God and Adam inescapably relational to each other, and diminished, if one can speak in these terms, the totality, the *shalom*, of the deity. Afterwards, in order to be the deity fully, God needed a response from Adam, the right response, the proper response, the expected and, not infrequently, the surprising response. Of course, we all know that Adam, our prototype, our model, did exactly what we always do. He disappointed God, gave the wrong answer, was obstreperous, contrary. Instead of becoming the covenantal collaborator, we humans became the opponent. And so the game was launched. The human enterprise was initiated, and the tension between the human and the divine, as is so graphically and perceptively portrayed in this first encounter between God and the human and between the human and God, unfolded in history, and continues to do so today.

Here we are really in the throes of a very painful dilemma. What is the basis of our understanding of who we as humans are meant to be, how we are intended to live, what values we are to shape and follow? Are we self-created? Are we the only beings engaged in the process of finding our own ultimates? Or is this endeavor beyond us, if for no other reason than that we humans are so very different from one another and are subject to such an enormous variety of experiences and developments of life and cultures that, of necessity, we differ sharply when left only to our own devices.

The question is whether being self-created is enough to explain the mystery that we discover ourselves to be. Our search and our need to answer the question of who we are leads us eventually to a nonhuman source. Clearly this becomes the crucial question for a person of *emuna*. In fact, it may be the very fulcrum of the question for the believer. The believer, so it seems to me, ultimately needs to assume that there is a nonhuman source of insight, of value formation, of commandment, or of *mitzvah*, to use the traditional word, that needs to be taken with utmost seriousness in the shaping of both the personal and communal life. Up to now, anyway, traditional religions have always made this basic assumption. For the believer, there is no possibility of an alternative, of an escape from it.

This basic assumption does not mean that people who disavow any possibility of the reality of the mystery of the divine are not capable of shaping a system of values that is highly respectable and workable. Such people live in a context in which whatever we have generally accepted as the ultimate values has become so well known and rooted that one could today proceed without testing their origin and validity by demanding that they be either lodged in or reaffirmed by revelation.

It is simply not easy to be a believing human being, in all of the depth this statement implies, without confronting the inescapable question of whether the mystery of the divine and the mystery of the human can relate to each other in such a way that the human derives some direction. The intent of describing Adam as having been made in the image of the divine seems to be that in contrast with all of the other items in the created order, the human has some unique affinity and characteristic relatedness with the divine. If that is, in fact, one of the principal assertions of our humanness, then the whole question of revelation flows from it without undue difficulty.

"Image of God" is a very difficult phrase, however. The word "image" is probably a poor translation of the original intent in the Hebrew word *tzelem*, but there may not be a better one. It is a word laden with enormous opaqueness, begging for human interpretation and understanding, and yet by its very coinage may be an intentional barrier to such an enterprise. It is a hint. It is one of those puzzling profundities of insight into the strangeness and uniqueness of the human, and equally into the strangeness and uniqueness of the divine. It leads us to think of ourselves and God as having such deep potential points of similarity and contact that they become the very foundation stone of our entire edifice of belief.

Jewish tradition says that God demands that certain values be both exhibited and made real in this created world. What is really necessary now is to immerse ourselves as deeply as we can in the actual performance of what we know is expected of us. It is not necessary to look for further instruction, or to wait for new directives, but to buckle down and do what we know needs to be done. And what we do is not being done just because we find it to be advantageous, or respectable, or even because it is what we have been taught to do. We do it because we accept it as being, somehow or other, the wish of the mystery of God to which we want to respond. This, it seems to me, is really the whole key of a position that no longer depends on ongoing revelation, but rather on the reciprocity of the covenant.

But it does depend on ongoing relation, and that relation is now flowing mostly from my side toward the mystery of God. To put it directly, God has done enough, we have not. God has given us a world in which to live. Human life is the evidence or consequence of God's creative capacity and will. We have received instruction, at least in such a way that we can apply ourselves to it with our minds and our hearts and our being.

The fact is that we, as humans, as Jews, have not done enough. What God has offered has been so partially accepted and responded to that we are continuously in a deficit position. Particularly since the Shoah, I believe that one needs to understand God as deeply disappointed, hurt, diminished, by the accumulation of evil, although God no longer responds as God once did, as recounted, for example, by the text on the flood of Noah. It is imperative for me to let God know that I understand that my role is crucial now. That I am the decisive element in the relationship becomes incontrovertibly clear to me as a result of the Shoah, which is the evidence of God's woundedness, God's helplessness

When seen in this way, reliance on the necessity of ongoing revelation can been considered a kind of postponement, or even an evasion, of the necessity to face up to the enormous responsibility that now devolves on us as humans, on me as a Jew, a post-Shoah human being in a world that is so often overwhelmed by evil.

The relationship between the human and the mystery of the divine comes out of *my response* because the omnipresence of God is not dependent on any further evidence of God's involvement through revelatory events. God's omnipresence, central in the creation of the world, including human life, my life, is so pervasive, so unmistakably clear that it is self-validating. God's helplessness is expressed in the fact that, contrary to earlier, especially biblical testimony, God no longer acts directly and immediately in given human events and history. This devolves the weight of the work on me. This is the fulcrum, the inner meaning, of this current moment in the development of the religious life. The relationship, the covenant, is damaged not by God's supposed absence, but by mine – not by God's inaction, but by mine.

Chapter Ten
The Nature of God

God said to Moses, "I will be what I will be."
(Exodus 3:14)

$\mathcal{R}$ecently I was at an interfaith gathering, a Christian/Jewish conversation. We prayed, as we often do, each in our own fashion, Greek Orthodox and Lutherans, Episcopalians and Catholics, and Jews. Every time we prayed, we regularly used five different names for the divine. I was aware, naturally, of the fact that Christians pray in the name of the Father, the Son, and the Holy Ghost or Holy Spirit. Early on, Christians found a formulation sufficiently direct and yet encompassing so that they do not have to search for anything else. It is an ingenious solution: thinking of God as human and divine at the same time. In parts of the Christian story, *homo* and *deus* are inseparably linked. And the determination of the Nicene and Chalcedonian church councils that this was the only correct formulation hoped to settle all kinds of internal stresses and strains and alternatives that were swirling around. Jews have never had anything similar to this juxtaposition of *deus* and *homo*, God and human. To us the problem of finding adequate words to speak about the divine makes it much more difficult for us to talk about God. This in turn leads to the multiplicity of approaches, of formulations of the divine, in the Jewish liturgy today, much of it derived from biblical times.

The human search for the words to describe God is reminiscent of the description of people in blindfolds trying to define an elephant. Where they touch the animal determines what they think the elephant might be. It seems to be a rope if they touch the tail, or a column if they touch a leg. Jews are confronted with the same type of problem, and just as in the story of the elephant, it starts with human deficiency. We start from the deficiency inherent in the accepted radical otherness of God from us as human. Of course in all of this we must remember the great rabbinic dictum that "Torah texts speak human language," and that human language is the only one we have. This said, Judaism has had to be very inventive. We have found all kinds of names for God.

Throughout the biblical texts, two major words are used for God. One is the word *El*, and its derivatives like *Elohim* and *Elohaynu*. The other is the Tetragrammaton, the four-letter word *Yod, He, Waw, He*, camouflaged into *Adonai*, so that no one would try to pronounce the proper name of God. In Jewish tradition, in the time when the altar was daily used to reconcile God and the people, only the high priest and his deputy knew how to pronounce this name. It was only pronounced once a year at Yom Kippur, and in such a way that only a few would hear it. The reason the deputy would also know it was in case the high priest died before having an opportunity to teach someone this, the greatest, perhaps the only real secret of Judaism. The name was lost when the last high priest and his deputy were slain while officiating at the altar by Roman soldiers on the ninth day of Ab in the year 70, when the Temple was destroyed by Titus's army. With that, the knowledge of how to pronounce the name was lost forever. There have been attempts to reconstruct it, and there are variants of such pronunciations in Jewish tradition. One solution to the puzzle had seventy-two letters.

There is a legend that from time to time there is a *Ba'al Shem Tov*, a "Master of the Good Name." The "Good Name" is the name of God. A Master of the Good Name has somehow been graced with the secret knowledge of how to pronounce the Tetragrammaton. Accordingly he is capable of performing miraculous acts. The greatest of these figures lived in the eighteenth century, Rabbi Israel, the so-called *Besht*, which is the acronym of *Ba'al Shem Tov*. When Rabbi Israel appeared in Eastern Europe in the year 1740, he seemed to have a secret power source. The lore of Hasidism, the movement to which he gave rise, tells stories about his being able to be in two places at the same time, interceding with God when there were dangers threatening the Jewish people, and performing miraculous acts of all kinds. He was able to do this for the simple reason that he was graced with a knowledge of the pronunciation of the Tetragrammaton.

Modern scholars use *Yahweh* as the pronunciation, a doubtful attempt to reconstruct the lost name. In biblical practice, elements of the Tetragrammaton were included in personal names. Joshua is *Yeho-Shua*, and *Yeho* uses three of the four letters. Isaiah is *Yesha-Yahu*, so that again the first three of the four letters are used in Isaiah's name. Jeremiah and Hezekiah are *Yeremi-Yahu* and *Yecheski-Yahu*. Typically, three or four parts were added to personal names both as prefixes and suffixes, and the pronunciation is *Yeho* or *Yahu*, or the like.

The names Yeho and Yahu are quite different from Yahweh, but whether one is better than the other cannot be ascertained. Moreover, the various names cited above are all incomplete because they use only three letters instead of four, and it is possible that the third letter could have been used in a different way in organizing the pronunciation.

Certainly, the name Jehovah is a misreading. Jehovah is a set of syllables created by the rabbis, who superimposed the vowels of the word *Adonai*, which means "Lord," and is the counterpart of the *Dominus* or *Kyrie* of Christian tradition, across the Tetragrammaton, in order thereby to keep it unpronounceable. But knowing this has not stopped many people from speaking the name Jehovah, although it was intended as a preventive camouflage.

There are other names for God, like *Shaddai, El Shaddai,* and *Tzoor,* meaning, respectively, "Powerful," "Powerful God," and "Rock." The rabbis went beyond these. Sometimes they called God *Makom.* This name comes from the root *kom,* which means "erect, stand, establish." *Makom* is the noun derived from the verb *kom,* a regular word formation in Hebrew, where all nouns are derivatives from verbs. Literally, it means "place." Modern equivalents of this name include such formulations as "ground of being" and "substratum of all reality." *Makom* might also be taken to be the Hebrew equivalent of the word "existence," which comes from the Latin *existare,* or "standing out." So existence is something that "stands out." It is a curious possibility that the rabbis, profoundly influenced by the Hellenistic and Roman cultures in the time when the rabbinic movement began its remarkable unfolding, knew of the word "existence" and translated it into Hebrew as *makom.* Therefore, it might be a similar formation to the one that led Latin-speaking thinkers to attribute "existence" to God. In Hebrew, however, the word almost becomes tangible, because *makom* also means "where you are standing." It is more a tactile sense of place than mere existence. If you take existence in its original meaning, however, and with some verbal precision, it also means that which can be touched and which one can encounter physically.

Ultimately, because existence really has so tangible a spatial impact, that description becomes untenable and needs to be replaced by "being." It is misleading in connotation and meaning to speak of God as existent. God *is*, but God does not *exist*. We can say that God is a be-ing rather than that God exists. Therefore, the question "Does God exist?" is either imprecise use of language or a false attribution. Of course, when we talk about any of these matters, we need to keep some accuracy of articulation or else the whole enterprise of speaking about God is hopelessly flawed.

Another common name for God is *Shalom*, meaning "totality." Those who used the word in this way may have meant that there is a total serenity, a total undisturbedness in God. This image is perhaps more a product of human imagination and wishfulness than the reality contained in the sacred texts, which speak of God as disturbed, upset, moved by deep passion and emotions.

God is also called the *Bore Olam*, "Creator of the World." Sometimes God is indirectly referred to as the Giver of Torah, the *Notain Torah*. In any number of prayers we refer to God as *Harachaman*, "the Merciful One," or *Bore P'ree Hagofen*, "Creator of the Fruit of the Vine," or *"Hamotzee Lechem min Ha'aretz*, the One "Who Makes Bread Come from the Earth." God is the *Osay Shalom*, the "Maker of Peace."

God is also called *Ein Sof*, meaning "Infinite." This name derives primarily from the kabbalistic movement that surfaced in the twelfth and thirteenth centuries in Spain and southern France, and then traveled eastward through southern Germany and eventually into Poland. *Ein Sof* is found in the *Zohar*, the core text of the Kabbalah, which was probably composed by Moses de Leon sometime in the twelfth century in northern Spain.

All of these and many others are terms that we have used in order to draw from the human sphere something that might at least faintly resemble, or in some way come close to, what we might want to say about that which is ineffable, beyond our human wording, beyond our capacity to articulate. To say this differently, we have to use so many different ways of referring to the divine because it is impossible to find words adequate to define what we mean when we say "God." If it were simple to talk about God, there would be one word.

These names also reflect a conscious awareness of the presence of God. It could simply be that the omnipresence of God needed different appellations depending on where God was perceived, or where God was sought and found, whether in food, in drink, in creation, or in relationships to others, in time and space.

The rabbis, noting these two major groups of appellations for God, interpreted the various usages as denoting different divine characteristics. The majority of their opinions interpreted anything that has to do with *El*, like *Elohim*, as always pertaining to the remote God, the powerful God, the judging God, the ruler of the world. On the other hand, the Tetragrammaton, the Adonai form, is the near God, the supportive, loving, nurturing, forgiving God. However, there is also a minority opinion that declares just the reverse. Their *Elohim* interpretations depict God as close, nurturing, loving, forgiving, while their Adonai versions refer to the dominant, powerful, judging, and punishing aspects of God.

It is fascinating that liturgically the two terms have often appeared together, particularly in one verse from Deuteronomy, which has entered the liturgy with such prominence that it is found in nearly every service, the *Sh'ma*. It says *Sh'ma Yisrael Adonai Eloheynu, Adonai echad*, or freely: "Pay attention, Israel, Adonai is our Elohim, is our God, and that Adonai is unique, is singular." This passage is often called the watchword of our faith, as the single clearest articulation of monotheism. Therefore, it is repeatedly used liturgically. In fact, a Jew is supposed to recite this verse three times a day: in the morning, in the evening, and just before going to sleep. There is a special *Sh'ma* recited on the bed. So if one recites it regularly, that would be twenty-one recitations a week or over a thousand times a year. In a lifetime, that really adds up. The enforced recital of this biblical statement of the nature of God is commanded and included in the liturgy not only because it identifies the Jews as the first promoters and adherents of monotheism, and therefore also of the challenge and assignment to guard it, but also because it is so hard to live up to.

Polytheism is so much more comfortable, and is a much easier theology than monotheism. In polytheism there is a god or a goddess of virtually anything and everything. So whatever you want to do, you have a divine protector or champion to do it. That goes for theft and infidelity and murder, whatever – even war. On the other hand, if God is singular, then absolutely, unavoidably, your moral system will say yes to some things and no to others. In polytheism, you cannot have that kind of definitiveness. It is only in monotheism that ethical codes can be established in which some things are right and some things are wrong, because there is only one ultimate referent, one ultimate source.

In a monotheistic system, one of the great understandings of the relationship of the human and the divine is the imitation of God, the *imitatio Dei*. It is enshrined in Leviticus 19:2. "You shall be holy because I, Adonai, your God am holy." This call to holiness clearly sets out one of the basic demands for God-pleasing, God-acceptable human behavior. It means that God represents in God's own being, as humans understand it, a set of values that we are bidden to imitate. The absolutely necessary, underlying assumption for our ability to imitate God comes out of the same passage in Genesis that says that we are made in the image of God. If we were totally different from what God is, imitation would be impossible.

The whole question of what "holy" means is controversial. The most frequently agreed upon definition or understanding is "being separate, special." This distinction is one of the great underlying understandings of the Torah story of creation, that is, to make a differentiation, to be able to discern, to discriminate. To be separate from the totality is, in a sense, to be able to discriminate, to make a distinction between that which is acceptable and that which is not acceptable. The creation story is the basic story of separating light from dark, heaven from earth, dry land from water, eventually that which is human from the rest of the created order, and finally, the created order from God. The created order is understood to be, is portrayed as being, God's work; it is, therefore, to a great extent God's self-disclosure. And again, this view is taken from the way we are. What we do, what we say, what we create, is a reflection of our own selves. We are in it inextricably, unavoidably.

As noted earlier, one of the words that the rabbis used for God is *shalom*, not meaning "peace" in this instance, but instead meaning "totality, unfracturedness," the ultimate vision of what we might call holiness. The question, then, is, how can we attain it? Obviously the created order is not holy in itself. Some of the kabbalists said that creation is a self-inflicted contraction, a sacrifice, or abandonment, of the totality that God was before creation. Thus creation only becomes possible because God withdraws, as it were, part of the totality, the ultimate holiness. The result is not totally holy, but it has the potential for holiness because creation flows from the source of the holy.

There is a very beautiful and highly suggestive image drawn by the Holy Ari, one of the great masters of the kabbalistic movement of the sixteenth century in Safed in Galilee. In this view, creation is a scattering of all the sparks of the original flame of holiness into every aspect of what we consider to be reality. It is the human task, not only to recognize these bits of the original, now fractured totality of *shalom* which are embedded everywhere, but also to liberate them, to free them. These sparks then can be reunited with the original, now diminished supernal flame. The end will come when that work is complete.

This is compatible with the understanding and perception that whatever has a beginning will have an end.

One of the greatest merits of this idea is that the act of bringing the creation to completion is up to us humans. It is up to the Jew in the first place, because these images and ideas rise from an understanding within segments of Jewish tradition. Eventually, however, this is the act, the opportunity, and perhaps even the ultimate destiny of all that is human: to reunite the infinite number of fragments of the holy, the holy "sparks," and thus to reconstitute their original "flame."

In addition to the nuances of the creation story and the myriad names, Torah provides us with some very explicit statements about the nature of God. A good example is the answer that God gives to Moses' question concerning God's identity in Exodus 3:14. Some translations insist on putting God's answer in the present tense, "I am that I am." In the Hebrew grammar, however, it is in the future tense: "I will be who I will be." The translation "I am that I am" is under the impact of the need to establish God as everlasting, immutable, not subject to the degree of interaction that "I will be who I will be" virtually invites, or certainly permits. There is something that speaks of substance in "I am that I am." When used in this way, it is the assertion: This is what I am, and there is nothing you can do about it, nothing that any relational connection would in any way make a dent in. I am that I am. Period. End of subject.

The difference between "I am that I am" and "I will be who I will be" is significant. "I am that I am" says you have got to take me the way you find me. That's it. "I will be who I will be" implies that there is the possibility of variation, of development, maybe even of contradiction. "I am that I am" excludes contradiction, leaving the human bewildered and with the sole responsibility of possibly cleaning up any and all the contradictory statements in the sacred text. If I start out with "I will be who I will be," then a human understanding of God at any given point or situation can be slightly different from that understanding at another point or in another situation. It invites an understanding of a God who in relation to the human has leeway, has the possibility of different kinds of responses or challenges, has the inherent quality of changeability.

"I will be who I will be" leaves open the possibility, if one can even talk in this way, of change in God, of God's being open, willing, and capable of development within God's self, so to say. Therefore, God is not immutable, not static, but dynamic, in process. Support for this characterization can be found in the biblical texts where God is surprised, where God does not know what God is going to find. What else would account for such a phrase as "God gets angry"? If God does, it effectively acknowledges what the biblical text continuously insists it is our ability to do, that is, to surprise God by what we do or do not do, by our willfulness. "I am that I am" does not permit these possibilities, or makes them highly unlikely. "I will be who I will be" asserts the option that we as humans affect God and that God is not so total, so self-sufficient that humans are negligible – without any impact, without any effect on God. And there is no question that the opposite is asserted vigorously throughout the Bible.

The classic biblical text asserting that God is affected by human action is in Exodus after the golden calf episode. Moses is in total despair, in deep depression over his personal failure as a leader and teacher. He has failed to marshal the people's souls sufficiently so that they would reject idolatry. Obviously the golden calf episode is a regression to what we must assume were Egyptian religious and cultic practices. Moses thinks that he has failed totally, not only because he is the representative of the people toward God, but because his whole function is in radical question. In his despair, he asks God for reassurance.

Moses is quite new in his leadership role, and he may no longer have been sure that he understood God. Calculating the time that it might have taken for him to negotiate with the Pharaoh for the release of the people, the seven weeks that it took to get to the mountain, and the "forty days," if it is an accurate figure, that he was absent receiving the commandments, Moses' encounter at the burning bush may have happened only six months earlier. In such a short time frame, it is understandable that Moses might feel unsure about this God.

He experienced God in Egypt as a powerful force, punishing the recalcitrant, the unyielding. On the journey through the wilderness, he experiences God in the rescue from immediate danger, and in the provision of nourishment. So bit by bit, Moses learns aspects of this God that were formerly unknown to him. In these early stages, Moses can never fully understand God, and it is not difficult to empathize with him as he is confronted by this devastating problem. He assumes that he has been ineffective, to the point where he pleads with God to reassure him lest he be unable to go on. Moses needed something from God to restore his capacity to continue what God had commissioned him to do at the burning bush: to be the people's liberator from Egyptian bondage, to bring them to the holy mountain, to become their guide toward the covenant between God and the people, and to be the conduit of what then issues from that event, namely a whole set of commandments, of laws, of values.

One could and should read the Exodus saga as a near-disaster for God, who profoundly misread the character of this people who had now become God's stake in the future of humanity. Having gone out of Egypt only a few weeks earlier, they were just not ready. It might even be said that we, the people, may never be ready, not to this very day. Minimally, we must feel a sense of a lack of completion, a lack of sufficiency in living up to the profound challenge of the Covenant.

So Moses is in need of reassurance, and that reassurance comes in the form of a self-disclosure by God to Moses. There is a tender scene between God and Moses depicted in Exodus 33:23, where God tells Moses, "I will put you into a crack in the rock, and I will put my hand over you as I pass so that you cannot see my front, but you can see my back."

This is a very telling description of the fact that nobody can ever be in the unshielded presence of the divine. One always gets only an outline, a glimpse of familiar features, but never the total picture. Once we see a person's face, we can know the person; however, when we see only the back, we are not so fully certain. There remains a vagueness, an indistinctness, the possibility of error. In this perhaps clumsy way, the biblical account says that we cannot ever be totally in the presence of God.

The Torah text records that God identified God's being in the following words to Moses: "Adonai, Adonai, a God compassionate, gracious, long-suffering, full of love and truth, who shows love to thousands, who forgives transgression and sin, and who holds guiltless, but not totally" (Exodus 34:6–7).

This self-disclosure is not meant only for Moses. According to the rabbinical understanding, this self-disclosure is so basic and true that it is also used liturgically. We pray it, recite it, several times during the liturgical year. Traditionally it is recited three times in front of the open ark before the Torah scroll is removed on certain holidays. This in itself indicates what the rabbis thought about these extraordinary verses of the Torah. This self-disclosure by God is used liturgically in its entirety, except that the rabbis chopped off the last phrase, which suggests that God will "not totally forgive" or "hold entirely guiltless." The rabbis end the quotation after "God will forgive" transgressions and wrongdoing. In the Torah text of the actual encounter between God and Moses, God adds that we will *not* be held totally guiltless. The rabbis took a profound liberty in this instance. They felt empowered. They quote only partially because that is what they wanted to say and teach through this liturgical passage.

This tender, gentle, loving scene between God and Moses is very different, for instance, from the one that Isaiah highlights, when he hears the *kadosh*: "Holy, Holy, Holy." The Trisagion ("Thrice Holy"), as this invocation is termed by scholars, is not only a highpoint in the main rabbinic prayer, but also a key element at the heart of the Christian mass. The statement in Isaiah is not God saying something about God, but what the angels are singing, proclaiming. In contrast, God's self-disclosure to Moses is both moving in its contents and rare, if not unique, because it is recorded in God's own words. God's self-description is positive, loving, affectionate. Moses needs this encouragement in the moment of his own despair, and this description is obviously provided in order to encourage him to think of himself as allied with a Being from whom he can receive nourishment, support, encouragement.

God's self-disclosure is remarkable, expressing God's loving, caring features. The first adjective in the list, *rachum*, comes from the Hebrew word *rechem*, which means "womb." So God is depicted as acting with the same kind of care that a woman has for the baby in her womb, which is the ultimate picture of total nurturing, caring, protecting, and loving.

Rav is translated as "full," but that is not the usual meaning; it could mean "big," "great," or "powerful." *Chesed*, although it is not the word that people usually look for as the word for "love," is the Torah's word for "love." Another Hebrew word for "love," *ahava*, is more like *eros*, and *chesed* may be more like *agape*. But this is playing with words. We are told that we are supposed to love God and the word used is *v'ahavta*. The word used is right from the same root as *ahava*. However, modern biblical etymology has accepted *chesed* as the word for what we might translate as "love."

Love is linked to *emet*, "truth." One possible understanding might be that love is not absolute: love and truth must be joined together. There must be a justification, a basis for love in the sense that while it is a primary capacity and function of being, both divine and human, it needs to somehow be put into reference with facticity. That is, love has to have a link with such elements of reality as give it a basis on which we can stand and through which we can grow. It cannot just be esoteric. Nor should it be just an emotional feeling, because that can be misleading. Rather, the very linking of *chesed* and *emet*, of love and truth, in God's self-disclosure indicates that there has to be a factual base, a basis in truth, something we can hold on to. From this solid base, we can justify an enduring love, give love content, rather than it being a pure feeling.

In other words, love grows out of and is linked with such essentials as are accessible to the method of establishing facts and truth that we normally use, the interpretive, the rational. So the whole intent is to not allow love to become a romantic expression, but instead to have a love grounded in experience and in an appreciation of what is real or possible, whatever is subsumed under the equally large-roofed term "truth."

If God is filled with this love and truth, two things become immediately apparent. The first is that this love is available to us, and that is why God says it to Moses, so that Moses would be relieved of his despair. Then second, of course, the other way around also applies: that we ought to imitate God and should also be loving.

Love is not intended to be an absolute, because no absolute is possible for us. We are talking here about what God wanted to tell Moses. The idea is that love needs to be bonded with, tethered to, truth, whatever truth is – and who knows that? Truth is a very difficult concept. The question "What is truth?" is very disquieting. What is implied is that there are so many different ways to get at the truth that truth is not absolute but relative. And this may be implied also in the linkage of love and truth, that love must be relational and not just a subjective outpouring of some interior feeling. It is okay for God to speak of truth, but when we do, we need to be aware of its relativeness, and for that reason we are deprived of a firm, unbreakable base on which to stand. While there may be some things that are sufficiently true even for us, such that we need not doubt or question them any longer, there is also no doubt that there are aspects of truth that are fluid, unfolding, and developing.

The word *alafim* added on means "rendering love to thousands." The rabbis were intrigued by this phrase too, and one of them interpreted it as meaning that "thousands" must be at least two thousand, and that the punishment for faithlessness goes only into the third and fourth generations of those who do wrong. Therefore the rabbis calculated that God's willingness to forgive, as over against God's inclination to punishment, is five hundred to one. God is five hundred times more loving than judgmental.

Sometimes a thousand is an exact measurement, but in this case it really means virtually endless: thousands as individuals and generations. Because it is clearly stated that the punishment goes to the third and fourth generations, "to the thousands" was then also understood, by implication, to refer to generations. It means that there is no end to God's mercy and willingness to overlook and forgive. The intent of the phrase, what it hoped to convey, is the immensity of God's willingness to forgive, to overlook, not to reckon, and not to judge.

Avon v'afesha means "bears sin, transgression, wrongdoing." And *v'nake lo yenake* is usually translated as "holds guiltless and forgives," although it actually says "holds guiltless but not totally." Essentially, these statements combine to mean not to absolve without any consequences.

The formulation here of God's virtually endless, infinite capacity to overlook contradicts any notion that the Shoah was God's judgment. It is, in fact, the reverse: the understanding of God's being so willing to forgive that it is virtually impossible to use the theological construct that many traditionalists put on the Shoah, namely that it is God's punishment for a faithless, sinful people. Those who use this construction, that whatever happens to the Jewish people is deserved and is simply God's unvarying judgment and punishment, distort the understanding of this and other descriptions of God. *V'nake lo yenake* means to absolve but not without any consequences. But after the Shoah, it is now we who are called on to absolve, for it is we who have a question about God's functioning.

In fact, none of the biblical descriptions and understandings of the nature of God are capable of responding to the Shoah and to the obvious nonfunctioning of God in any rescue. So I am compelled to find a new image and to refer to antecedents in the Torah and biblical texts which permit me to construct, as my prevailing notion of God, the idea of God as a sufferer. A God who is not omnipotent can be found quite often in biblical texts. Therefore, I am not creating something totally new, but I am merely referring to aspects of Torah and other biblical and rabbinic understandings of God which Jewish tradition, on the whole, has either ignored or overlaid.

God's self-disclosure implies that the Shoah is a major break with tradition. The mainstream of Jewish traditional understandings and rulings is not incompatible with this reading of God's nature as compelled by the Shoah. It is implicit in many scriptural passages, though they are ordinarily or historically downplayed or ignored altogether. It would be an interesting question to try to discover why this is so. Why has the power status of God, especially the royal image, prevailed to such an extent? What is it about this image that so satisfied and captured the allegiance of our forebears that to this day it is the main simile used for God?

Perhaps there is a psychological ground for all this. Perhaps the need to have all power concentrated in one figure, in one point of reality, reassures us. Since we now speak primarily about God rather than an earthly king, it reassures us that the "divine king" would always reliably function in such a way that one can form one's own life in relation to that assumption, and therefore have ultimate certainty. This may be seen as the best tool for cosmos against chaos.

My need to depart from this picture rises in relationship to the Shoah, where the "King" does not function as the protector, rescuer, father of his people as kings should and are assumed to be and to do. But my willingness to depart from this image is also an outgrowth of a truly human understanding of where the power really resides. I believe that to a large extent it resides in me. It means that I am not totally dependent on a centralized point of power. This in turn means that I no longer base my whole existence on the ONE who is the embodiment of all that is assumed to be right and good and just. Instead, it transfers the responsibility for living in that way to me.

This changes the relationship fundamentally. One is no longer an *eved*, a "servant" or "slave," which is the same word used in Hebrew for "worshiper." In Hebrew the word for "worship" is *avoda*, which is also the word for "slavery" in biblical terminology. The curious coincidence of these understandings, correct translations, and uses of these words is more than accidental. The word "worship" is an indication of a relationship of the low to the high. "Your worship" is a title of very elevated status when applied to human beings.

It is also intriguing that in Christian liturgical practices there is a type of building called a "basilica." A basilica is the place of the *basileus*, the Greek word for "king." There is the "throne" of St. Peter; and in all churches there is a thronelike seat on which the chief officiant or primate is seated. Another example is the "bishop's seat," an elevation, a physical arrangement, indicating the power structure. The very structure of Christian houses of worship reduces the attendant individual to a lower status because of the very high ceilings, which are not really elevating. Instead, they actually function to reduce the status and stature of the ones who are down on the low level of the floor.

Synagogues are traditionally different in this regard. However, modern architects, very often without realizing what is happening thereby, are erecting churchlike buildings for Jewish religious worship. In contrast, for example, the traditional Sephardic arrangement of the synagogue is a rectangle, with the reading desk in the middle. This arrangement is indicative of an understanding of the place of the individual person in a synagogue structure, which unfortunately Askenazic Jewry has not accepted. It is a much more adequate and correct consequence of the understanding that we are not approaching a holy, elevated spot which is assumed to be owned by a king – and if not by a mortal, then by the divine king.

These items provide a clear indication that these kinds of images are not superficial. They are so deeply woven into the texture of our theological and liturgical life that they are overwhelmingly dominant.

It is unfortunate that God's self-disclosure to Moses is not used more often, especially when it comes to interfaith conversations and dialogues. More often it is the other version of God in the Torah that is used, where God is being judgmental, angry, irascible. This is especially true in contrast to the God of the Christian Gospels, who is pictured as all-loving and forgiving. This construction, which grew out of the conflict between early Christianity and rabbinical Judaism, is only a partial truth, but it has hardened into a perception that is expressed even by Christian people who have no particular hostility toward Judaism. They have simply been taught, or perhaps in reading the Gospels come to the conclusion themselves, that Jesus expressed a new version of the loving God.

This issue also touches the phrase "love your neighbor as yourself" (Leviticus 19:17). "Love thy neighbor" has gotten worldwide address as one of the great teachings of Jesus. Many people, past and present, have thought that Jesus made this up and do not realize it is a quotation from the Torah. Jesus was, after all, a rabbi who knew Torah. So in this regard, the origins of Christianity are inseparable from the main body of Jewish teaching.

The other remarkable thing about God's self-disclosure to Moses is that there is no direct reference to the Jewish people. It might be expected that a God who had entered into a covenant at Sinai just days earlier might have referred back to it, might have indicated that this was really how He wanted to appear to the Jewish people, or indicated that this was the Jewish people's legacy or precious treasure. We might say that the absence of such reference is due to the fact that this was a personal, intimate moment between God and Moses, God's response to Moses' desperate need.

Of course, all the articulation of the wording of the biblical text needs to be understood and accepted as the product of the human mind under the impact of the presence of God, and this explains that whatever we say about God is inescapably, unavoidably couched in human terms, a reflection of ourselves, for we can do no other. Like "in the image of God" in the creation story, the text "I will be who I will be" is haunting. It is difficult to firmly grasp what these phrases mean. On the one hand, they exclude any "likeness" in the sense that God is to be understood in terms of my humanness, that is, the physical or the emotional or the religious sense of whatever verb or adjective we use. But at the same time, there is this mystery, this paradox, that the total otherness of God is not absolute, that there is something in God that speaks to and is evoked from human wonder, response, doubt, questions, disagreement, challenge.

It is worth noticing that at this point Moses has already told God off. Moses has already told God that He cannot pursue His angry intent to wipe out the whole Abrahamitic root. It is interesting that this feature ignores the great event in God's life as we read it out of the Torah in finding Abraham, who unconditionally entrusts himself to God's call and thereby becomes God's possibility of establishing a new relationship with humanity. This covenant, a relationship that had never before been attempted in this fashion, is endangered by the threat of the total destruction of the sinning people. God is willing to get rid of this people that is understood to be the Abrahamitic heritage and to start anew with Moses.

Ultimately, Moses was confronted by that which defies words, the ineffable, the mystery. That is still true even for us. Today's discoveries and scientific conclusions lead us to understand that in the formation of the universe with a big bang, the tiniest variations at that moment would have created an entirely different universe in which humans would never have appeared. Our existence depends on a very limited environment and the confluence of innumerable physical and chemical factors. So today we can refine what we call creation, but we are still confronted with the same unanswerable questions: How come? Whence? Why?

Of course, one could simply take the position that it is beyond the current constitutive being of a human to give any kind of ultimate answer to these questions. Therefore, we will simply refrain from talking about it, from speculating, imagining. For those who can live with this self-imposed limitation, it is right as far as it goes. There is, however, an additional step possible to a believer, because we have a capacity that seems, according to the best of our understanding, to be unique to us as humans – the capacity to have *emuna*. By this we mean that we can take our stand, maybe even an ultimate stand, in something that is not definable, not provable, not rationally discernable. Nothing else in what we call the created order appears to have that capacity. It is one of those additional endowments and capacities that is enveloped by the sheer miracle of the appearance of a human. And if this is an endowment that we have uniquely, why not use it? In fact, we may have been given this strange capacity so that we would use it.

A similar, comparable capacity would be language. We know that communication exists in creation in many different forms; some are very rudimentary, others are quite highly developed. We have a capacity for subtlety, nuance, and creative enrichment of speech. Not only would we be foolish not to use the gift of speech, but in fact we would be unable to understand ourselves as distinct were it not that we have been granted its use. Perhaps we are even compelled to use it. If speech, or the making of music, or any artistic capacity is specific to humans, unique in the complexity and level to which we have risen, then why not follow the invitation of the gift of *emuna* and not make an artificial stop, saying "Beyond this I cannot go"? The capacity of taking that additional step is a truly human achievement. Being a believer is that step. No need to call it a leap, because there is nothing desperate about it, there is nothing so daring about it. It is just another unique gift.

Having faith is not restricted to our relationship to God, it is also basic to our relationships with each other. Over and over again, and sometimes against all evidence, we are capable of trusting in each other, a capacity we need to stress and to celebrate. This leads into the realm we call the divine, or the numinous, or that to which we put the noun "God." It is not a luxury, it is a necessity.

In actuality, it is unlikely that we know more about the nature of God than Moses did. We articulate it differently, but our understanding may not be fundamentally different from his or advanced beyond it. We are just using different words. In all of this, we imagine God somehow to be like we are for the simple reason that there is no other way that we can imagine anything. Of course, the capacity of imaging, of having faith, of believing, is totally linked to our humanness. There is nothing else that informs it. So we continuously and unavoidably speak of God, think of God, imagine God, in terms to which we can relate.

There is a danger in trying to correlate our humanness too closely with the divine, to which we can only hint. To identify something of God from our human vantage point may be a transgression, because sometimes we get to the point where we think we can define God. Anybody who defines holds power, because the definer "sets the limit." If we say what God is, then we have defined God, and then God is what *we* think and allow God to be. We need to stay aware that God must be much more than anyone can say at any time. Unless God remains mysterious, God may become so familiar that we will think ourselves capable of using God. Or we will get to the point where we do not even care anymore because what we know so well becomes so familiar that it ultimately loses its attraction and even its value.

Chapter Eleven
Fundamentals After the Shoah

Surely this great nation is a wise and understanding
people.

(Deuteronomy 4:6)

The Shoah was a radical discontinuity, a break with the past
in many crucial aspects, particularly of the fundamental experience of *emuna*, and therefore also with how we speak of
that belief, especially in the liturgy. It is necessary, however, to
acknowledge that there are some firm posts that have with-
stood the necessity of radical reshaping in the aftermath of the
Shoah.

First and foremost, a "religion" without a belief in God
is not recognizably, or in any form effectively, entitled to the
designation "Jewish." Or to put it differently, there is a verse in
Deuteronomy (4:8) in which Moses declares to his people that
the acceptance of Torah is what makes them a nation, a people.
It is understood, certainly by both Moses and his hearers, and
then by us, that Torah means the relationship put in words
between the mystery of God and the human community. So
Torah is then the binding element. It is the covenantal text, or

as some have said, the *ketubah*, the marriage contract between God and the people.

There is no other way to identify the Jewish community except by this fundamental recognition. Of course, this fundamental recognition carries with it many other ramifications. A monotheistic understanding of God precludes any representation, even ultimately any human articulation, of the God who cannot be represented by anything "in the heavens above, or in the earth below, or in the waters beneath the earth" (Exodus 20:4, Deuteronomy 5:8), to use the statement from the Ten Commandments. It is a God who is incomparable, who cannot be likened to anything in the created order, the reality in which we ordinarily not only live but also by which we identify other items of existence as well as our own selves.

It is true, in a very technical way, to say that God does not exist, God is. And there is a difference between these two verbs. Existence always presumes that there is a trace, an actuality in a sensate fashion. It is something that can be seen and touched. However, that is not what monotheism in its depth can predicate of God. This is the real difficulty of monotheism, which over and over again demands of its adherents a belief in a being that cannot be corroborated in any direct fashion by our senses. As humans we are totally the product of our senses. We are the ultimate sensate being. God, according to the depth of understanding of monotheism, is meta-sensate. This immediately creates a major challenge for most human beings. We need both continuous reinforcement and the joy of having relational contact in a way that confirms our own humanity and is accessible to us through our senses, thereby rooting our identity in something beyond ourselves.

If being human is antithetical to the assertion that God is beyond the senses, and, therefore, cannot be grasped by that which makes us inescapably and totally human, we introduce not only a tension, but also a grave challenge. Perhaps being "made in the image of God" is an attempt to comfort us, to somehow reduce the ultimacy of the Divine Otherness, that Total Being different from what we are. And yet in a very curious way it also hints at the fact that we ourselves are more than just the product of our senses, that there is the capacity of transcendence, imagination, thought. All of these assertions and our experiences of ourselves hint at the fact that there is an additional factor that is not totally reducible to the mere sensateness of our being.

The fact that the monotheistic God has these unique characteristics explains why our ancestors, and perhaps we ourselves, are continuously seduced by, attracted to, and even involved in idolatry. The making of an image, the creation of something accessible to our senses, is so incessant a demand that even devout and totally convinced monotheists are often shaken by the seduction of the tangible image, the "idol." The Torah, the whole Bible, is a record of the struggle of our ancestors against idolatry, against the necessity for the comfort that comes from imagining God as so much like ourselves that the distance between the mystery of the ineffable, incomparable deity and ourselves is narrowed. Nonetheless, and this is the crucial aspect of being a Jew, one is bound to assert, believe in, and live in relation to a Being that is in some specific, basic way totally different from what we know ourselves and experience ourselves to be as humans.

Also untouched by the Shoah is the traditional understanding that in some unimaginably complex and mysterious way, reality is the work of God, the result of God, and is to be understood as the gift of God. God as Creator is the very cornerstone of the Jewish understanding of the nature of God. It is for us the arena of our existence, the unmerited gift that makes us possible. It is only when we recognize it in this fashion and respond to it in this way that the relationship of the Jew to God can be rooted and anchored firmly.

The Sabbath each week is to recall and reemphasize this aspect of the deity. The very institution of the Sabbath becomes an indispensable ingredient of the awareness both of the utter Otherness of God and, paradoxically, of the authorship by that very God of everything that we are, and can understand, imagine, strive for, love, and accept.

The institution of the Sabbath goes all the way back to and before Sinai. It was and is a revolutionary idea in that it demands a total change of life and of function for everyone, including both stranger and servants. Eventually in the history of the Jewish people it is used as the time when, because a person is other than a working animal, one can devote oneself to an entirely different mode of existence. It is a time when one can expand the mind, participate in discussion, feel elevated to the position of a sharer rather than one who is continuously under the heel of the master. The Sabbath is a dangerous institution in this regard, and some, recognizing its revolutionary character, have actually accused the Jews of purposely injecting it into the life of a society that was not at all prepared or willing to have such a different sense of time.

Sabbath has to do with the whole notion that one intentionally attempts to arrest the rush of time, at least as much as we humans can, to give time a different coloration, a different shape. Time is now no longer a virtual enemy, not a taskmaster; now time is a friend, a helper. Having obtained a different status for at least that one day, one can look at the flow of life and the flow of time in a much more affirmative, quiet, and elevating fashion. The Sabbath prohibition of work is intended to lift the human being out of what often is the rut of necessity, which has often been a hard form of responding to, understanding, or being subject to time. In a way, on the Sabbath a person becomes the master of time rather than its slave.

One possible, and often quite noticeable, consequence is a whole change in personality. One has a different character that day. Quoting talmudic sources, the Hasidim used to say that one gets a "Sabbath soul," a very special kind of personality. The truth in this understanding, and also the special way in which the day is linked to God, is based in the fact that even God observes the Sabbath after the Creation.

This is another, obvious example of the fact that we have nothing else but our own experience to inject into deity. We assume that God rested, most likely because we ourselves want to rest. Therefore, it was easy to introduce it into the deity because we noticed that the institution of the Sabbath really is a sacred moment, and has a quality of the holy to such an extent that it is inescapable that we share it with God. Whether or not it was God who instituted the Sabbath, at the moment when the Sabbath became the characteristic mark of Jewish religious life, it was immediately sensed that this furnished a most remarkable, insightful link to the holiness of God.

It is difficult to know exactly when the Sabbath was instituted. On the way to Sinai, there is a story about somebody not observing the Sabbath properly. One of the ten words, or commandments, related to the Sinaitic, revelatory experience, simply says, "Observe the Sabbath." So it must already have been part of life, a life that is now authenticated or deepened in its importance by being understood as a direct intent of God to the Jewish community or anybody else beyond it.

There is also something else that we need to understand, especially in terms of Christianity. The move from Saturday to Sunday as the sacred day of the week was decreed by the Council of Nicea in 325 C.E. It established Sunday as a day emblematic of, and anchored in, the celebration of the resurrection, rather than in a cessation from work. This gives Sunday a different character than the Sabbath as described biblically. Sunday as Sabbath deemphasizes the cessation from work aspect and introduces the fundamental creedal element of the Christian faith in terms of the death and resurrection of the

Savior, though some Torah aspects of Sabbath observance were retained.

There is no reliable evidence of the institution of the Sabbath as a functioning element of Jewish life prior to the exile. What Jews did, how they observed the Sabbath is simply not a feature of the texts. There are no descriptions of how Jews observed the Sabbath, even whether they did so, or whether the Sabbath had already become the cardinal element in the rhythm of life. The very fact that one does not have to go to the Temple in Jerusalem on the Sabbath, but only need go three times a year on the pilgrimage festivals, throws the weight of observance back into each community, each family, each person. The Torah is clear about the obligation to come three times a year to the Temple in Jerusalem, and it speaks of the Sabbath and of the special offerings brought on the Sabbath in the Temple. What that meant, and how it really worked itself out in the actual weekly structure of life in those days, is not at all clear. What is clear is that the books of Ezra and Nehemiah state that special measures had to be instituted to guarantee Sabbath observance by desisting from commerce.

The modern Sabbath observances need to be understood as an outgrowth of the rabbinic development, as contrasted to the biblical. There may not have been a total break with the past in the rabbinic development, in that the rabbis may have latched onto practices and traditions that were in vogue prior to their own formulation of the rules and regulations and the apportionment of functions on the Sabbath. Nonetheless, the way we now understand the Sabbath to be observed is clearly a rabbinic development that primarily took place sometime after the destruction of the Temple, and it remains fundamental. We are living in a time when, for a variety of cultural and economic reasons, the Sabbath really no longer functions as such. The cessation from work is far less noticeable today than it was in some generations past, and this may well have significant consequences.

The relationship between God and the human is not an easy one. It is fraught with continuous tensions and bewilderment, even as it is with the ever present possibility of great joy and fulfillment. It needs to be stated as clearly as it can be that these are our understandings, our human definitions and words, our human grasping for an explanation that can be discussed and lived. Without this search for and acceptance of such words and images, and their radical consequences, a Jewish understanding of God and relationship to God becomes impossible. The singular God is a continuous unmet challenge to anyone, particularly to the Jew, to whom it was given to reach this understanding, apparently as the very first in the human family.

When we talk about matters that remain untouched even after the overwhelming tragedy of the Shoah and its radical discontinuity with so much from the past, we need to take a critical and searching look at the moral system. Monotheism is the basis for a morality that is beyond human control. Here, and, I would say, fortunately, we find something that can remain intact. Moral choices are also divinely sanctioned in polytheism, but they are so varied and even inherently contradictory that a consistent moral system cannot arise. It is only if there is a single source of everything that there are clear, ultimate choices between the permitted and the forbidden.

It is exactly the understanding of the singularity of God that forms the basis of the either/or foundation of the moral challenge. Contrary to anything else we know in Judaism, where it is usually couched, in the relationship of both/and rather than either/or, that in moral terms there are no exceptions to the either/or, though there are highly nuanced discussion of possible variants. Something is either permitted or forbidden, and it can be traced as permitted or forbidden to what we assume to be, understand to be, and accept as being the intention of God as it comes to us out of our covenantal relationship with God and God's revelatory function. It is precisely because God offers God as covenant partner and we accept this offer by dedicating ourselves as co-partners in the covenantal relationship that we also inescapably accept the consequence of those demands, some of which we call morality.

This is true even though God may now be perceived to be in need of reassurance or, as we might put it, help from the human side, in order to assuage hurt, loss, disappointment, and grief for what God's creatures are doing to each other in the world that we assume God never intended to be so abused. Paradoxically, in connection with this aspect of God as sufferer instead of as a triumphant power, one of the great gifts we can return to God is our adherence to and performance of the moral law understood as rooted in God. This could be understood as an assurance to God that no matter how frail, or how disappointing, or how flawed, neglectful, or even obstreperous the Jewish covenantal partner has been and is likely to continue to be, there is also in us an awareness of our moral obligation and a willingness to assume it. Nor is this exclusive to Jews. Anyone and any community similarly bound to God participates in that relationship through their acceptance and performance of the moral law challenged similarly.

If we frame our adherence to the moral code as one of the healing gifts that we offer back to the God who originally gave these gifts to us, then it is clear that morality becomes a sacred act, a recognition of the holiness that is its basis. Morality is not, then, anything done in expectation of a return gift, or a reward, or even some sign of divine approval. Quite the contrary, it becomes another way in which we can let God know that we are here for God precisely because we are willing to perform those acts which we understand as, and therefore assume to have been, God's intentions for us.

This viewpoint lifts the entire question of moral behavior beyond the cause-and-effect sequence so tightly clamped onto the human scene and certainly onto Jewish tradition. The performance of the moral act was always under threat of punishment, on the one hand, or expectation of reward, on the other. We can raise morality to a level of greater purity than just some sort of arrangement in which we engage in the hope that it will be to our benefit. Let us live the moral imperatives for the sake of God, on behalf of God, in an attempt to reassure and heal the Sufferer, who is wounded as a result of the Shoah and other cruelties – those vast areas of injustice and misdeeds on the part of humans one against the other.

This discussion leads back to the most basic and pervasive function of God, that of Creator. It is not so much that God as Revealer or Redeemer is ignored. Rather, it is just that God as Creator is not only primary in terms of the flow of events, but also is primary in terms of our understanding. Even revelation is ultimately an outflow of God as Creator. Revelation is in this regard an aspect of the Creator's understanding that the creatures need guidance, correction, help in order to be the creatures God had hoped for. In order to fulfill the potential of being the covenant partner, the human partner needs continuous injection of insights, directions, challenges, refinements. Were there no human beings, then there would be no need for any of these considerations. Indeed, there could be none.

Two of the great Pharisaic masters in the early development of rabbinic Judaism were those giants of the Torah, Hillel and Shammai. Both of them developed schools of disciples. The Talmud relates that these disciples engaged in the discussion of a very controversial, even startlingly basic question: Should God have created Adam or not? Or to put it even more directly, did God make a mistake in creating us? According to the talmudic record, the schools debated this issue for something like two years. We need not assume that they did so to the exclusion of any other disputes or discussions, but it must have been a recurrent, nagging theme during that time. At the end, the schools came to the stunning conclusion that it would have been better for God not to have created Adam. Or to put it differently, they concluded that God made a mistake.

This is bold. This is full of *chutzpah*. And yet aside from the daring that this statement implies, it also implies nearness and relatedness, because such a statement presumes that humans have a right to say this about God, that humans need not cower in abject servitude before the Master, that they are not slaves. Rather, they are really partners − to be sure, junior partners. Partners can disagree. In fact, implicit in the whole notion of partnership is not only the possibility, but even the expectation, of disagreement, of challenge, of diversity of opinion. Otherwise it isn't a partnership. To be covenantally related to God permits, or even demands, at least the possibility from time to time of radical disagreement.

So the disciples of the great masters engage in a prolonged debate and come to the conclusion that God made a mistake. But that is not the end of the story. The disciples go on to say that as long as we are here, as long as Adam was created and the human, the Jew, came into being, it is up to us "to be very careful with our acts." That is to say, it is now our condition to be extraordinarily sensitive to and aware of the results of our actions. To put it differently and in this context, morality is understood to be our response to the loving gift of God of our life and being. It is now our indispensable and truly human, truly Jewish, answer to God's creation of the human. Morality is not a separate issue, unrelated to the basic understanding of the Jewish tradition of God's being.

One could even say, and I think this is one of the profound, traditional insights coming out of the talmudic literature, that the *mitzvah* system is intended for one overarching purpose: to refine, to gentle the human being. In the rabbinic understanding, there is a wrestling match going on within each of us, a wrestling match between the propensity toward good and the propensity toward evil. The *mitzvah* system, while helpful, can be perceived as very onerous. In fact, tradition speaks of the "yoke of the commandments," a clear indication that the intention inherent in the *mitzvah* is to control, channel, direct the human being, in this instance, the Jew, in a way that he or she will act properly.

Removing ourselves from and going beyond the reward-and-punishment aspect of the *mitzvah* system also flows from the Shoah. Now we adhere to the system because there is a Commander who gives the commandments, and we are returning to the Commander the awareness that we are under commandment. Instead of neglecting the intention, disregarding it, or acting willfully against it, we are attempting to respond affirmatively, maybe even joyfully. In this way, we somehow create assurance, joy, affirmation, healing for the Commanding Source.

This notion of the yoke of the commandments is a very stark picture. Rabbinic tradition was under no illusion that humans are managed easily, that one can bend the tender twig and it will stay in the proper shape for the rest of its existence. On the contrary, rabbinic tradition was always aware of the many seductions and the incessant stream of opportunities that tempt us to disregard our values and go willfully our own way. Therefore, one of the most pervasive and hopefully effective aspects of the whole Jewish understanding of the covenantal relationship is that our response needs to be so much more than verbal, more than liturgical. Rather, it is really our lived life and the quality of life which is the return gift God wants, and now perhaps needs more than ever before. We need to be reminded of the quality of our response, of our failure to make our response adequate to our awareness of the enormity of the gift that we have received and represent more frequently than

once a year at Yom Kippur. Indeed, one of the conscious intentions of the liturgy is to remind us of these facts.

The miracle of being human is overwhelming, immense,
limitless. Not to understand this, and to be deaf and blind to
it, as our routine existence so often induces us to be, is one of
the causes of additional grief to God. This is surely the symbol
and actuality of our own deficiencies. The fulcrum of Jewish
tradition lies here. The best and indispensable evidence of the
quality of our humanity, of our understanding of the miracle of
being human, of being a Jew, is in the act of performance.

Of course the miracle of being a Jew is heightened, as
against that of being some other type of human being, for the
simple reason that we have suffered a history unprecedented
for the recurrent pain, suffering, persecution, rejection, defamation, and murder inflicted on us. As great and as indispensable a gift as the disclosure of the singularity of God may have
been to the whole future of humanity, it also has exposed those
of us who are its witnesses to continuous opposition, calumny,
rejection.

Perhaps the frequent proclivity toward anti-Judaism is ultimately to be traced beyond any other, ancillary causes to the
fact that we taught the world the moral consequences of the
singularity of God, and therefore became their primary witnesses and supposed exemplars. Many, perhaps unconsciously,
have never forgiven us for bringing this insight into the world
and to the consciousness of humanity. Yet the ultimate purpose
of what we call religion, religious systems, and communities is
to be witnesses and teachers of the inescapable consequences
of the monotheistic divine singularity. It has not been an easy
journey for the Jew. The Shoah was horrific, the monstrous
most recent chapter in this dangerous, perilous journey.

Polytheism is so much more comfortable. It is a much easier environment for the human to live in. Monotheism imposes
demands which inherently, instinctively, the human is not built

to accept and to follow readily. It takes an act of will, vigilance, training, and the awareness of difficult, sometimes uncomfortable tasks to perform, choices to make of the way to live.

The question is whether it is worth it. And while perhaps many nonobservant Jews today would not go through the process of making such an analysis in a step-by-step fashion, nonetheless, many would rightly perceive being a witness, being a Jew, as too great a burden. There is a Yiddish proverb, "*Shwer tzu sein a yid*, It is difficult to be a Jew." This saying is not merely a reflection of imposed poverty, restrictions, ridicule, and rejection, it is also the truth about the inherent and very real burden of being witnesses.

There is a tradition that when, upon awakening, one recites the *Sh'ma*, the affirmation of the singularity of God, the watchword of the monotheistic belief assumption, one thereby takes upon oneself the "yoke" of the divine rule. Jews are bidden to do this every day for as long as they wake up. Therefore, one can have a certain degree of understanding and perhaps empathy with those who say it is too much. The burden is too great. The price is too high. There are easier ways to live that are less demanding and ultimately less painful.

We should not forget that the Greek word for "witness" is *martyros*. It must be understood that a witness may well be the person who puts his or her very life on the line in order to assert, and continue to assert, the uniqueness of God. But to be witnesses to God, while a strange kind of role, is also very powerful. Once one understands that this is the opportunity and expectation, then to be such a witness also becomes the source of deep fulfillment. So witnessing is both burdensome and dangerous, but also a very high rung on the ladder of human fulfillment.

There is a footnote here, although it is much more, – a talmudic, midrashic commentary on the phrase in Isaiah that goes to the effect "You are my witnesses, and I am God" (Isaiah 43:12).

A talmudic sage spins the phrase this way: "*Only* as long as you are my witnesses am I God." So even witnessing is not a one-way street, a single act. Again, it entails the possibility of reciprocity.

Even God's own being is affected, perhaps radically, by our willingness to witness to God. What would happen if all Jews were to take an oath never again to speak of God, to think of God, to do anything about God? Is it too great an arrogance to say that this would affect God? Or let us even go further: what if all humanity should decide by a resolution that God was no longer to be addressed, thought of, involved in the ongoing life of human beings? Does not God depend on our awareness of God in order to be effective? Is not the story of the creation of Adam – and this is its genius – an assertion that without Adam, God is really not the kind of God that God wanted or even perhaps needs to be?

Giraffes, field mice, roses, orchids, crystals – all are lovely aspects of God's creatorship. But, at least as far as we can assume at the current level of our knowledge, they do not have an awareness of all this, or the capacity to respond or to refuse to respond. Therefore, even in witnessing to the creation, there is an indispensable, implicit reciprocity. It produces an effect on the deity.

This is astounding. It again shows that the covenant is truly a power-sharing relationship. For to refuse to witness, to refuse to be there for God, *is* in the power of the human being. And it is the recognition of this power that really is part of the religious moment. The moment is not a once-and-for-all event. It is merely an example of that which occurs regularly, and the possibilities for which are incessant.

The morning recitation of the *Sh'ma*, the acceptance of the yoke, the acceptance of the relationship, is institutionalized in another way as well. Jewish tradition says that we should say a hundred *brachot*, or "blessings," a day. What is the intent of saying a *bracha*? It is to be mindful of the involvement of God in whatever the blessing aims at or points to. Whether that is lightning, or food, or a person, whatever the occasion may be that elicits the response of a blessing, certainly part of the intent is to again become aware of the involvement of God in all of reality.

So God is omnipresent, which is the only one of the three "omnis" that has escaped the Shoah. Neither omniscience nor omnipotence is, to my mind, any longer possible in statements concerning God. But omnipresence remains, certainly in a giving fashion, and sometimes in a receiving manner, sometimes joyously, sometimes grievously. When some of the Hasidim said that there is not a single item or action in the created order that does not potentially speak of God, they correctly meant that there is this all-pervasive possibility of sensing God even in the least expected and seemingly totally unrelated moments of every day.

The third fundamental of Judaism that survives the Shoah is the synagogue. I consider the synagogue to be the single most important gift that the Jewish people have made, both to the institution of religion and, beyond that, to the depth of the world's religious life. Without the synagogue as a model, there would not have been a church or a mosque. It is worth discussing how the Jewish people moved to a Temple-based religion and then away from it.

According to our texts, the Temple on Mount Zion in Jerusalem was clearly an institution modeled after the patterns of the surrounding cultures. If the texts are at all true, and there is no reason to doubt it, King Solomon asked his friend, King Hiram of Tyre, to send him architects and masons and other skilled craftsmen in order to build the Temple. This indicates that there may have been as yet no such talents available within the Jewish community. Also, the only kind of a Temple the Tyrian architects and masons could have built was one of the type with which they were familiar and had built for their own people, essentially a pagan solar temple. Thus, for instance, the whole orientation of the Jerusalem Temple from east to west was based on solar considerations. And there are traces in our traditional literature indicating that our ancestors were aware of this.

In about 165 B.C.E. after having recaptured Jerusalem, the Maccabees refurbished the Temple, which had been abused by the Syrian conquerors. Listed among the acts of the restoration of the Temple was the hanging of burnished copper and gold shields on its eastern wall. Now the only plausible explanation seems to be that this was done in order to catch the splendor of the rising sun's rays to make it appear that the whole Temple was aglow, almost aflame, with the miracle of the resurrection of the sun from its apparent nightly death.

A passage in the Mishna, in the section called *Yoma*, which deals with Yom Kippur, states that while "our ancestors used to bow to the east, we now bow to the west." Again, it would seem to me that these are traces of a practice that had to do with the phenomenon of the sun's arrival each morning as a harbinger of life, light, and all the implicit and explicit values that are framed in such a statement.

Some modern scholars claim that the story of the Tabernacle in the desert is an *ex post facto* story told to justify the building of the Temple in Jerusalem. Interestingly, if, in fact, our ancestors built a Tabernacle in the desert, it too had an east-west orientation, showing the influence of the orientation of the major temples in Egypt. Not only is it likely that the Temple in Jerusalem was not built on the model of the Tent, but that the Tent was a fictional *post-factum* creation in order to give the Temple authenticity as part of the earlier foundational chapter of the people's emergence, not only onto the stage of history, but as covenant partners of the singular God.

It is also quite clear that what happened in the Temple in

Jerusalem is in no way basically different from what happened in all other types of temples at the time. Temples were considered to be the residence of the god in whose name and by whose power they were built. There needed to be attendants to make sure that the majesty of the deity was properly recognized and served, and there was a need for a very elaborate etiquette and set of regulations that only those who were highly trained and designated to know and enforce them were entitled to practice. The central purpose of the establishment of sacred buildings and precincts was not only to provide a residence for the deity, but also to have a designated place where gifts could be brought to the deity, an action which needed to be done in a fashion regulated by those who alone were licensed to offer these gifts, these offerings to the various deities.

It is very difficult for a God who is a unique, singular God to be the supposed resident of a given place and accessible only in a given place to an extent quite different and more effective than any other place. If God is the creator of the universe, if God is the God of all human beings, then it is difficult to concentrate the essence of God's presence in a tiny point on the globe, or in one specific space in a given city, or, even more precisely and definitely, in a rather small cubicle. The purpose of the edifice was in itself a *tour de force* that ultimately could not withstand basic question and review.

What I am really saying is that the Temple was inherently a nonmonotheistic establishment. It was a concession to the need of the people to have something concrete, something visible, something to which they could go, someplace to which they could point. The Temple was a place where they could believe that the omnipresence of God was so highly concentrated that they had, by way of their deputies, licensed access to it. The Temple needed to be totally regulated, but nevertheless it was a possible access to God.

This is inherently a contradiction to the monotheistic idea

of God. God should be everywhere, and anyone should have access. There is a biblical verse expressing this notion: "In every place where I will allow My name to be mentioned, I will bless you" (Exodus 20:24). Prior to the establishment of the Temple and the priesthood, Abraham, Isaac, Jacob, and others brought their own offerings to altars they themselves built wherever they thought was a proper, acceptable place. In a way, the Torah interprets the sin of the golden calf as God's becoming aware that the people need God palpably, concretely present, resident. The motivation for the building of the Tabernacle is for God "to dwell among them" (Exodus 25:8). They need to build a suitable residence for the God who up to that time was not felt or accepted as being among them.

Why was this necessary? Because just a few weeks after the greatest event in Jewish history, the revelation at Mount Sinai, the descent of God to the mountain, and the mountain being in total uproar, God disappears together with Moses. The mountain is totally still. The heavens are serene. And a group of newly escaped former slaves was left leaderless in the desert, not knowing where their leader was, not knowing where the God whom they had accepted as their liberator had disappeared. The panic that set in when the recognition of this abandonment, as they saw it, sunk in and gripped them, led them to demand that the only leader who was left, Aaron, make an idol. Characteristic of the Egyptian acculturation, they made a calf, a bovine. After all, the chief animalistic symbol of Ra in Egypt was a bull.

The reading of the text indicates that this act so upsets God that God wants to destroy the whole people. Moses dissuades God with the strange argument that such an act would be bad for God's reputation among the nations. God would seem to have been unable to manage this obstreperous people whom God had freed and to whom God had revealed not only divinity, but instructions.

As I read it, and the Hebrew text is very clear, this is a moment of discovery and education for God, who now realizes that God must "dwell among them," become present, become immanent. In order for God to do so, the people needed to build a proper house for the deity, similar to what was done in every other culture in the world at that time. So, to begin with, the whole notion of a Temple was a concession to the impossibility for this nation, newly created and a covenant partner, to live the full implications of these two facts. The concession took the form of physical structures and cultic practices almost indistinguishable from anything other religious systems had evolved into doing a long time before the Jews entered history.

We need to understand that the battle against the impact of assimilation with surrounding cultures was really never won, and certainly not before the Babylonian exile began in 586 B.C.E. According to our texts, Solomon dedicates the Temple to the unseen God, which was intended by him, and by the others who participated in the glorious event, to be the incorporation, the very embodiment, of the monotheistic understanding of God (1 Kings 8). However, even in Solomon's time, this is soon tainted. Not only did some of the wives he married bring their own cultic practices into space assigned in the Temple for their own chapels, but Solomon himself erects idols to three deities in the self-same Temple.

The whole history of the Temple in pre-Babylonian exilic times is one of continuous infestation by idolatry and its practice, very often at the instigation and under the championship of the ruling monarch. There were only two or three leaders in the whole list of kings, beginning with Solomon through to the exile in 586 B.C.E., who were monotheists to the point where they tried to deestablish and sometimes actually destroy the idolatrous features of the Temple. Such efforts were never permanent. These reforms occur from time to time simply because the bulk of the Temple service is always tainted with idolatrous practices. The references to this in the Tanach include a description of women coming to the Temple to worship the Queen of Heaven and emerging from cubicles in the Temple with markings on their foreheads.

The Temple cult was a deviation, a contradiction from the inherent understanding of what the singular God needs from the worshiper, from the devotee. Some of the prophets, of course, understood this. They criticized and sometimes even satirized the behavior of people who came to the Temple and sometimes even ridiculed, and therefore rejected, the offering cult. It was not until the destruction of the Temple under the onslaught of the Babylonian Empire that a review and change occurred.

First of all, there is no more Temple, no more altar. No longer is any one place the supposedly sole licit area in which God could be worshiped. Moreover, many of the priests are taken into captivity into Babylon and can no longer function as priests because it was clearly understood that the only place where the worship of the Jewish God could proceed legally was in Jerusalem on Mount Zion. In exile, these priests were out of a job; they had no function. What happens therefore during the exile is a significant, fairly radical shift away from the altar.

The only religious item the people may have brought with them in exile were sacred texts, the scrolls. No longer could they maintain their specific identity as a people who worshiped God by means of the cultic exercises performed for many centuries. Now all they had were sacred texts that recounted some of these practices and told part of the story of the beginning of this people, even of the whole world. We cannot know the exact nature of these texts – whether they had the whole five books of Torah, or parts of it, or scrolls of some of the prophetic texts. No one really knows.

We know that in the Temple Levites chanted hymns and psalms. Apparently they could not perform even these marginal accompanying aspects of the offering cult in exile. Psalm 137 indicates the Babylonians actually taunted the exiles to sing the hymns of God, the psalms. They replied that it was impossible on strange soil, indicating that in their theology, God was limited to the territory of the land of Israel, the sacred land. It is interesting theologically that God cannot be addressed except in God's own land. "How can we sing God's hymns in a strange land, on a strange soil?" (Psalm 137:4). In their perception, without the altar on Mount Zion, there could not be a legitimate approach to the deity.

Under these circumstances and conditions, something happened that I consider to have been the seedbed of the institution we ultimately came to call the synagogue. In the absence of the altar and therefore of the offering cult, the texts gave the Jewish exiles in Babylonia the only remaining binding element for their religious life. In other words, what they now needed to concentrate on, and what formed the glue holding them together as a separate, religiously identifiable people were the sacred texts – Torah.

There are indications that point to the likelihood and importance of these texts. In the fifth century, among those who eventually returned from the Babylonian captivity, was a figure named Ezra, who is usually identified as a scribe. However, the Hebrew word is *sofer*. This word is correctly interpreted as "scribe" because it can mean someone who is literate, someone who can read and write. But I would like to take a much narrower definition, because I think the right interpretation may be that a *sofer* is someone who knows the *sefer*, that is, the holy book. So Ezra was not just somebody who could read and write. Ezra was an expert in the sacred texts. He was an intellectual, a man knowledgeable in the written word, who apparently had found a place in the life of the Jewish exilic community. May we not infer that such sages, or "book men," did not function in the pre-exilic Jewish community as long as they were living in their own land and had the Temple and the priests serving on their behalf? Certainly there is no evidence of them. Ezra was clearly not a priest. So out of the Babylonian exilic experience comes a man who is known as the "book man," as the scholar of the book, *biblion* in Greek, or *biblia*, the Bible, as we call it to this day.

The Babylonian exile may have directed some of the Jews who lived there toward the texts as their primary communal element, as well as the primary way of probing life, approaching God, and finding the meaning of the universe and the human condition. The text became the primary way of being faithful to God when offerings were no longer possible.

In connection with a discussion of offerings, it needs to be understood that such offerings were universal. Every religious culture of the time had offerings. But sacred texts, and the study and understanding of those texts as the binding element between a community and their God, may well have been unique. We do not know for certain why the people came to depend, possibly quite enthusiastically and joyfully, on the reading of the texts, the discussion of their contents, and the invitation to imagination that comes from the texts, as the central feature of their religious life.

But we do know that something extraordinary happens during the Babylonian exile. Before the exile, the religious life of the Jewish community was one-track: Temple-centered, altar-centered, priest-centered. A small minority of the Jews in captivity return after the exile, and now there is a two-track Judaism. The Temple is rebuilt by 516 B.C.E. The offering cult is restored, and the priests are functioning again. The priesthood, headed by the high priest, had an elevated status in the postexilic time compared to its preexilic role. In fact, the high priest becomes the top of the societal pyramid because there is no king, no secular ruler, since the community was subject to the Persian imperial system. But alongside the priesthood, the altar, and the Temple, there is now this innovative concentration on texts.

Ezra, when he returns, decisively becomes the organizer and shaper of the new commonwealth by holding a convocation for the purpose of the reading of the texts. It is clear that the people to whom he read from the text had never before heard it and were smitten by its contents. It is hard to know whether this means that during the exile and the absence of the upper strata of society, those who had remained in Jerusalem were untutored, or whether it is possible that the mode of religious life before the exile consisted of a total and exclusive concentration on the altar, the priests, the Temple, and the offerings. There is very little evidence in the Torah itself of any regular, organized, consistent reading or study of texts as far as the people were concerned. While the people may have done this in the Babylonian exile when they could not offer up the ordinary, regular means of reconciliation between God and humans, to do so in Jerusalem and therefore in the country would have been an apparently unprecedented experience for them.

After all, the ordinary person had no significant role in the Temple. Only priests, who were priests by virtue of being born male into the right kind of family, had any access to the really important sacred functions. All the ordinary person could do was to bring the offering, hoping that it would be accepted by the priest stationed at the gate to examine it before it was brought into the Temple. It was not possible for a lay person to know which, if any, of the animal parts were his in any given offering being taken to the altar in solemn procession by the priests. There were certainly multiple offerings made each day, and it was most likely impossible to identify one's own animal as being offered up at a given moment in time. So the role of the lay person in the Temple setup was minimal.

The book of Leviticus served as a manual for priests, an instruction text as to how to function in their new role. Before the Tent in the desert and the Temple on Mount Zion, there had been no functioning priesthood. Abraham certainly was a Jew in every sense of the word. Abraham built altars and brought offerings, but there was no Temple, no priesthood. The whole offering cult was really based on the assumption that it was necessary for the deity to be assuaged. The deity needed the continuous evidence of human faithfulness as expressed through the bringing of gifts. This was clearly part of the reward-and-punishment construct.

It is taught in the rabbinic development of Judaism that one performs religious duties for their own sake. The ideal study of Torah is not done in the anticipation of reward or in the fear that one will be punished for not studying. The highest level of Torah study is for its own sake – *lishma*. When one is engaged in study and discussion of words and text, it is, of course, easier to feel the possibility of being liberated from the clamp of reward and punishment than if it is a question of bringing gifts to a deity who requests them, a deity who needs a gift as a sign of the human fulfillment of obligation. The omission to carry out such an obligation obviously implies an immediate dire consequence, whereas the opposite is rewarded. In fact, if these gifts are brought continuously and correctly, then the deity will be friendly, supportive, and in a kindly mood.

However, when we start listening to a text and are encouraged to ask questions about what we are hearing, or reading, and if there are experts, teachers, scholars, who engage us in the examination of the texts, something novel and exciting happens to us. All at once we become an indispensable part of the action. We are drawn into the process of study, of hearing, of reading, in a fashion that no cult offering can even minimally approach. So it is easy to understand that the concentration on texts must have been a remarkable opening up of their human potential for the people who engaged in it. They must have felt, and perhaps for the first time, that they were not just passive participants, but active in the religious endeavor to search for the meaning of God and God's intentions for the individual and the community.

Some individuals may already have known the stories that form the history of Judaism, but the Torah is not only stories, it is also law and ethics. There is material in the sacred texts that invites participation without hindrance to the searching mind, the questioning spirit. People thus caught up in a totally new experience, an experience at that time unique to the Jewish community, must have felt a liberation of person and elevation of status that the Temple mode, the altar, the priest, could not offer them. Quite on the contrary, in that system they were totally at the mercy of those who had a monopoly on the means of salvation. By contrast, they now became fellow searchers, true participants in the quest for understanding, for truth, for inspiration. It must have been an exhilarating, liberating, experience the like of which we probably will never fully understand or grasp, for the simple reason that we have lived now for more than two thousand years in a text-oriented civilization and religious life.

When the Temple was destroyed again in the year 70 by the Romans, Jews now had another track, another way of expressing themselves religiously, and one that has proven not merely to be a substitute but, in fact, an invigorating, vivifying, electrically charged methodology for living a religious life. It was a genuine alternative to the Temple cult. Despite the absence of real evidence on which to form a definitive decision as to the exact time when the synagogue came into being, it is clear that this newly found means of being religiously faithful and active through study of the sacred texts would have led to the formation of participatory assemblies of people. It is plausible that the people would have clustered around persons they recognized as scholars, experts, teachers. Such a scenario is a plausible explanation of the development of the synagogue. Of course, there is the additional clue that there were synagogues in the Greek world. It seems likely that their development was another evidence of the influence of Hellenism upon Judaism in the Mediterranean world. Hellenism deeply influenced the entire civilization of that whole part of the world with the coming of Alexander the Great in the latter half of the fourth pre-Christian century. After all, the very name "synagogue" is Greek.

The transition of the synagogue from a place of study to a place of worship was an outgrowth of the division of the country into twenty-four districts, each of which was obligated twice a year to furnish the minimum number of animals that had to be offered up at the Temple each day. Groups of people in various districts of the country would convene at the same time that their deputies would be in Jerusalem furnishing the offerings for the week. The custom apparently sprung up that while the delegations were in Jerusalem, the home folk would gather at the time that the offerings were brought, in the morning, and at dusk, to co-celebrate. They would do this by chanting hymns, psalms, and perhaps there were some who could even compose a prayer. They may have gotten into the habit here or there of reading sacred texts related to the offerings being brought. Unfortunately, we have no records, and much of this is just conjecture.

On the other hand, it is a fact that when the Temple was destroyed, Judaism did not disintegrate, unlike the fate of other temple-based religions. It might be said, in terms of the Jewish tradition at the time, that the heart of the religious life that had been shattered and torn out was put back and healed by the synagogue. The synagogue was apparently sufficiently developed to fill the enormous void caused by the destruction of the Temple and altar.

The synagogue is not merely the successor of the Temple. It is a totally new, enormously enriching, and dynamic means of living a religious life. The elimination of the altar and its functioning priests ended what was thought to be the sole, indispensable, monopolistic path to God. The replacement is, as it is sometimes called, the "offering of the lips," that is, the words of the worshiper. This replacement raised the status of the individual, who now was allowed to speak to God directly without the intermediation of an ordained and therefore solely licit functionary.

To me this elevation of the individual to a functioning component of the community became the real seedbed of democracy. Historically, Athens is usually identified as the starting point of democracy, but the democracy in Athens was elitist. One had to own property in order to vote. Someone without property, which would have been the situation of the vast majority of Athenians, had neither vote nor voice. But in the synagogue everybody is equal before God. There is no inherent need for anyone to act as a conduit and, therefore, to take the place of the individual in the unfolding of liturgical, hence religious, life.

However, without some structure of liturgical life, the synagogue would have been chaotic. It would probably not have been able to survive as a functioning institution. In Judaism, we have always placed the emphasis on the group, on the community, not primarily on the individual. The synagogue certainly is an expression of a group of people; in fact, there need to be ten adults in order to establish the quorum, the *minyan*, which is the minimum number of adults for the conduct of the authorized order of service.

So the synagogue functioned, and continues to function to this day, in two paradoxically opposite ways. It is an example of the both/and norm that runs through Judaism so continuously. It raises the individual to a status never before obtained, in that every person is considered qualified to face God directly. At the very same time, the synagogue insists that we have to do this together, as a group. The nature of the synagogue, the essential quality of the synagogue, is really paradoxical.

While there are people who yearn for the reestablishment of the Temple in Jerusalem and the re-institution of a functioning priesthood on a rebuilt altar, this is to me anachronistic and totally undesirable. The synagogue Jew, devoted to prayer and study, devoted to the words in whatever form, is the true embodiment of the original intent of the covenant and is the link to the Sinai event. At that moment at Sinai, there was no altar, no priest, no Temple, no offering. There was a word, there was a sound, and there was a reception of the word by the pledge to live out its meaning.

The Temple has always been an interloping interference in the genius of the Jewish understanding of the religious life. So I do not yearn for, or pray for, the restoration. I might mourn the destruction of the Temple for the simple reason that these were grievous wounds inflicted by enemies. But the synagogue is the living embodiment of the real genius of the Jewish way of searching for God, trying to be faithful toward what one understands to be the intent of God for human beings.

Fourth and finally, after monotheism, the Sabbath, and the synagogue, the cessation of the Temple as the sacred center and focus of the religious life gave the home a focal role in religious life that most likely it never had before. The fundamental importance to Judaism of the home, sometimes called a miniature Temple, is an idea that is too often neglected or not even understood. In a way, the home becomes a successor to and substitute for the Temple, with the dining table being an altar, and father and mother being the priests. It is believed that the Divine Presence enters into the home. Religious practice is developed within a home setting that may never have existed when the Temple was built and functioned as the sacred center. Not only is the individual elevated in the synagogue, but the home now becomes equal to the synagogue, the successor to the Temple. The real center of Jewish life is in the home; the synagogue, with all that it represents, is an adjunct to the home. The notion that Jewish family life is elevated above that of the surrounding environment and cultures could well be traced to this – the significant role, religiously speaking, which Jewish family life had in the community.

To some extent this could explain and may partially excuse the fact that the synagogue became a male club in which women had very little, if any, participatory role. On the other hand, in the home, the woman was really in her element. She was the queen of the house. Her function was nurturer, healer, and the one who had the responsibility of making the home fit for the kind of religious life that was expected to be conducted within it. This responsibility raised her to a position that she could not have had as long as the Temple was the all-absorbing focal point.

This supremacy in the home goes even further, because the woman has also the cardinal role in the sexual life, in the regulation of the periods of intercourse, in her obligations and opportunities to ensure the ritual purity of her own person and of the whole home. It is she who deals with the dietary laws and really is in charge of the preservation of the fitness of the home as a place for the expression of religious elements from morning to night, every day of the week, throughout the entire year. Not only is the home now a parallel to the synagogue, it is for the woman the equivalent of the synagogue.

There is a rabbinic statement that women are exempt from any *mitzvah*, any obligation, that has to be performed at a given time, such as regular services, because they are engaged in works that are the equivalent of what the religious content of the rest of the *mitzvah* system was intended to represent. These are really extraordinary kinds of consequences, and they have shaped Jewish life decisively.

The idea of *shalom bayit*, the peace of the house, the unfracturedness of the house, the harmony of the house, is more than just an appeal for human relations of decency, sensitivity, compassion. It also verbally relates one's house to God. It is an ideal in Jewish life to strive for *shalom bayit*. Therefore, it is also one of the deplorable facts of our contemporary Jewish life that some of the magnificent and deeply moving values and ideas of this tradition are either unknown to some Jews, maybe even to many, and no longer function as a compelling element of family life and structure. In this regard, the immersion of Judaism into the general culture has damaged it and led to an adulteration of what could be the identity of the Jew in our time.

The notion of sacred space, when understood in this fashion, is tied inescapably to the flow of time. We meet at certain times around the table. We observe sacred seasons and holy moments and events together as a family. The interesting thing is always that the main focus of Jewish life, the main arena of Jewish ritual life, is the home and not the synagogue. The synagogue is an adjunct to the home, but the home is the main place in which Jewish life is intended to function and needs to function.

There are many Jews who consider the Temple Mount sacred because they have adopted a stratified position with regard to space. There is certainly a strong component within the Jewish tradition that draws these concentric circles with the Temple Mount at the center. The land of Israel is more holy than other lands; within the land of Israel, the city of Jerusalem is more sacred; within Jerusalem, the Temple Mount is more sacred. It is understandable why this was done when it became necessary to create a single sacred space eliminating all others. In polytheism there was an immense proliferation of sacred spaces because the gods and goddesses have the capacity to appear and be present to their worshipers and could be worshiped just about everywhere. One of the portentous consequences of worshiping the Single God was the concentration of sanctity to a single space, a single place on the globe.

However, Judaism has twice survived the destruction of that sacred precinct and the people's removal from it. What we ought to learn from this is that God is available wherever any of us search for God, reach out to, pray to, hope for God. In other words, the history of my people can teach me that there is no monopoly of a given place on the globe in which God becomes more available, and toward which, as a result, my whole orientation from a religious point of view should be directed totally. The omnipresence of God is not only a basic aspect of the singularity of God, but becomes the extraordinary component of God that makes it possible to approach God, to be reaching out toward God anywhere, under any circumstance, in any place. This is a central, basic, most remarkable understanding.

The concentration of God's presence and availability in only one particular location has idolatrous overtones and leads to the deification of that which is not God. Omnipresence, God's availability wherever one seeks to reach toward the divine, is the indispensable ingredient of my own religious understanding. When Jewish tradition sanctified the home, the table, the parents, as a replacement for the now no longer available Temple, altar, and officiants in Jerusalem, it not only managed a catastrophic development of historic proportions, it was also a radically new idea of the relationship of the human with the divine.

Chapter Twelve
Worship in the New Millennium

Adonai, open my lips and my mouth shall speak your praises.

(Liturgy)

Liturgy means "the work of the people," and worship is that work. Worship is our repeated assertion and evidence of the awareness we have been given, in a totally unmerited fashion, the world and life itself. Repeatedly, we are not only impelled to give evidence of this awareness, but to reinforce within ourselves the articulation of it. As human beings gifted with language, from time to time it is necessary to state in unmistakable and perhaps captivating words that which moves us, that which constitutes us in the most profound fashion. And thus our basic stance should be one of limitless gratitude and, to use Heschel's great phrase, "radical amazement" – amazement at the very root of our being at the receipt of these gifts.

Each of us needs regularly to give expression to this basic constitutive fact of our existence. So for me worship becomes a necessity, not imposed from the outside, but welling up almost without any effort from within my own perception of who I am,

214 | HINENI — HERE I AM

of how deeply I have been gifted with depths of possibility and actuality that are beyond description and total understanding. When I think of my own body and the absolute, sheer limitless complexity of my physical being, I cannot help but be in a continuous stance of wonder and gratitude. So my worship is my return of my thanks to the mystery of God, to whatever level I have risen in understanding who I am, where I am, what the possibilities of my existence might be, what I might perhaps have done or could do or need to do.

Of course, in a way one could say that one's whole daily life ought to be a form of worship. That is certainly a very lucent possibility: to understand oneself as an ongoing act of worship is a window into the mystery of being human. Such a concept, when fully understood, would be a guide to a type of life that to our detriment and shame most of us do not live. But it may also very well be that if one actually tried to live constantly in this type of aware condition, it could be both a continued spur and a real hindrance. The very demanding nature of living our life is likely to take over to such an extent that it deadens the resolve of living up to so maximally devout a possibility.

Sometimes I really am afraid that those who immerse themselves in, and therefore insist on, the formalities of the liturgy, even if performed irregularly, thereby feel excused from and not compelled to live out what worshipfulness is intended to convey in the rest of their daily routine or lives. This is always a danger. Of course one should not use this potentiality as an excuse for desisting from liturgy, but at the very same time we ought not to be too harsh in our judgment of people who do not participate in organized worship on a regular basis or perhaps at all. Sometimes, the life they lead is more of an expression of an awareness of God than can happen in a formalized liturgical setting. I think of people who deal with the poor and with the distressed, of people who are able to convey beauty and art, of people who are so totally engaged in life that one could think of their life as the equivalent of a formal liturgical setting. Indeed sometimes they are even a better example of the worship due to the Source of these enormous gifts with which we are endowed.

Here however, we come to a typically Jewish problem, namely that Jews are intended to pray in community. When you intend to do anything in community, you have to find a common element. Since Jews are verbal, attuned to listening as the primary experience, the necessity of finding a shared communication form is unavoidable. Here we get into trouble because we then clearly bump up against the fact that the verbalization of one period or of one group may not be sufficient or adequate for another period or another group.

I know of a present-day rabbi who wanted everyone in the congregation to feel like a tree, rooted, growing, having branches, and being open to the world, to the air, the sun, the rain. That was that rabbi's religion. To me, celebration of the physical for its own sake is idolatry. It is okay to recognize the physical as God's handiwork, as a reminder of the otherwise unapproachable and inarticulable, pervasive presence of the deity. When it comes down to being totally oriented to the individual self, it may be very nice and very helpful, and it may make people feel good, but it isn't Jewish. We are not primally oriented toward the individual per se. Rather, the individual is a component of a community.

The trend toward individualism is certainly responsive to an overwhelming tendency in our society, the almost complete focus and concentration on the individual, not on the community, not on relations with others. If you tell me that you take Buber's approach, that the individual is only an individual if there is an "other," yes of course, that is Judaism. I can only be "I" if there is a "You." But that is not what this current kind of individualism is: I feel good; I unfold myself; I don't need an other, indeed, there is no other; I can do this all by myself. The

Talmud says that the only way to God is through the other –
other humans. But what is being said now is "Be yourself, fulfill yourself. Go into the depth of your own being." The whole
emphasis is what is too commonly known as spirituality. You
can fulfill yourself when you are unhappy, in conflict, torn, in
pain, puzzled, unsure, for you will find all the answers inside
yourself.

This is the result of our profound reliance, our concentration, on the psychological, which has certainly become a
hallmark of our modernity. Freud and his collaborators and
successors certainly opened up a whole new way of looking at
the self, of analyzing the self, of dealing with the self. I am sure
that much of what they found and taught about is valid and
of great help, but what is happening in our civilization is that
it has led to a virtually exclusive concentration on the self in
contrast to what is the heart of the Jewish tradition, and that is
the relational – the both/and, not the either/or.

None of us has an individual covenant with God. The covenant was made with the whole people at Mount Sinai. Before
that it was with individuals, Abraham, Isaac, and Jacob, but that
has been supplanted forever. Now we are introduced by the
circumcision ritual into the patriarchal covenant, the covenant
with Abraham, because that was the first one. But we do not
have an individual covenant with God, we have a covenantal
relationship with God as a result of our being part of the covenantal community which is the partner with God.

Of course, there is an individual response to the Mystery
of God. Judaism is very hospitable to this, and inconceivable
without a celebration of the individual, but always again within
the framework of the community. Because modern Reform
Judaism is much more resonant with and receptive to the
streams of civilization in which we now find ourselves, we are
influenced by the cultural celebration of the individual. So, for
instance, in Reform Judaism it is often assumed that all of us

have a right to make up our own minds about everything. This leads first of all to diffusion, and second, very often individual decisions are made without understanding the elements from which Jewish tradition formulated its earlier decisions and therefore its responses to the challenges of life. What is really the problem of our modern Judaism is to find the confluence of traditional competence and knowledge with openness and a receptivity toward what modernity offers in its own unique and unprecedented fashion. And time and again that is an acrobat's act on the high wire.

An individual Jew needs to do the homework necessary to get to that point or be willing to consult those who have already done so. In contrast, there is an illusion, based on misinformation, that everybody has equal competence to make decisions. This is even true of some of my colleagues. We were at a retreat a while ago where one of my colleagues was involved in the totally traditional methodology of praying: *davening, tallit, tefillin,* and so on. Someone was upset with him and went up to him after one of the services and challenged him.

This person asked him, "Don't you realize that you are a Reform rabbi?"

He responded, "Reform means choice. This is my choice."

The answer was both glib and wrong, because Reform does not mean that everything can find its place under its umbrella. That understanding of Reform Judaism is a misuse of a kind of limited, circumscribed freedom that modernity insists on and which I find congenial and attractive. It stands in contrast to the ultra-traditionalist position in which the individual has almost no choices because one is told what is incontestably right, and what is the only right way. You had better not deviate or otherwise you are in trouble. Neither of the these two positions on either extreme are acceptable to me.

Again, I have individual responsibility, to be sure. The community is is made up of individuals. But individuals get their standing, character, identity within the community. The community, the *mishpacha*, the family in a very extended fashion, makes someone who he or she really is. This is why one is born a Jew, but, for instance, is never born a Christian. One has to be made a Christian, either by the administration of certain rites or, at a certain time in one's development, by voluntarily and very consciously adopting that particular way of life and believing.

I have a notion that many of the people who are turning to Buddhism are using it as a counter-valence to the enormous emphasis on the self that is the central feature of our Western culture. The key to Buddhism is that the source of all error and evil is the self, and therefore that what is necessary is to learn how to get rid of the self, no longer to be ensnared by it.

Individuals can attain Buddhahood, which I am sure must be very difficult to accomplish, by stripping themselves bare of what we would consider to be self-identity. I once spent a couple of hours with the Dalai Lama. He came across as a real personality, but that may not actually be the key. In other words, even when one is able to eliminate the selfhood, that does not mean that one is no longer recognizable as a distinct person. It is desire, it is attachment to what is designated by Buddhists as improper, invalid, that needs to be eliminated.

The ideal of the Buddhist might be retirement into some cave in which one will spend years of one's life in total self-absorption in order to get rid of the self. This could never happen in Judaism. Equally, the monk abjures some of the ways in which ordinary people are permitted to live in order to achieve the ideal life as lived in monasteries and convents.

Even if the monk or hermit may be praying for the world, the question is whether that is a sufficient address to the commandment of *tikkun olam*, whether one could "fix up the world" that way. I must tell you that my skepticism, even more my rejection, is again based on the Shoah. In the death camps, as we can imagine, billions of prayers were said, and none of them were either answered or effective in the sense in which the one praying had intended or hoped it to be. The whole question, then, pertains to the effectiveness of prayer in the solution of the world's problems, in meeting the challenges the world poses to us. It is a very real question, and not only to me.

I find it exceedingly touching and moving when over and over again some of my Christian friends tell me that they have me in their prayers. Not only would it be totally ungracious of me to reject that or to make any comment upon it, but also I am really touched by their obvious solicitude. This was true when my wife, Lotte, was having an operation. I know that some of my Christian friends were praying for her recovery. Again I say this was deeply moving, because it expresses a degree of concern and outreach that is truly vivifying.

But if I were to say to myself that any prayer for her or me would have had the effect desired by the one praying, I would have to ask what happens to the overwhelming number of prayers that do not result in the desired outcome. If a prayer works in a given instance with me, if it did indeed work, wonderful. But what about all the others in similar conditions, better or worse, on whose behalf prayers have also been recited both by the person in need and also by others, family friends, clergy, from which there was no positive result? I wonder, really, whether this form of prayer has the validity so regularly assumed and asserted. I wonder if the studies showing that people who are prayed for heal faster are in any sense objective and valid.

We certainly do not know what the effects of a given prayer act may be. We simply do not know whether there is any measurable, tangible result from prayer. Of course, I am aware, for example, that until the second half of the nineteenth century nobody knew anything about radio waves. They were there all along, and we simply didn't use them, or we used them without knowing what we were doing. So I retain a certain amount of openness toward the prayer question, but I must also say that the assuredness with which I see so many people using this category of religious observance and practice I just cannot share. Sometimes I wish I could, because I know it means a lot to the persons who are doing the praying and who are being prayed for.

Oftentimes I have had a member of the congregation say, "Rabbi, pray for me."

I have to reply, out of the truthfulness of my position, "I'll pray *with* you. If there is any prayer that has to be said, you have to do it, because I have no more access to what is presumed to be the destination of such a prayer than you do."

I would never arrogate to myself the power and privilege implied in the notion that I am a more favored vessel than anyone else through which my prayer would flow to its destination. That I reject. But as an indication of how inconsistent I am, I pray every night. And I include individuals in my prayer. It is a total inconsistency that comes out of my upbringing when I was young, and thus out of sentimentality or irresistible habit.

This reminds me of a professor of Talmud I had in seminary. He was already retired, but some of us took private lessons with him, and he lived in our dormitory. He was an expert on superstitions and often was able to unmask them. Once we took a walk, and there was a ladder leaning up against the wall. I was just about to walk under it, and he yanked me back and led me around the ladder.

I said, "Professor Lauterbach, why did you do that?"

"You must never walk under a leaning ladder. It is bad luck."

I said, "You, who are the expert on these superstitions and have written learned essays about them, you are saying *this*?"

He replied, "Why take a chance?"

Consistency is a highly desirable aim to strive for, but it may not always be profoundly satisfying.

Of course, according to the Talmud, no service is complete unless it includes a time in which people can express their own personal and private thoughts and needs. In the traditional liturgy there is always a silent prayer that makes room for the individual to create and express personal needs, thoughts, wishes. This is a fixed part of each authentic liturgy. However, there is text provided even for the silent meditation, which may often mean, and perhaps more often than not, that the worshiper uses the prepared text rather than what the intention behind the creation of the silent prayer had been. Thus we come to the whole question that communal worship is not inherently individual even though, of course, the praying community is always made up of praying individuals. The Jewish answer to this problem lies in the understanding that the "people's work" with God needs formal settings, that the people need to say the right things in the right way and at the right time.

At the very same time, Jewish tradition, for instance, also says that one is supposed to say a hundred blessings a day, a blessing for every conceivable circumstance, such as meeting a friend, going on a trip, concluding a successful negotiation, seeing a beautiful woman. There is a blessing for everything, an action that is always individual because it depends on your own experience of life at any given moment. A blessing always contains language with which one praises God and therefore thanks God for whatever has occurred. It is the awareness of the omnipresence of the deity that is at the basis of and motivates these many additional blessings.

In other words, the liturgical life is really not totally restricted to given times and a given form. In addition to which you can never stop people from uttering their own words, their own aspirations, their own cries of the heart. I believe that one of the differences between modernity and that which preceded it is that in the past the omnipresence of God was felt, addressed, and recognized more intensely and more readily than in our modern frame of mind. Questions concerning the artificiality and compulsory nature of the formalized liturgy did not really obtrude in the same fashion in the past. It is to those of us who may waltz through our daily routine without ever really giving any thought to what might be "behind the curtain" that the call for a formal liturgical setting becomes such a distinct interruption of our normal routine, and such an irruption into our lives of something we really have not considered a need or option. This still does not deal with the fact that the need for communal worship, and therefore a need for the coinage of words, immediately introduces insurmountable problems.

It was not until about the tenth century c.e. that an order of liturgy became more or less universally accepted in Jewish life. Nothing had replaced the authority structure that ended with the destruction of the Temple in the year 70 c.e., and the eventual loss of both a religious and administrative center in the land of Israel. The result, as discussed previously, was the development of the synagogue as the people's place, where there is no need for priests. There is no need for anybody except those who come together even temporarily for the purposes of assembly, of study, of worship. The synagogue is an ingenious new way of stating and making possible the covenantal relationship.

According to Jewish tradition, any ten adult males can form a synagogue wherever a *minyan* of people would be, whether in a field, in a basement, in a home, or on a ship – wherever. This is not merely a substitute necessity imposed upon the Jewish people. It is a radical reshaping of the whole notion of how one relates to God, how God is available, and how God becomes possible for humans. The synagogue is not the Temple. It is a house of study, of assembly, and of prayer. Nor is it a building; it is an assembly of people. Therefore, any of the prayers in the

Jewish tradition that yearn for the rebuilding of the Temple and the reestablishment of the altar and priestly cult are, to me, a misunderstanding of the new possibilities resulting from the destruction of the Temple.

The memory of the Temple now destroyed was not only deeply implanted in Jews and to this day in the liturgy of the traditional community, but it was also transmitted through the Jews who became Christians into the earliest layers of Christianity. And it was then transmitted to those of pagan background who eventually became the vast majority of the Christian community, beginning in the second century. The synagogue was either already established as an institution or was in its incipient form for centuries before the destruction of the Temple in 70 C.E., so that the alternative of the synagogue as over against the Temple in Jerusalem had already become a feature of Jewish life long before the Christian era. Nevertheless, young Christianity wedded itself more to the Temple modality, in terms of altar and priesthood, than to the synagogue model, although Jesus, as a rabbi, seems to have been more oriented to the synagogue than to the Temple.

Christianity changed the Temple mode in two ways. First, one could be a priest no matter where one came from biologically, and second, it took the mobility of the synagogue and made the church to be wherever people were. Instead of monopolizing one single spot as the only licit place for approach to God, as was the Temple on Mount Zion, the church, like the synagogue, followed the people.

One possible explanation for the reliance of Christianity on the Temple model is that the synagogue model was so new that it really had not yet established itself as a totally effective alternative, radically innovative mode of serving the religious person's needs. The link may also be to the pagan practices of having altars and priesthoods, so that the link between that memory and memories of the Temple in Jerusalem among the earliest creators of Christianity may well have merged into a pattern that has become standard.

The Temple model requires a priest, and there are important differences between a rabbi and a priest. A rabbi is really not an intercessor, is not a privileged channel toward and from God. The rabbi's main function is to teach and to model the truths and aspirations of the Jewish way of life. The rabbi does not dispense religious functions in any privileged or graced way. Though ordained by virtue of learning, the rabbi remains a lay person who may or may not make the rabbinate a means of livelihood. Inherently, a congregation could function without a rabbi, although optimally a congregation would want a teacher if for no other reason than because study is a *mitzvah*, a fundamental commandment.

The military defeat of the Jewish nation by the Roman Empire in the first and second centuries led to the wide dispersal of Jews throughout the then known world and to diffusion and variations of all kinds. Under the limited means of communication then existing, very often local communities developed their own styles, almost an independent kind of existence simply because there were no recognized centers of authority. This despite the fact that the Babylonian academies, Sura, Pumpedita, and Nehardea, did function as reference points of such authority for those who accepted them and had access to them. Not surprisingly, it was exactly at this time that the only real schism in Jewish life occurred. The so-called Karaites split off from the Rabbanites and created an alternative in Jewish life and practice that came to an end only in our own time through the destruction of their remaining religious communities by Nazi armies operating in the Crimea.

So, especially then when it came to liturgy, there was the possibility and the danger of such wide diversity that commonality might have gone by the board. It was under these circumstances that the responsa methodology was helpful, with telling results. Communities inquired of the Babylonian seats of learning, among many other concerns, what the right way of the liturgy might be. Sages in the tenth century outlined it, and from then on their outline became virtually universal and cemented Jewish liturgical life into a common framework, and this despite the fact that the major "coinage" of the liturgy had roots going back as far as the era of the Great Assembly in the fifth pre-Christian century.

In a way this process paralleled, although in a different fashion, the work of the Masoretes, who in the ninth century developed the authorized text of the Hebrew Bible, the Tanach. This too became necessary among other responses, because there were variants in the transmitted texts, sometimes of considerable extent. Therefore the danger of schismatic developments, which again were the result primarily of the loss of a controlling authoritative center, were always present. So in this period, both for the biblical texts and also the liturgy, an authoritative statement was effectuated that brought order and commonality into the now far-flung Jewish communities.

While the Tanach is inviolate, the liturgy was intended to be more malleable. It did not work out quite that way because there was a tendency to circle the wagons, to make sure that everybody more or less conformed, and that the unity of the Jewish community, which was now in a really diffused Diaspora, would be preserved by way of a common sacred literature, and a Siddur, a common order of worship.

It is remarkable that the Jewish community was willing to submit itself to this kind of control, structuring, discipline. The other side is that the verbal content, once fixed, became as inviolate as the sacred texts of the Scripture. Woe to anyone who made a mistake in the words, their sequence or omission. It was the role of the *chazan*, the cantor, to know the liturgy and to conduct it, to pronounce it properly, to know all the intricacies of the variations between an ordinary day and a Sabbath and a holy day, and the various seasons of the year, all of which were characterized by a plethora of variables. This pertained also to the chants and their variations, in which the *chazan* was expert.

Changes in the liturgy constituted one of the distinctive innovations brought about by Reform Judaism. In fact, its main deviation from the past is liturgical, and it is an ongoing process. We have had several revisions of our worship literature, and no end is in sight. All of which leads again to the problem that is inherent when the liturgy is the unifying element of a community. How can it be achieved? Does someone living on Park Avenue in New York City express ideas in the same language as someone in a kibbutz on the Golan? How can an adequate common language be found for someone who believes that the ultimate truths were given in the past and others who are convinced that the current advancing edge of modern life is bringing us incisive and fabulous new information and knowledge? How can one bridge the gap between these assumptions and stances? It is exceedingly difficult.

Often the only consensus that can be reached is that the Reform movement has failed to agree on even a fairly indefinite kind of theology, and in the absence of consensus, those who work on this believe the liturgical wordings need to reflect a wide range of positions. For example, in recent proposed revisions of the prayer book, an attempt is made to have only one service. This is in contrast to the current Siddur, where there are eight Sabbath eve services and five Sabbath morning services. In order to have only one, the creators of the new Siddur tried to gauge where most members of the Reform movement, especially most of the younger members, might be tending.

Apparently they are interested in a more traditional wording rather than some of the theologically induced changes in the liturgy that have up to now been the hallmark of the Reform movement. Thus an attempt was made to reintroduce the assertion of a physical resurrection. Equally, there has been a reintroduction of a section of Torah text which indicates a cause-and-effect relationship between our faithfulness and the assurance of good crops, rain in its season, and the like. Now I am sure that in the earliest stages in the development of our religious life, way back some twenty-five hundred or three thousand years ago, these may well have been very effective means of teaching and of corralling the people's adherence to what was the revolutionary understanding of God and life that monotheism demanded. But are we not past that stage?

Generally speaking, recent liturgical creativity is directed more toward a recapturing of what we deviated from in a fairly radical way in the nineteenth century than toward what seems to me to be the necessary point: to radically confront the theological and liturgical needs of the post-Shoah world. For me in particular, some of the traditional wordings that preceded the Shoah are totally unacceptable as a result of what happened in the Shoah. To speak of God as the always functioning savior of the people, or as absolute power, the reigning monarch of the universe, is simply totally incompatible with the experience of the Shoah.

I struggle with the language of prayer, and find it difficult to participate wholeheartedly and meaningfully in this type of shared formal worship. I do so simply out of solidarity, but often I have to undergo a sacrifice of integrity when I do. I always hope that there are many others who feel as I do and therefore would be prepared to create new liturgical material that can more adequately express our post-Shoah experience, liturgical material that would reflect the fact that God can no longer be spoken of in the same terms used by those who assumed that God was always right and we were always wrong, that whatever befell us was always just punishment for our own sinfulness.

All of this language was perfectly understandable as an attempt on the part of our rabbinic sages to create a framework within which Jewish existence could be safeguarded and continued. But that was before we were consigned to death on the basis of nothing else but the biological condition of our birth. Before the twentieth century, we dealt with enemies who fabricated all kinds of reasons to hate us and therefore to punish us, often also by inflicting death. However, no one previously ever conceived of us as the ultimate biological evil which had to be destroyed for the sake of humanity. Therefore, anything expressed in relation to our experiences of disaster prior to the Shoah simply fails to adequately address the key issue in the Shoah. Without such an expression, such an articulation, there is not only a gaping hole in the wording of our liturgy, but it often becomes stultifying and even ludicrous.

To me the whole sequence of cause and effect as mirroring God's function in the life of humanity and the Jewish people is untenable, obsolete. The idea that we are acting because we know what needs to be done, and want to commit ourselves to action for its own sake, is not only preferable, but is absolutely a necessary stage of development in our religious understanding of ourselves and of God. So the reintroduction of some of these now-obsolete notions is to me almost like a counsel of despair, an admission of defeat in response to modernity as we experience it.

By modernity here I mean that increasingly we understand something about who we are as human beings, how we function, and what motivates us. Of course, there are levels in all of this. Many people still raise their children by threatening and punishing them, and possibly this is still an inescapable phase of a child's growth. But most people today have finally come to a point where, given the stage of development of the child, they would rather reason with the child and induce proper results, not by threat of punishment, but by explaining the value of the desired act, the propriety of it. This approach would induce in the child a collaborative response rather than a fear-driven one.

Instead of trembling in front of a God who is ready to punish or to reward, we need to understand our own relationship to the mystery of God in a new and different way similar to the one we take in the rearing of our children. This is something that we have discovered and learned in the last century with increasing intensity, and we need to transfer it into the section of our being that is called religious.

A return in the Siddur of Reform Judaism to prayer forms that are antiquated and outlived in terms of language and ideas would be a terrible disappointment to me. If it is really true that we can no longer find sufficient agreement in our Reform movement on the key elements of our covenantal relationship with the mystery of God, then the greater wisdom may be to keep a Siddur where there are choices that can be made by the officiant or by the congregant or both. The very multiplicity of the ideas incorporated in some of these multiple structures and liturgical modalities is a learning experience. It certainly will teach those who are sensitive to and care enough about the wording to pay attention to the fact that in Reform Judaism there is a variety of positions, that we are not interested in, or capable of having, only one mainstream notion. The liturgical and theological life may be enriched when exposed to variation. We are not talking about wild experimentation, nor is that found in the prayer book as we have it now. I recognize, however, that the conclusion that we should maintain these choices may not only be unpopular, it may not meet the needs of the Reform rabbinate and the Reform movement as a whole.

On the other hand, I feel deeply that most of the Jews I know, including my rabbinic colleagues, over and over again either shy away from an examination of the Shoah as a radical discontinuity or have never even thought of it in that way.

They just accept the Shoah as one more great calamity that has befallen our people, who were certainly acquainted with grief and disastrous events in the past. The uniqueness of the Shoah is often not understood or accepted, and therefore neither are its consequences. Yet the consequences are profound.

Chapter Thirteen
My Brother Joseph:
Reconciling Jews and Christians

> I am your brother Joseph, the one you sold into
> Egypt!
>
> *(Genesis 45:4)*

When the late Archbishop Joseph Bernardin came to Chicago, seventeen or eighteen years ago now, he immediately asked to meet some of us who were considered to be among the religious and civic leaders of the Jewish community. At that meeting, in a way that immediately captivated everybody who was there, he repeated words that Pope John xxiii had used when he met a delegation from the American Jewish Committee in Rome soon after his installation as the head of the Roman Catholic Church. He said, "I am your brother Joseph." This statement was meant to be not merely a biblical reference, but a powerful declaration that he considered us related to him in a way that only close family members would claim and understand. It is easy to grasp that he won everybody's heart at that moment. And subsequently it became very clear that he was interested

232 I HINENI — HERE I AM

in reaching out to those who were not Roman Catholics, and particularly to Jews, not just as a job function, but really as part of his own identity as a prince of the Church. He understood or drew conclusions from the Second Vatican Council with a clarity and purposefulness that up to that point I had not found in anyone else, let alone anybody at such a high level of authority and power in the religious world.

Bernardin became a cardinal soon after he came here. Among his initiatives, he founded a Council of Religious Leaders of Metropolitan Chicago. Very quickly, I was invited to join the council, and I became its president rather surprisingly soon afterward. Indicative of his own intentions, the cardinal attended most of the sessions during his reign, which was quite a commitment of time because in those days we met monthly. It was clear that he had the sort of a mind that could pierce through unimportant or obstructive issues down to the very heart of a matter almost in an instant. He had the gift of being able to clarify matters and show anybody willing to be involved in this kind of process what was really the important point. That gift helped his whole function as a peacemaker in his own church and with others, because he was able to clear away the rubble of any obstructive issue, or sometimes even just unimportant, deliberately defeatist matters.

I do not remember at all how we came to become friends. I do remember I once invited Bernardin to come to Emanuel to speak at a Sabbath-eve service to the congregation, which he was gracious enough to do. In those days I had a little room off the *bima*, or platform, in which I robed myself before going out for the service. Bernardin brought the gown that he needed to wear that evening and robed with me in the little private room. And then he said something that totally astounded me, and until now was virtually a secret that I kept to myself.

He said something like, "Herman, when you are in the room with me, I feel particularly at peace." I don't remember his exact words, but that was their gist. I could not understand it, because until then I had only rarely been with him, certainly not regularly. Never from my point of view had there been any kind of special relationship between us, let alone one that would have engendered what I considered to have been a very intimate disclosure. Needless to say, it not only stuck with me, it introduced into me the idea that I could have a very special relationship with this extraordinary person. So over the years, in totally unstructured, unintentional, unprepared ways, working together on various matters, particularly on the Council of Religious Leaders, it became very clear that the more often we were with each other, somehow this sense of relatedness deepened.

Then in 1994, under the auspices of the American Jewish Committee and the Jewish Federation, a pilgrimage to Israel was proposed which Cardinal Bernardin was eager to accept. Eventually there were fifteen of us, eight Catholics and seven Jews, two of whom were rabbis, and the other five laypeople from the two sponsoring organizations. I was included, even though at the time I did not have an official position that would have automatically made me a part of the group. The cardinal let it be known that he wanted me along at his special request.

The Hebrew University had invited him to give a lecture while we were in Israel and was giving him an academic honor. Bernardin had prepared a major paper on the church and the Jews. I would call it a breakthrough paper.

On a visit with him, he said, "I've prepared this paper, and now I have to send it to Rome to see what they say."

About three weeks later he called and said, "Come over, I want to show you something."

I went down to his study on Huron Street, and he showed me a letter that had come that day from the Vatican, stating that there was nothing in the paper he proposed to deliver that was not in consonance with the current Vatican stance. He was really excited, because it was a very courageous paper in which he took as much responsibility or more for the Church's thoughts and actions than anybody ever had done with respect to anti-Semitism and everything that happened as a result of it. And the Vatican had okayed the paper.

The pilgrimage was only possible because Israel and the Vatican had come to a diplomatic solution of their relationship. The Vatican had accepted the State of Israel diplomatically; therefore, this was not a private visit, it was an official visit. We even went to see the president of the State of Israel, Ezer Weizmann.

We met in the cardinal's residence a few weeks before our departure to go over the program. There was one thing that powerfully occurred to me, and I spoke up. What had struck my eye was that in the early morning of the Friday of the week we were there, we would walk along the Via Dolorosa and end at the Church of the Holy Sepulcher. It was very clear to me when I saw this in the program that there would be difficulties for us, because it would be, inescapably so, a deeply religious event and experience for the Christian members of the delegation. Since the program certainly included any number of major religious services that Cardinal Bernardin and his Catholic delegates were either eager to perform or that were necessary to perform in terms of masses and so on, I told him that in all of these matters, we would want to be there as observers, but obviously not as participants. And therefore, we would offer the same kind of status for any of them when we visited or participated in any of the services that were part of the Jewish program. Bernardin immediately agreed that this was the way it had to be.

In Jerusalem that Friday morning, we left our hotel about 6:00 A.M. in order to be there before any other visitors began to throng the Via Dolorosa. There was a Franciscan monk in charge of all of the stations of the cross, and we went ahead and walked with our Catholic co-delegates through the stations. At each station there was a prayer and an explanation of the prayer and the station. Almost instinctively I drifted to the very end of the procession, I guess simply because I did not feel it was my religious ceremony. As I came around the last bend toward a little square that in three or four steps leads down to the entrance of the Church of the Holy Sepulcher, I saw that the delegation had already moved toward the entrance. But Bernardin was standing at the top of the steps, and he was obviously waiting for me.

He put his arm around my shoulder and said, "Herman, I cannot tell you what it means to me to have gone the same street that my Savior and Lord walked."

To this day, a chill runs through me when I think of his words. First, of course, it was an obvious sign of his deep friendship that he, who should have been at the head of the delegation leading them into the church, was instead waiting for me, who was straggling behind all the others. But second, I had never quite understood viscerally the enormous importance of Jerusalem to Christians. I had always known intellectually, of course, that Jerusalem was sacred to three religions. There was no question that I had known this, but I had known it on a level of pure intellect. Now I began to understand how deep was the faith of my friend Joseph in the Lord whom he worshiped. The impact of the experience on his life as revealed to me by this dear friend just overwhelmed me, and still does.

It is my observation that most Jews do not understand how deeply Christians are affected by and involved in Jerusalem. There are lots of reasons for this. It is part of the estrangement of Jews from Christians, part of the millennial disfiguration of Jews as human beings that has been the legacy of so much of Christianity. Anyhow, it was a most moving experience for me.

When the National Conference of Catholic Bishops convened in Chicago, Bernardin invited me to attend a meeting.

They were discussing nuclear war and the church's stand so that the Catholic bishops could come up with a statement, a policy, regarding nuclear weapons and nuclear war, and thereby influence national policy. He said, "If you are interested, I will issue you an invitation to come to one of the sessions."

Bernardin presided. All of the country's four hundred and some bishops and cardinals were there. I just sat in the back row watching the scene, absolutely overwhelmed by his capacity to bring divergent or even opposite positions closer toward a middle ground. The discipline with which they spoke! They were given three minutes, and that was it. No matter who you were, three minutes. I was impressed by the deftness with which he directed the flow of the conversation despite the controversy. There had been talk before the conference convened that this would be one of the toughest issues they would have to discuss, and there was a possibility of not coming to a conclusion on the matter, at least not at that session of the conference. Finally, after about three hours, with an issue like this, with four hundred some personalities in the room, Bernardin led them to an overwhelming consensus. The resolution they developed was very heartfelt.

I was president of the Central Conference of American Rabbis at one time, and had one or two major debates come up during my term. I was not nearly as successful as Bernardin, nor could I invoke anything near the discipline that he could. Of course at the Central Conference, we always had time limits, and we always had someone who would announce the point at which there were only thirty seconds left to the finish. But that did not stop anybody.

A classic instance of this involved Rabbi Alexander Schindler, who at the time was president of the Union of American Hebrew Congregations. Schindler was one of the proponents in a debate, and he had three minutes. When he did not stop at three minutes, I interrupted, "Alex, your time is up."

He said, "But Herman, I'm in the middle of a sentence, there is a comma here – and I should be allowed to finish my sentence."

There was inordinate applause, and he went on for three minutes more always saying, "Comma…, semi-colon…"

Of course everybody howled. But it is typical of the lack of self-discipline of the rabbinate, in contrast to what the Roman Catholic bishops were willing to subject themselves to.

Of course, the cardinal and I had any number of subsequent opportunities to be with each other. One that sticks in my mind was when the archbishop of Canterbury had come on a visit and was speaking in an Episcopal church on the South Side. Both Cardinal Bernardin and I had been selected to respond to his sermon. We were waiting in the hall to proceed into the church, and I was standing behind Bernardin. I noticed that his robe was dragging on the floor.

I said to him, "Joseph, are you shrinking or something? What's the matter with your garments?"

He said "Yes, I am shrinking, and I haven't had a chance to have all of my garments hemmed properly."

I dismissed it at the time, but the more I thought about it, the clearer it became to me that something must be going on in his life. I gingerly inquired from some of his inner circle of priests, one or two with whom I was also close. They said that they thought that he was unwell in some way. Then I heard that he had fallen on the steps of his residence – his private rooms were on the second floor – and that he had to call for help because he could not get up. Before long, we learned that he was struggling with pancreatic cancer, and after awhile it became evident that he was losing the battle.

During this time Bernardin called and said, "Come and talk to me."

I went to see him, and he told me that he was facing the ultimate. He was totally serene and unafraid. In fact, in a manner of speaking, he was even looking forward to what he thought might happen to him after death. He told me about the arrangements he was making for his mother and other intimate things, deep glimpses into his faith life and into the exceptional, splendid person he was.

In the months before he died, President Clinton decided to give Bernardin the Medal of Freedom. Unbeknownst to him, someone in his entourage insisted that I come to Washington for the ceremony. They had been given an opportunity to make up a guest list, so I was invited. Bernardin was already having difficulty climbing up the platform. Four or five people were given the medal that time. I admired the beauty of the ceremony, its rightness in some way. Marines would hand the president the medal and ribbon, and the president would put it around each recipient. The president spoke to each of them, and each then gave a short reply. It was just beautiful and memorable.

When the ceremony was over, Bernardin descended from the platform. Members of his family were there, well-wishers, and so on. So I waited again until some of the crush was over, and I went up to him. You should have seen his face. He embraced me and expressed his absolute deep satisfaction that I was there for him at that time.

Then, when it was quite clear that he had only weeks to live, he went to Rome to say goodbye to the Pope. On the trip back on the plane, he outlined his funeral down to the smallest detail, including such items as what kinds of flowers, which hymns. He had already designated his friend, the cardinal from Los Angeles, to be the lead officiant. Everything was specified: where the coffin would be, how many days, what garments he would be clothed in, and so on.

I got a call from one of his priests, who also unfortunately died shortly after the cardinal, saying, "Herman, the cardinal has a request of you."

I said, "Oh?"

"On the second day of his lying in state in the afternoon, in the cathedral, he wants you to conduct a religious observance for the Jewish community."

I was speechless. I knew that no rabbi had ever done anything in a church in an official religious matter, knew that most of my traditionalist colleagues, if not all of them, would not even enter a church, let alone even be present for a service in a church, let alone do anything Jewish as part of the service.

I said to my caller, "I have to think about it."

I called a few people, like Maynard Wishner, Rabbi Knobel, and Jonathan Levine, then the area director of the American Jewish Committee, all of whom had been on the Israel trip. I may have talked to one or two others also. We wanted to develop something that would be a product of and representative of the Jewish component of the trip to Jerusalem. I did not want it to be a specifically liturgical event, because I did not want to offend the traditionalist components of the Jewish community and Jewish world. Although I expected that they might object, I did not want to be provocative. I realized that a purely liturgical event might not be altogether right for Catholics either. We met and came to the conclusion that what we would do was that the seven of us who had been on the pilgrimage would each write something or say something taken from our traditional texts. I think I was the only one who was totally free to speak. So we constructed something that had a somewhat liturgical character.

Eight or nine days before Bernardin died, he called me again and said, "Come and talk."

I went upstairs because he could no longer come down to his study, and again we talked very intimately about his life, his expectation to see his God. We embraced as I left after about an hour, and he said, "One more thing. In my will I have set aside this Lladro figurine of a rabbi that was given to me by a dear friend, and now I want you to have it as a memento from me."

I was close to tears as I left the residence. A few days later there was a phone call telling me that the cardinal had died, inviting me along with some family and friends to come to the residence to see him. I had previously met his sister, who had been there for some other events I had been invited to share. I went down to the chapel in the residence, and a small procession formed. I put myself toward the end. We went in by a far door to file past the bier. A young person, a nephew I believe, touched the cardinal's hand as he passed the corpse. Then as he went on, I did the same thing. Here was the hand that I had shaken, that had always been so warm and receptive, now stone cold. Stone cold. I shudder to this day.

At the funeral, the cathedral was so full of people; they were standing in the aisles or along the wall, and hundreds were outside watching on television screens. It was broadcast all over the world, I am told. There was a last-minute hitch. We were in the robing room being assisted by our Catholic friends, when I think it was Maynard Wishner said, "If this is being broadcast worldwide, we are going to arouse controversy if we are wearing robes and prayer shawls. The ceremony is going to be overshadowed by controversy." So at the last minute, to the great dismay of the priests, we just went out in business suits and had no identifying accouterments. There was an overwhelmingly positive response to our participation. Being part of that event was the most difficult ceremony I ever participated in.

It was clearly understood that Joseph Bernardin was at the cutting edge of the improvement in the relationship between Jews and Christians. Again, as in so many other ways, he was able to bring along a lot of people simply because of the power and clarity of his mind and the sheer purity of his intentions.

So there was something very special in this man. The word is often misused and abused these days, but he had charisma. There was a grace about him that was just remarkable. To watch him with people at a public event was fascinating and uplifting.

Bernardin was not at all afraid to look into the cracks and take on the difficult issues. He had a capacity to be conciliatory that brought people of divergent opinions and stands to some common ground. He could look at the other side and say, What is there about this that could be true? He would almost say it in such words; certainly his attitude would convey the fact that he took totally seriously the positions other people held and made no claim whatever that his position was the only possible and the only right one.

One other thing Cardinal Bernardin did for me personally was to appoint me a laureate of the Roman Catholic Church. He had a lovely dinner for me at a hotel in Skokie, and said beautiful things. The award is one of my most cherished possessions.

Losing him was hard for me, but I deeply rejoice in Bernardin's friendship. It is astounding to me, and even to this day not totally comprehensible, that our relationship should have developed. It was a total surprise, and one that really has shaped a good deal of my life. His influence opened my whole being to an understanding that it was possible for someone at the highest levels of the Roman Catholic leadership to be, not just institutionally open to Jews, but to have really the ultimate interior capacity to be a brother, to be an "other" for a Jew. The presence of Joseph in this world for whatever time he had, and the fact that he helped articulate a new position for the Roman Catholic Church to the extent that he could, is something that remains with me, remains with all of us, as a precious memory and legacy.

Since that time and in part because of my relationship with him, I have been even more open to the vastness of interfaith experience. Though it seemed the right thing for me to do at the time, I regret the defensive posture I fell into, for example, on our visit to Jerusalem. I always felt so marginal toward other people's religious practices that I never allowed it to enter me as an experience, to become something to which I was more than just present. It would also, however, be fair to say that I am not always able to shut out whatever memories of the past I have. And those memories can stand in the way of any openness toward worship performed by non-Jews in my presence, because it so often elicits, almost instinctively, the memories of what such practices signaled and meant in the past.

The destruction of the Temple in the year 70 C.E. was interpreted by early Christians as God's rejection and abandonment of the Jewish people. Therefore, the New Testament and the New Covenant and the new Israel, as Christians often called themselves, were a replacement for the old, with which God had become fed up. Historically this has been the major position that Christian theology had assumed vis-à-vis Judaism. We were always considered to be stubborn, blind, perverse, and sometimes also even satanic, devilish, willfully obstructive. All of the medieval accusations, such as the blood libel or the host desecration, the poisoning of the wells – all of this could only come out of a background in which it was assumed that Jews had missed the boat and continued willfully to ignore the real truth, which was available to them and offered to them continuously, sometimes under rather severe and strange conditions. This allowed Christians to feel that they were doing God's work in keeping Jews in a reduced and degraded condition.

The notion of two covenants began to work its way through, especially in Christian circles, in the mid-fifties of the twentieth century. This notion holds that the "old" covenant has not been superseded, is not abrogated, has not lost its validity. That is a major statement to make, because of the polemics beginning at the end of the first, and during the second, third, fourth, and fifth centuries, in the growth of young Christianity. The "new covenant" became the only valid statement. The fact that now the two-covenant position is not only possible but has been declared officially by the Roman Catholic hierarchy to be valid, and is in fact the new official position vis-à-vis Judaism, is extraordinary, especially in view of the many centuries of hostility and defamation.

Unfortunately, there is not enough happening on the Jewish side. In early 2001, a proposal was formulated by three or four Jewish theologians under the Hebrew term *dabru emet*, "let us speak truth." Some of us were invited to sign on, which I and some others did. This proposal calls on Jews to seriously study and recognize the truths of Christianity for Christians. There has been controversy in the Jewish world about this declaration. Nevertheless, it is an incipient and growing recognition that our position with regard to Christianity has been distorted by our experience over the centuries as victims of Christianity. We have really never given ourselves a decent chance to examine Christianity for its own sake and in a dispassionate fashion. It just has rarely happened up to now.

There is progress. Some Jewish scholars are considered New Testament experts and are teaching New Testament in university religious departments. All of these are new developments. It is the recognition of the enormity of the Shoah and its growth within a Christian environment that has finally begun to turn the tide in this regard.

Cardinal Bernardin felt that we needed to re-examine the split that separated the Jews and early Christians to better understand that which unites us, as well as that which divides us. This is an effort that his untimely death did not allow him to pursue. Over the years, I have attempted not only to do some research, but also to do some thinking about the first century, because in every sense of that word, it is obviously the moment in history when the breach occurred.

To begin with, Christianity was a form of Judaism. All of its early adherents were Jews. It was only in a partial way, toward the end of the first century and then massively in the second century, that non-Jews entered into young Christianity and thereby changed the character of this new community, eventually so radically that in fact the departure from mother Judaism actually became a protest against it, a focus of hostility.

The first century, then, was really an extraordinarily important moment in time which we need to understand better. Such an effort is ongoing now among some Christian and Jewish scholars. Hopefully the results will be to abandon the former way of hostility and suspicion of one against the other and to replace it with an openness and a search for a kind of relation with each other that is worthy of our being believers and religiously oriented and motivated people.

During the first century Rome was the ruler of Judea. This domination had begun in 68 B.C.E., in the first pre-Christian century, when the Roman general Pompey, stationed in Egypt, was called in to settle a dynastic quarrel between two Maccabean contenders for the throne of Judea. Since both had adherents, and they could not work out a compromise, they called on the Roman general to settle the dispute instead of fighting it out in a bloody civil war. Pompey then picked one, and from that time on Rome had the final say as to who would be the king of the Jews.

Why would the Romans be so interested in Judea, this little bit of territory on the eastern shore of the Mediterranean Sea? The answer is Egypt. Egypt was an absolutely indispensable ingredient in the maintenance of the Roman style of life. The Roman mobs needed *panem et circenses*, bread and circuses. The Roman emperor could easily furnish circuses, but bread was a different story.

By this point in history, the population of Rome had grown and there was a huge proletariat. Proletariat is an interesting word that comes from the Latin word *proles*, which means "offspring." These were people who simply produced children and had no other real function in society. The proletariat was always difficult to handle because they were demanding and easily led to violence, especially in the city of Rome.

In order to maintain an adequate supply of food, Egypt was absolutely necessary, because the delta of the Nile is the single most fertile piece of land on the planet. The Nile brings all kinds of alluvial matter from East Africa and deposits it onto its flat delta. The climate is capable of producing two, three, sometimes even four crops a year, making the delta the granary of that part of the world. And Rome therefore needed to conquer and secure Egypt in order to maintain a supply of grain in order to provide bread for the otherwise often unruly and ungovernable mobs.

Everybody wanted Egypt because of its fertility. Even the emperors of Mesopotamia, what is now modern Iraq, whether they were Assyrians or Babylonians or Persians or later Alexander the Great, all launched campaigns, some successful, some not, to attempt to incorporate Egypt into their own imperial structures. For their part, the Romans were never able to completely control Mesopotamia. Time and again they tried, and for a few years here and there, they were able to control it militarily against the eastern peoples who were encroaching on its territory. Mesopotamia was also desirable for a simple reason conveyed by its name, "Land between the Two Rivers," namely the Tigris and the Euphrates. The fact that there were two rivers and efficient systems of canals meant that crops could regularly and reliably be grown in sufficient quantities to ensure enough food for both the people and the armies.

But the Romans never were able to fully secure the eastern boundary of their empire, even as late as the fourth century. Therefore, the land of Israel became the bastion that protected Egypt from any assault from the east, because it is the only land bridge by which one can go from Mesopotamia or other Asian centers into Africa, into Egypt. It is a rather narrow strip of land, at places only a few miles wide, because there is a trackless desert and mountain ranges to the east which in ancient times nobody really wanted to try to traverse, certainly armies could not. Any approach to Egypt from the east had to be made through the narrow funnel that was the land of Israel. Therefore Rome was totally committed to retaining sovereignty over the land of Israel, because it was in fact a necessary protection of its granary in Egypt.

So from the middle of the first pre-Christian century onward, no Jewish king assumed his throne unless the Senate of Rome had given consent. The one who is best known to all of us as gaining power from this arrangement was Herod the Great. Herod had grown up in Rome as a hostage for his father's loyalty to the Roman Empire. His father was the prince of Idumea, to the south of the kingdom of Judea. In order to make sure he stayed loyal to Rome, the eldest son was taken hostage when he was what we would now call a teenager, although in those days that disease was unknown. In any event, he was a young man who grew up with the flower of Roman aristocracy. By all accounts, he was a very winsome fellow, excellent in the martial arts, sports, and whatever young male aristocrats did in those days in the Roman world.

The throne in Judea became open because there was no direct male heir of the Maccabean line, who themselves had been appointed because no king of the Davidic line could be found in the middle of the second pre-Christian century. Herod had no difficulty in being installed as the king of Judea. He married Mariamne, the remaining princess of the Maccabean dynasty, but eventually had her murdered in a jealous fit, as well as their two sons, who were drowned in the palace swimming pool. Herod knew he was hated by the Jewish people, and when he lay on his deathbed, ordered that the heads of the Jewish families in Jerusalem be imprisoned and executed on the day on which he died so that there would be mourning in Jerusalem. Fortunately the order was not carried out. It is clear that he was always considered to be an outsider, an imposition by the Romans of someone who was originally Idumean.

When we think about Jewish life at the beginning of the first century, it is important to keep all this in mind. It was a terrible period for the Jews. First there was Herod who died in the year 4, followed by Roman procurators who were sent to govern the land because they had the reputation and, of necessity, the skill of keeping the place quiet. Their only instructions were to make sure there was no disturbance of the Roman hold on the land and to exact the greatest amount of taxes. This laid the groundwork for Pontius Pilate. In the Gospels he is sometimes depicted as a gentle, sensitive, wonderful man. In reality, we have the Senate minutes as to what led to his appointment to be the procurator of the land of Judea. He was known as one of the most ruthless administrators of any territory, as the Senate intended.

Again, it was strategically of supreme importance to keep Judea not only secure but tranquil. Therefore, anything that happened in the land of Israel that in any sense threatened the Roman position and presence was a matter of the utmost and sensitive importance for the Roman governor. Anything that even smacked of disturbance, let alone rebellion, would be ruthlessly dealt with, because if somebody had somehow the aura about him that he was the "King of the Jews," that was tantamount to raising the banner of rebellion. In fact, that was the official reason why the Romans executed Jesus of Nazareth. This "crime" is stated on every Roman Catholic cross to this day, I*esus* N*azarenus* R*ex* I*udaeorum*, "Jesus of Nazareth King of the Jews": INRI – the identity of the criminal and the crime.

The first century was a time of profound disturbance, of unrest. People were asking themselves: What is God doing? Is this the time we have hoped for, when the great redemption will take place? There had been no king of the Davidic dynasty since 586 B.C.E., some six hundred years earlier. Was this the time when God would somehow reveal the supposedly hidden descendant of King David who was the only one entitled to be the king of the Jews? The *mashiach*, the anointed one, the *Christos*, which is the Greek word for the Hebrew word *mashiach*.

It is understandable that the worse things got, the greater was the yearning and the conviction of many that this was the time known in Hebrew as the "birth pangs" of the Messiah. Somehow there had grown up a notion that when things got so bad that they could not possibly get worse, that was the time when God would send the Redeemer. There was an aura, a feeling of expectation, percolating through some segments of the Jewish population, among those who studied the texts, who hoped they could find through a cryptogram when God would in fact bring about the so long deferred redemption.

Part of the expectation resulted from the ending of the Maccabean line, because when the last of the Maccabean brothers to survive the struggle against Syria was installed in about 140 B.C.E., they were told that this descendant could only rule until a true king of Davidic descent was found.

So we get a sense of the feelings of people who are under severe distress, who are suffering from a foreign and brutal domination, who are heavily taxed in the most abusive way. The tax collectors just simply went into one's home and took whatever they thought was the equivalent of a tax obligation. The way this was usually done was that the procurator would find a wealthy Jew with whom he would make the following arrangement: You pay me X million sesterces, which are the taxes for this year, and then you go ahead and get the money from whatever source you can. Of course the Jewish tax collector then used whatever means his Roman friends would make available, and they were often brutal. He went to a farmer and took, let us say, two sheep. There was no recourse. Where could you complain? Who would listen? What institution was there to which you could turn for justice? You were under foreign occupation and the taxes had to be paid or else.

This paints a clear picture of a community in distress. During this time, and under these circumstances there were a number of rabbis whose charisma – and that is a good Greek word to describe the very special attractiveness of their message, of their person, of their whole presence – led to a kind of whisper at least among their disciples: Is our Master the one whom God is sending? Are we fortunate enough to be in the company of a Master who will eventually fulfill the deepest yearnings of the Jewish community?

During this period, over a couple of centuries, there were four or five claimants to the Messiahship. The last one was called Bar Kochba, the "Son of a Star." That was not his real name, but it is indicative of the mystique that grew about him. He was able to rally the Jewish nation to another terrible war against Rome only sixty years after the bloody defeat in the year 70. So in 132, he raised an army and once more engaged the Roman Empire in a three-year war. This war was so terrible that a book recently written by a historian at the Hebrew University said that the bloodbath the Romans instituted when they defeated Bar Kochba and his armies was by percentage a larger loss in blood and life than even the Shoah. The Roman emperor, Hadrian, was so incensed by the very fact that the Jewish people had risen against Rome once more, that he gave orders for the city of Jerusalem to be totally destroyed, plowed over. Salt was sown so that nothing would grow there. He erased the name Jerusalem and renamed the site Aelia Capitolina so that even the name would be lost. He looked back hundreds and hundreds years in history to the Philistines, long departed from history, and instituted the name Palestina so that there would be no mention anymore of Judea.

Despite the enormity of the stress, this was not a time when

Jews and Judaism were moribund. On the contrary, this was a period of vigorous intellectual and religious discussion and controversy, albeit often fueled by despair and anger. It was a time of seeking for news ways of understanding what it meant to be a Jew. Experimenting and searching ultimately became necessitated by the fact that in the year 70 the last and only altar the Jews ever had in the Temple in Jerusalem was destroyed. The last high priest and his second-in-command were hewn down by Roman soldiers as they officiated at the altar. The Temple and altar have never been rebuilt, despite the incessant prayers of members of the traditional wings of Judaism, who three times daily pray for their rebuilding.

The soul of the community, its very heart, had been torn out. The main religious life had been centered in the cult performed by priests, who could only be priests by genealogy, by biology. If your father was a priest you were a priest; you could not be a priest any other way in Jewish life. They were the only ones who were entitled and ordained to officiate at the altar daily thereby to reconcile God to the people and the people to God. This was the major structure for religious life in Judaism at that time, with possibly a minor role for the synagogue.

There is a lot of controversy in Jewish scholarship as to when the synagogue began to make its appearance. Somehow, in the centuries prior to the Roman conquest in the year 70, a new institution had begun to appear and to flourish. The synagogue was a "coming together" of people. Whenever there were people there could be a synagogue. A specific building was not essential. The guiding spirits in the synagogue were cantors and rabbis, teachers. A rabbi is nothing else than a teacher, not some kind of a special channel of grace or anything like that. We are, as our ordination says, entitled to "teach and to judge"; that is what a rabbi does and is. The rabbis were thus also the judges of the religious courts which dealt also with the civic and social issues of life.

To this day, Jewish communities of any size retain or maintain a *bet din*, "a house of judgment." The minimum of such a court is usually three rabbis, and to this day in certain circles in Jewish life, primarily, of course, in the more traditional ones, issues are brought to this court rather than to the civil court because then the issues are decided by Jewish law and stay within the family, as it were, rather than becoming part of the life of the general population. This occurs most often in the traditional community, and is sometimes also observed in Conservative circles. While this is very rare in Reform communities, it does occur. For instance, if we have someone who is not born a Jew, but wants to join our community, then this has to be done in the presence of three rabbis. So we form a *bet din* for this purpose even in the Reform movement. At the *mikva* there will be three rabbis in order to receive the hitherto non-Jewish person into the family of the Jewish people.

But basically the court system in ancient times was established by people who lived according to the laws that are in the Torah and their interpretations, and it was understood that the king or the leading stratum of authority would operate within the legal confines of the laws found in Torah. Therefore, in Christian circles very often the Pentateuch is called the Law, which is a misnomer because Torah is much more. The word *torah* does not mean "law," though law is found in Torah. It has various meanings and teachings which can be legal.

Therefore when, sometimes in a combative fashion, the idea of God in Judaism is depicted as the God of stern judgment, in contrast to the idea of God in Christianity as the God of love, this is an extraction from the fact that God is the source of the judicial norms, the laws by which Jews are supposed to live. When, for instance, the law says "Thou shalt not steal," this is not just a moral maxim, although it is that also, but then, and this is particularly the work of the rabbis, the question is now developed, What do you mean by stealing? What is theft? Under what circumstances does something happen that is called theft and therefore causes certain consequences? The consequences are already either indicated directly or implicit in certain statements of the Pentateuch, the *Chumash*, the compilation of five. *Pentateuch* is the Greek translation, for it also means that which is "five."

Jews of course had a judicial system. Eventually, and certainly under the rabbinic effort of structuring things, and searching for precise meanings, and again part of the evidence of the influence of the Greek milieu, there were three levels of institutions: first, the *bet din*, composed of three; second, the court of twenty-one, which was responsible for capital cases; and third, the supreme court, the Sanhedrin, with seventy-one members. Curiously the supreme court had a Greek name. *Sanhedrin* is a Greek word referring to an arrangement of chairs. Thus the highest court of Jewish life had a Greek designation.

In addition to judging, rabbis are to teach. What did our ancestors who began this tradition, this new calling, teach? The books. In Greek – *ta biblia*, anglicized as the Bible. Rabbis became the teachers of the sacred texts. They studied, first by attaching themselves to a master, and then becoming ordained.

The rabbinic method was to either have a *yeshiva*, a "place to sit," where students would study, or a master would take students and travel from community to community, where they were either invited or tolerated, depending on who they were and what message they brought. This is how rabbis functioned. Jesus fits into this mold without the slightest friction. In fact few rabbis had stationary *yeshivot* serving as the only place where they taught and where their students came to listen and work with them. Many of them went from place to place.

This is a feature of Jewish life that did not die. Itinerant rabbis in Eastern Europe were a well-known and highly regarded feature of Jewish life. These were people who would come to a community, stay for five or six weeks, deliver their message, pack up, and go on to the next community. Even in America, in some of the smaller communities, we have circuit rabbis. This form of rabbinic life is nothing so startling or unique that one would have to say that in that regard Jesus was a deviant

What eventually developed in a *yeshiva*, the "sitting around," was that students advanced down the rows; the more advanced students sat toward the front, the beginners in the back. A student was given permission by the master to change his seat, to advance a row. Finally, when the student was in the front row, he would be ordained by the masters and become a master, a rabbi, himself. He then went out and started his own circle. Eventually a systemized ordination process was developed.

All of the enormously exciting but in many ways disturbing and frightening impact of foreign cultures of occupation in the centuries preceding the birth of Christianity generated a number of major responses. Of the two most important, one was the Sadducees. This movement was essentially made up of the people who clustered around the royal court and were in the top ranks of the priesthood. They were the political and social elite. Therefore, they had a position with regard to scriptural texts that reflected their own sense of identity and power. For instance, because of the influence of the Greek way of life, many Jews who had been totally pastoral and agricultural now began to live in cities. No longer living on the land, this shift in social conditions required a different arrangement of social interrelatedness; relationships, the whole fabric of society changed. A whole new roster of occupations and skills developed that had not been needed in rural society, where each one did most everything for himself or by a member of his household. There was no legislation in Torah that reflected city life. New laws were needed about how to live in the cities, how to be an artisan, how to live in a market society. The Sadducees felt that since they were the power elite, if new laws were necessary, new responses to radically different forms of life, they were empowered to formulate them even when Torah did not furnish them.

The second major group, the Pharisees, took an opposite position departing from the basic assumption that the sacred texts were related to God, and thus that since God was in the texts, they must have already provided answers to even formerly unknown conditions. The question is only whether one was prepared to take the sacred texts as of final importance and to persist in searching for the necessary answers out of the texts.

The Pharisees said that the texts could never be obsolete. There can never be any condition of life that is not already somehow cryptogrammed into the texts. What one needs to do is use one's intelligence and ingenuity to find in the texts the possibility of answering whatever new questions arise. And so they said, "Dig in it and dig in it. Everything is in it." One of the great Pharisaic leaders established thirteen principles of interpretation. He said that if those thirteen rules were followed, all necessary answers could be found in the texts. The reason there are Bibles still being read today is that the Pharisees refused to let the texts become obsolete items collecting cobwebs on the shelves in a museum or library.

The fact that the text is malleable is an almost irresistible invitation to all of us to be exegetes, to start looking searchingly at it. In fact we read the text differently every time we come to it, because we are different people every time. All of us in some fashion, noticeably or sometimes unnoticeably, are different because we are alive. Because we are different, we respond differently. Every time I look at a picture, I see it differently. Every time I hear a piece of music, I hear it differently. Otherwise there would be no sense in hearing it again, or in rereading a book.

Jesus may have been more extreme than other rabbis, in terms of some unusual opinions, but he was a Pharisaic rabbi, raised as a Pharisee, and reasoning in a Pharisaic mode. There is the well-known story that he went into the synagogue to read from the text and astounded those who heard the interpretation he gave even as a young boy. He was supposedly twelve years old at the time. If he had not been in a Pharisaic environment, this would not have been possible. People went to the synagogue to hear a new message, and here was this man attracting crowds because he was saying things that nobody had ever said that way before, or perhaps because he was saying them in a captivating fashion.

In the Talmud, which is the great work in which rabbinic lore and activity are compiled, there are six or seven thousand names and opinions registered over a period close to a thousand years. It is an encyclopedia collected and edited from about 400 B.C.E. to about 600 C.E. There are two Talmuds. The more authoritative one is from Babylonia. After the Romans were finished with the Jewish people in the second century, Jewish life in the land of Israel became so difficult, so reduced that the main thrust of the scholarship and leadership centered in Babylonia, in modern Iraq. The second is the Jerusalem Talmud. It is smaller and did not achieve the kind of authority that the Babylonian Talmud has to this day. The Talmud is adversarial in style. It is remarkable, for instance, that even the opinions of a rabbi who ultimately declared himself to be an nonbeliever, an atheist, are preserved along with the others. He had certain experiences that led him to say there can be no God, yet even his opinions and teachings have been preserved.

There is a question that has been raised as to whether Jesus' name is anywhere in this vast compendium, this sea of learning. There are some who think it is. This is a really controversial issue that has been raised again recently, perhaps inconclusively. Nonetheless, that Jesus was a Pharisaic rabbi does not depend on his being mentioned in the Talmud or other literature.

The substantial break by nascent Christianity with traditional Judaism occurred because of Paul. He had been raised in a non-Jewish environment in Tarsus. Although trained in the Pharisaic methodology, Paul had not been ordained a rabbi. By his own words, he was one of several individuals who were assigned to counteract any possible sectarian deviations from the mainstream of Judaism. On the way to Damascus to carry out his mission, he had a fundamental experience which turned him from a persecutor into the greatest adherent and advocate of the *evangelion*, the New Good Message. What was the Good Message? It was that the *Mashiach*, the *Christos*, had already come in the person of Jesus of Nazareth. And then Paul, who because he had lived in a non-Jewish environment and therefore knew non-Jews much better than most Jews did, came to a very significant and, in terms of its final consequences, enormous conclusion. He concluded that the acceptance of this new variant of Judaism by non-Jews would be difficult, if not impossible, as long as males had to be circumcised and people had to keep the dietary laws, *kashrut*, the kosher laws.

Paul, in a typically Pharisaic exegetical manner, interpreted certain verses of the Torah in such a way as to give him the authority to abolish the requirements for both circumcision and dietary restrictions, thus making it possible, by removing the barrier, for masses of non-Jews to accept his new interpretive teaching. How did he do this? This is a fascinating, wonderful example of hermeneutics and exegesis. Paul said that Abraham was a man who followed God totally, a great man of faith, the first Jew. If Abraham could be the first Jew prior to Sinai, prior to the giving of the Torah, which demands both circumcision and the dietary laws, why cannot we be Jews without them? This is typically Pharisaic methodology. The Sadducees would have never taught this way.

This is what Paul did. It was ingenious. The consequences are epochal and led eventually to the texture and structure of the whole new system of belief that eventually became known as Christianity. The break with Judaism primarily occurred because of the genius of this man who was not even a rabbi. Jesus' brother James and the group centered around James would not go along with some of the changes Paul instituted. These changes were a daring deviation.

But the point needs to be made that Paul's decisions were totally within the structure and the methodology that the Pharisees had developed to deal with texts. It was simply the use of method by a great genius to confront a new condition of life and to find an answer to it that he could anchor in Scripture. To a Jew, if something was not found in Scripture, it was alien. And in the early formative decades and new generations of nascent Christianity, everything still needed to be bound to or related to Torah. Eventually notions developed in Christianity that could not be found in Jewish Scriptures and traditions – most significantly, ultimately, the deification of Jesus.

Even after the meeting in Jerusalem, Paul still saw himself as a Jew. First of all he preached to people in synagogues in the Mediterranean world. Who else would listen to him? Some non-Jews who had become uncomfortable with pagan worship and theology clustered around the synagogues of the Mediterranean world. For these people, polytheism had run its course and was increasingly unsatisfactory. They were deeply moved by the monotheistic religion. While they did not convert, they came to the synagogue, listened to the exposition of the Scripture, and became part of the community, at least on the fringes. It was among this group in various cities in the area around the Aegean Sea, but also then in Rome, that Paul found his first following and adherents.

Another factor helping Paul in his itinerant teaching career was the existence since the third pre-Christian century of the Greek translation of the Jewish Bible, the Septuagint. Many educated members of the Greek-speaking population of the Mediterranean world had heard of or even read Jewish biblical texts available in Greek. The remarkable availability of an alternative to mythology and polytheism should not be over-looked in tracking the growth of early Christianity.

Beginning this discussion of the similarities of the two systems of belief ought not to lead to the idea of the ultimate value of a single religious community. Such an idea may not even be desirable. The retention of specificity both for Christians and for Jews is desirable, even necessary, for we have our own histories, memories, values. Without clear delineation between the religions, there might be a tendency to go too lightly in declaring these differences to be unnecessary or unimportant. Diversity is good, fructifying, and energizing. It benefits both religions and the leading edges of both communities to know more about each other, to be influenced by some of each other's notions, and even to be willing to accept here or there correction from the other.

Ultimately we must recognize my somewhat startling position: we are all in the earliest stages of our development of being human. Based on this perception, surely our religious understanding is part of the novelty of being human on an earth that is billions of years older than anything we can even slightly identify as hominid. Therefore, I expect that in the next fifty million years or even as soon as fifty thousand years, not only will humans develop into something that cannot now be projected or anticipated, but also that whatever religious understandings we have now will have expanded, changed, and developed into totally unanticipated and unpredictable forms. It is curious to me how short-range most religiously observant people imagine the story of humanity to be.

It is impossible to know what religion will be like fifty thousand years from now. What concerns me is not this uncertainty about religion, but that so few people can really conceive of the human enterprise as capable of lasting that long. There seems to be a built-in expectation of an early end, an eschaton, whether naturally or catastrophically. That is one of the most dire prospects, because I am afraid that under the impact of such impatience about putting an end to the human unfolding, somebody will find a means to do it. And by now we have developed the means of achieving this catastrophe.

My hope is that we will not think of ourselves as standing at the final stages of insight into the sacred, into the mystery of reality, into what we call God. To me, it would be strange to think that my descendants would have the same ideas about God that I have, and this comes from the simple fact that I am totally wedded to the notion that everything I know, or that anybody who has preceded me knew, is to a large, even decisive extent culturally determined. It is the inevitable part-and-parcel of our understanding of our reality in all of its forms. For example, when one thinks of the earth as flat, and the sky as a globe with the stars affixed to it, on the basis of that available knowledge one constructs a three-story universe, with a netherworld underneath one's feet, and then that idea shapes one's entire response to the totality of being. Whatever appears to be part of God, of whatever else is involved with that realm of inquiry, is totally dependent on our own understanding of who we are, where we are, of what our understanding of reality consists. For such a perception, up is always good, and down is bad.

I am always reminded of the second commandment, which prohibits anything that would be a likeness of God, of that which is in the "heavens above, or the earth beneath, or the waters beneath the earth" (Exodus 20:4). This was the full range of our ancestors' understanding of the world in which they lived. It was a totally satisfying understanding on the basis of their capacity. But for me to be stuck with that understanding is impossible. Moreover, whatever derives from an understanding of that kind is in need of correction, expansion, replacement, maybe even total rejection here or there.

If our general cultural condition is inescapably woven into

whatever we know or conceive of the totality of our reality, then I would expect that humanity in some indescribably far-off future will experience a similar expansion, change, rearticulation. Think of what happened to our vocabulary just in the twentieth century as a result of Darwin, Marx, Freud, Einstein, Buber. Each of them and all of them together created new wordings and new concepts that are now so deeply woven into our whole vocabulary and mode of expressing ourselves that somebody who lived before and was untouched by these geniuses and their discoveries could not and would not speak that way.

Yet even these are not the last word. There certainly have been serious challenges to Darwin's understanding, and not from opposition to Darwin, but from within evolutionary biology. And the same is true of every one of these leaders and innovative thinkers. Freud, for example, today is largely modified by new insights into the workings of our psyche. Marx's analysis has been challenged severely. Both Einstein and Buber are being modified.

If there is life elsewhere in the universe, it does not give me pause. I am completely convinced that whatever we think about God is totally related and inescapably linked to our being human, that is, to our being on earth. I do not know whether dolphins have any notion of some kind of God-ness, or for that matter, of violets. I know we humans have this capacity, and that is really remarkable. I think we ought to be aware of the extraordinary consequences of the discovery within us of a gift that nothing else in creation possesses. We have the gift of *emuna*, trusting, believing.

From all I have ever heard, or read, or learned, this gift is unique. Now some say that it was a mistake, that whatever led to the development of the human this way was somehow wrong, was a flaw. I like to go the other way, maintaining that the very fact of our having this capacity certainly permits the conclusion that it is for a purpose, that it has a unique use. Therefore, *emuna* is not only not an aberration, it may very well be the single most important of the two or three most distinguishing features inherent in being human. Just as a highly developed capacity to reason and to speak are endowments that come from our predecessors in the evolutionary chain, the capacity to believe seems to be the most extraordinary and unique of these talents. It is a talent that apparently has no precedent. Speech and intelligence we find in rudimentary fashion in some more or less pre-human stages of development and in other beings. I doubt whether faith and belief have any kind of precedent. It may very well be, therefore, the single most extraordinary characteristic defining the specificity of being human.

This leads me to posit that whatever we understand by *emuna* and its capacity to give us understandings, values, truths, insights, perceptions, may well be a hint of the direction in which the true future of the human adventure lies. We are told that we are only using a minor fraction of our brain capacity. This could be translated into saying that we are only beginning to know how to reason, and that some future development of the human species may double or multiply the use of the brain's capacity, thereby leading to more exquisite and perhaps unimaginable states of being.

We know so little about our brain that we do not know for sure whether or not there is a region in it that is the locus of the capacity to have *emuna*. Perhaps this capacity is not even in the brain, but in the totality of our specific constitution as a living creature. Whatever it is, it may well be that *emuna* has an aura of novelty and capacity to unfold and may be the most distinctive feature of being human. So while I understand why some have looked at it askance and have thought of the exercise of *emuna*, the use of belief, as a flaw, it could very well be just the opposite. In fact, for me it is the opposite. It is the assertion of a human capacity that is precious because it is unique to our species, and the future result of which is unimaginable. This may be so even when the capacity of having *emuna* can be distorted, abused, falsified into a caricature of our potential.

Here again I proceed from the assumption that we are at the very beginning of an understanding of ourselves, of a recognition of our own nature, to the point that to draw final conclusions from what we now know to what may be tens of thousands or millions of years hence is hubris, an arrogance that we ought to reject totally. We are just beginning to be human. We have only been around five or six million years, which is very little in terms of cosmic time, of God's "time."

This perspective leads to an awareness that I only have a fragment of the total picture. The fragment is good enough. It contains enough of what I can believe and defend as valuable, perhaps even offer to others to consider. However, to claim that it is the only valid perspective, the only truth, is not only excessive, it is destructive. Claims of that kind start from an understandable but faulty recognition that we often want to make whatever we know or whatever we are to be, the absolute: "Ours is the only true understanding. Anybody else is wrong." "If they are not with us, they are against us." Therefore, it is an inherent drive in many religious systems to make everybody "like I am." This drive assumes that there is a capacity for such extraordinary truth in what I understand, what I know, what I commit myself to, that everything else becomes inferior in comparison with it. Such an assumption, such a stance could easily be destructive of even the bit of truth that I might have, and so it has been throughout history.

Thus I am wedded to the two-covenant position, but also to the whole enterprise of reaching out to others not of my belief system in order to enter into conversations and explorations that would provide us with insight into one another's basic assumptions and allow us to compare them. Such an enterprise might even lead those who are wedded to certain beliefs to reexamine them under the impact of inquiries made by someone outside of the system. All of this I hold to be ultimately necessary to make certain that the human family on this globe can eventually come to a noncompetitive stance and relation that will do away with some of the most destructive evil from which humanity has suffered, and is suffering so egregiously – religious enmity.

We are at a beginning of the effort. We are doing things now with a scope and intention that have never been done before. Again, to expect immediate, startling results would be a misreading of ourselves and others. We are at the beginning, and this is the major truth of our time. This may be the single greatest hope I have for the creation by our descendants of a different kind of humanity and global community in the centuries to come. We are also under the threat of the opposite – unimaginable vast powers of destruction. I think we are at a stage in mankind's march toward whatever future it has where some of its options have narrowed. This adds an urgency to the enterprise for lessening of friction quite beyond mere curiosity or hope. And there are groups, perhaps many of them, all over the world, working in that direction. It is a far-off vision, but it is the one most urgently worthy of our commitment.

Chapter Fourteen
The Time to Come

He will reign on David's throne and over his kingdom,
establishing and upholding it with justice and righ-
teousness from that time on and forever.

(Isaiah 9:7)

If the issue of morality is totally rooted and subsumed in the
human sphere and condition, then ultimately it comes down to
a power question: Who has the ultimate authority to formulate
and enforce the set of rules? Then the question of what it is to be
good has no reference outside a given human situation. Under
these circumstances, there is no measure by which to gauge
whether a given set of rules or values is truer than any others. For instance, the Nazis' contention that the Jews were like
garbage to be burned up and removed from the earth for the
well-being of the rest of the humanity, and Himmler's statement
that the ss officers doing this genocidal work were as moral as
anyone else – these "value" statements are then as valid as any
others. Thus it is posited that there is no system of morality is
really valid unless it is anchored outside the human condition
that, at least to the extent that those who commit themselves

to a given set of values are accepting it on the assumption that it originated not totally within themselves but in the encounter with a Being beyond them that we usually call God.

This position does not, of necessity, include a day of reckoning, because it could still be asserted, as it is in a strand of rabbinic teaching, that one is moral for its own sake, and not in the anticipation or expectation of a reward, which then would also imply punishment in the case of nonperformance. One is moral because of having committed oneself, as an act of belief, to the validity and compelling quality of that value system. And, of course, it is this act of belief that is the indispensable, inescapable contribution the human can make to the Mystery of the divine.

To reject that Mystery is to take a stand claiming human total self-sufficiency, and that inescapably leads to a competition for power. History has shown the most devastating kinds of consequences imaginable flowing from that competition for power. In the long run, any assertion of total human self-sufficiency is really a death wish, not just for groups, but for individuals. Individual success is temporary; one is only successful until somebody comes along who has bigger muscles or better equipment. The self-sufficient individual's position is subject to continuous combat and measurement of the means and exercise of power. Ultimately it is self-destructive, suicidal actually.

In reality, it is life-affirming to have a belief in the collaborative grounding of the system of values to which one commits oneself, to trust in the interaction between the divine Mystery and the human mystery, for we humans are also a mystery. On the other hand, any recourse to human self-sufficiency is simply an invitation for us to kill each other off, because sooner or later there will always be somebody who wills to do so. The assertion of such power is always an implicit challenge to someone to come along and display more enforcement power.

Time and again, in whatever time span we want to contemplate, it is possible to choose individual wealth, luxury, power. In any given life, the consequences of such choices may unfold in a fashion that seduces one into thinking that one may personally be immune from the negative consequences that are otherwise inherent in a faulty morality. And since there are enough examples of how this works, many people are inclined to try it. But there are also are plenty of examples of how it does not work. Certain monarchs, dictators like Hitler, Mussolini, Stalin, are all examples of lives that ended in a disastrous way. The aftermath of Stalin's life, just to take one with which we are very much familiar, would not encourage anybody to copy his choices. History is replete with examples of protagonists of utterly self-centered, self-enclosed moral authority, such as Franco, Pol Pot, even Emperor Hirohito of Japan.

Of course, because of the way human society and life are structured, it is possible for a given person to get away with such activities for a while. Slavery in the United States lasted hundreds of years, as did the oligarchical structure of society in which the people on the bottom were immorally rendered totally powerless. It takes a long time for such injustice to be corrected; indeed there are parts of the world where it is not corrected to this day.

In a very practical sense, it is legitimate to question whether the notion that one does something for its own sake is sufficiently powerful to control a whole society, or to imbue a whole society with its energy, its enthusiasm. A corollary question asks whether societies, as they grow, can be organized on anything but a reward-and-punishment level. This is the point where the practical and the theoretical come into tension, maybe even into conflict. In a small community, or a family, it is workable to have as the guiding impulse the notion of morality for its own sake, and to have all values conducted, lived, shared, because of their intrinsic appeal. What do you do when you have a city of a few million, and a country of hundreds of millions?

One of the deepest human impulses is for cosmos as over chaos. Chaos – uncertainty, lack of structure, lack of limits – is an experience that is not only frightening, it may also be the undoing, in a very real sense, of a human person. Apparently, law is absolutely necessary. The question is, on what basis shall laws be formulated?

To me, the key is that the law respond to the lived life. In other words, you do not make laws in a vacuum. The law is not a theoretical exercise, it is a response to reality, to problems that arise in the interplay between people, and this is the framework within which one stands, also, in the interplay between deity and humanity. Therefore all of one's existence, all of one's total response to reality, is ultimately reflected in rules and in laws.

All sets of rules begin with honest choices. The choice for monotheism is an enormous choice, a radical departure from what most human beings live by, even to this day, and whether they know it or not. Polytheism is a much more reasonable and also a much easier way of life. Monotheism is a very demanding, controlling, even uncomfortable way when one thinks of the human being as capable of an untrammeled multiplicity of responses. Monotheism is really the only basis on which one has to finally say yes to some things and no to others. The whole grounding of morality is inescapably bound up with and only found in a monotheistic system.

I am in a very risky position here in the sense that I do not accept the traditional formulation of knowing exactly what God wants, what God said. I need to formulate, sometimes actually change, my responses to our tradition, which states with incontrovertible certainty that it knows what God wants and has the text to undergird this assertion. At the same time, I am still standing within the tradition, although not in a stance traditionalists would assume. But certainly I stand within the tradition in such a way that I always identify with the religious tradition as the starting point from which I need to develop my own set of commitments. The struggle is that if culture and the lived life are, in fact, an indispensable ingredient in the formulation of this complex set of rules, then I need to take into account who I am now. I cannot live only the life of eighteenth-century Poland or of Israel two thousand years ago. While I will always be respectful, and need to know enough to know where to start, nonetheless I do not think I am bidden to and bound by total conformity to the traditional formulation. And that, of course, is what makes me a nontraditionalist, what makes me a liberal.

In a monotheistic system, in a religious setting like Judaism, there is an ultimate sense of relationship to a source other than oneself. To actually identify that source in the sense of a definition seems impossible, because defining it would imply that I am in the driver's seat, that I set the limit, I define the terms. The reality is that there is a Mystery in which I find myself and which surrounds, suffuses, and in many ways determines me, to which I want to respond, to which I need to respond, simply because otherwise I would be totally insensitive and ungrateful, neither of which I want to be. Our human need for precision, for definition, our fear of the unstructured, of chaos, our continued striving after structure, after cosmos, is because then it is something that we can control. This is our great need because we are so afraid of whatever is uncontrollable and therefore surprising.

That is why we needed the notion of the redemption of the world. As one traditional view has it, the Messiah will come in the seventh millennium, a sabbatical of thousands, so that the earth will be redeemed in a Sabbath of millennia. At the beginning of the last of these millennia, the Messiah will appear, reign for a thousand years, and thereby achieve whatever is necessary to bring on the completion, the fulfillment, the end. The Greek word is *eschaton*; the Hebrew is *kaytz*.

Christianity has inherited this view of time, although in a

much more urgent manner, because for Christians the decisive redemptive event has already begun, is already in motion, and is somehow, as traditional believing Christians have always felt, working toward an end in the not too distant future, perhaps even imminently.

Jewish tradition has maintained the historic experience of the continued absence of the Messiah, his delay, because the expectations linked to the him simply have not yet been fulfilled. Therefore the notion developed in traditional circles that the Messiah is at the disposal of God, and the appearance of the Messiah will be a revelatory act of God, whereby God will relieve the tension between a judging God and a sinful people to effectuate redemption. In due course God will forgive all premessianic history. In that forgiving act, God will send the Redeemer so that whatever had befallen the people and so painfully pursued them until then will then be removed and changed into well-being, into *shalom*. This certainly is part of the messianic construction – not all of it, but certainly a major part. Again, it has to do with the reward-and-punishment perception of God.

The question is whether the notion of Messiah is still valid. The messianic idea developed in Jewish life in response to the experience, as it was interpreted, of the punishment of exile, of the absence of a native ruler, of God's displeasure, or worse, directed against the people. God's withholding the evidence of reconciliation and healing was then focused into a being called Messiah. Since the Hebrew word *mashiach* basically means "anointed one," and is applicable to both the king and the high priest, it is clear that the original intention of any notion of Messiah was the rediscovery of a true, authentic king, who according to some versions of this perception was held hidden by God, waiting for the right time. The *kairos* sends the prophet Elijah as the advance agent, the announcing messenger of the Coming. Tradition focused all of this into Passover and the lovely symbolisms of a cup for Elijah on the Seder platter, and the opening of the door to welcome the herald of the Messiah.

These developments are fascinating evidence of the capacity of the Jewish people for stubborn faithfulness. There is no other community in the world that, despite all evidence to the contrary, so devotedly clings to such religious propositions. Think of the millions of households on Passover, all performing the same rituals, all having a cup that is not drunk, all opening the door at the given point in the latter part of the observance of the festival. And perhaps not just going through motions, but also really investing Passover with an aura of the messianic. This is astounding, especially in view of the claims made by Christianity that the messianic event has already begun. For close to two thousand years, Jews have stubbornly clung to their own position, although they have suffered for this refusal, egregiously and painfully. Yet overwhelmingly, the expectation or belief in Messiah is still a major part of the Jewish hope to this day.

Since the belief in the coming of the Messiah is bound up with a staunch expectation of a fairly early end to humanity, it is impossible for me to accept it. Rather, I hope for a virtually limitless extension and future for the Jewish people and all humanity.

Time is an element that is specifically human. To the best of our knowledge, nothing else in the created order has an awareness of time. Animals do not seem to have a sense of time, although they respond to the stimulus of light and darkness, of climate, and the like. But in the sense that we understand time – as something that is measurable, that is predicable, that is in every sense of the word a component of our awareness of self – it is seemingly not to be found in anything nonhuman. Timeliness means awareness of death, not as an immediate moment, but as the anticipation, sometimes over decades, of an inescapable eventuality. Therefore, time/death is a component of our being to the extent that it seems to be singular, characteristic of the human, and has elemental consequences in living, thinking, and even the unconscious response to our reality.

Some think that the entire impulse to morality is a consequence of our understanding that we are going to die. The need to do something and to do it right and well because there is only so much time, because we do not have an infinite opportunity to do things the right way, is a need which in itself is a motivational aspect of being human and apparently is not shared by tigers and chimpanzees, let alone hawks or rose bushes.

Time is an immense understanding, and a recognition of the singularity of our own being. Therefore, for many the need to make time count is imperative, quite apart from the fact of counting time. Surely all our religious systems enshrine, somehow or other, a recognition of the urgency of the potential for being human simply because it is limited. Needless to say, in virtually every religious system this leads to the idea of an expansion of personal time beyond death. Most likely this is a result of the understanding that existence can be so short and experience shows that humans do not use time well. There is so much we should be doing that we do not do at all, or only do poorly. Moreover, often there is no reward for doing things right in life, so the expectation is postponed to a post-mortem form of being.

The impact of timeliness is enormous. It certainly leads to the assertion that God is beyond time, that God is eternal. This is one of the greatest differentiations between deity and humanness. Of course it is also true that in modern cosmology it is almost senseless to ask what happened before the "Big Bang," because the Big Bang is the coming into being not only of the cosmos, but also of time. Thus, one cannot ask what was before time. That is inherently a nonquestion unless one posits a multiplicity of universes, one of which may have preceded the one in which we are, others waiting to come into being after this universe no longer exists, others that exist coevally with ours.

We do have no way of knowing which of these choices are true because our being is totally and inescapably woven into the texture of this cosmos, at least as far as we can understand it.

Omnipresence is certainly untimely, that is, beyond time-liness. Omnipresence is a statement we make about God as a major differentiation about who we are because we cannot be in two places a the same time, at least not yet, quantum theory notwithstanding. Quantum theory offers a radically different understanding of how the world works that may eventually create a different understanding and reality of being human.

It is wonderful to live in a time when there are so many questions arising because we have made so many discoveries. Some of these new discoveries, and therefore the new questions they raise, are basic challenges to everything people have known, lived by, and therefore are comfortable with. Probably only a tiny minority of current humanity is acquainted with these new discoveries and the possible consequences of the far-reaching, hitherto-unimagined related questions and possibilities. These discoveries, therefore, also are a threat because we like the familiar. The familiar is where we are comfortable, where we can predict and therefore exercise a measure of control.

Control is one of the great needs of most human beings, because the unexpected, the surprising, can be so often upsetting and is a threat to that carefully stitched together bit of fabric that is our existence. New ideas and surprising, unexpected developments tend to tear apart the little bit of fabric, and we are dislocated. Then we need either to weave a new fabric or are left with tatters. The first of these options, while exciting, is too difficult and too burdensome for most. The second is painful. Yet it is not unfair to say that most human beings experience the tearing of their fabric and consider it to be so painful, so frightful an experience, that if we could, we would avoid it at all costs.

Control is the key word. And since control is obviously only possible within certain parameters, and is certainly different for human beings, depending on where they stand in the configurations of life and society, there are all kinds of deep-seated and emotional consequences. Concomitantly education is driven by great expectations of teaching the capacity to weave a new worldview, rearing people in the home or in school so as to endow them with the capacity to respond to the unexpected without being totally panicked or destroyed. It is a complicated process that takes time and unusual skill to evolve.

Creation remains the prime Jewish consideration and concern. Implicit in Creation, somehow, is also a finish, an end, a completion. Our ancestors who gave thought to this had a perception of time and space that was ultimately very limited. Certainly their spatial perception included a heaven that was a transparent globe of some sort, a flat earth, and some dark space underneath. Their idea of the physical reality of the scene in which human beings were placed could not but be circumscribed and limited. When they thought about time, they seem to have been similarly limited. Their perception of time was primarily founded on the flow of the seasons and the human span of life. Therefore, since human life certainly was circumscribed, people who in their experience were regarded as old were what we would now consider upper middle age. It was a rare experience for somebody to get to be seventy or eighty years old, and there is certainly textual evidence that this was considered to be extraordinarily rare. With the human life span so short, the application of that estimate to the whole question of what we mean by time, by duration, by the span of reality and life temporally speaking, was similarly limited. They could not have known that time and space are somehow phenomena of each other, which many now know coming out of the twentieth century.

At the beginning of the twenty-first century, we are living in a time when we know that we have received light from a galaxy 13.2 billion light years away. We think of the Big Bang as having happened around 13 billion years ago. When we begin to speak these numbers – and it is obvious that few of us have any idea of what they really mean when they speak of them – then the whole imagination of a "Sabbath of millennia" is so puny that it becomes irrelevant.

I sometimes startle my students by asking whether they have ever wondered whether the human enterprise might last five thousand more years. And when I notice surprise at this question, I say, "Well, let's get real. How about fifty million years? Does anybody here think that there will be humans around fifty million years from now?" And in all of my many decades of teaching among Jews and Christians, I have never found anyone who has ever thought about the possibility. It is clear that this perception has an immediate and devastating impact on the whole notion of Messiah. The traditional notion of a Messiah is a reflection of a highly limited understanding both of what the Messiah is supposed to achieve and also of the time frame in which all of this is to occur.

The end may well come when the earth falls prey to the dying sun, which, we are told, will expand and therefore heat up the earthly environment to a degree where it will destroy everything we call life. If we listen to the projections and expectations of some of the scientists in the pertinent fields, this may happen 3.5 to 4.5 billion years from now. Should this be true, regardless of whatever is the case now, whatever is real now, some exceedingly basic and radical notions concerning God appear.

What it implies is that the human enterprise as we know it is meant to be time-limited, that its total end can be imagined though it be far off. Perhaps for some it is desirable that the end be achieved soon, but it is not necessary. This has all kinds of implications. One, of course, pertains to our imaginings about

God in terms of God's function as Creator and Resident Ruler of the reality in which we humans find ourselves. It is possible, perhaps even necessary, to assign God an entirely different time frame, or no time frame at all, to think of an eternity of being, of divine timelessness. Such a possible end to human existence implies that the creative act of God, who supposedly is the ground, the cause, the Maker of our world, apparently had in mind to have this form of Creation exist only for a relatively brief cosmic time.

Traditionally, it is certainly not anything that can be thought of in millions of years. Our ancestors did not even have a perception of what a million is; there is no word for it in biblical language. It is a much more recent term. Yet a billion is just about unimaginable even for those of us who can say it or put up the necessary number of zeros, and we can even talk of even much larger numbers – trillions, quadrillions, and so forth. Our whole perception of reality, when seen under the perspective of time, has undergone a radical transformation.

Do I, therefore, look for the end of the world? No way! Not if it means an early end of the human phase of being. On the contrary, humanity is still in its diaper stage. We are, at best, toddlers, and it is not always clear that we have reached even that stage yet. Modern anthropologists suggest that we may have been around some four or five million years, beginning as hominids. This leads to the expectation that we are only at the very beginning of what it means to be human. If, in addition to this, one notes that the capacity of our brains is underused, with perhaps no more than 10 to 15 percent of its capacity actually functioning for us today, then the expansion of a future totally different from the so-called present in which we now live is not only possible, it is indisputable. Those religious systems that have somehow implanted within them a notion, a desire, sometimes even an urgent wish for an end of the human phenomenon, are just not in consonance with the latest available data about the reality and possibilities in which we find ourselves.

For that reason, I am not interested in a return of a scion of the house of David to a Jewish throne. Now many have explained the State of Israel and their participation in the effort of creating it, or their acceptance of it, as an advance step toward a messianic fulfillment. Those Jews who decided to take matters into their own hands and establish the State of Israel were justified, despite the opposition of ultratraditionalists who said that it was blasphemous because only God could give the signal for such an event. But in truth, such action is an anti-messianic event. It is gratuitous to think there is a messianic meaning to the establishment of the State of Israel, to the ingathering of millions of Jews who had no other way of living or who were determined to reestablish a Jewish autonomous national existence.

The Messiah is a real problem to me, and one that I have come to reject. This may be a dangerous, blasphemous position in some eyes, but I think it follows very consistently from my whole perception of my relationship to God. I do not expect God to provide anything more than God has already provided. Surely the Messiah is the clearest indication of an actual demand on the part of tradition for God to finally deliver an ultimate hope. The Maimonidean formulation of the demand, "I believe in perfect faith in the coming of the Messiah. And though he delay, I believe," is not only an indication of the Jewish capacity for stubborn faith but an implicit challenge to God to not hold back. The delay is understood to be totally God's act and will. And if I believe in the coming, if this is one of the basic principles that my monotheism has declared it to be, then I am bringing pressure on God to consider that it is supposed to be a compelling promise, either directly or implicitly, and time is an urgent factor, is now.

The delay is always placed on the shoulders of the people.

We are simply not fit, we are not faithful enough, not free enough of sin or of failure. Therefore, there is a principle in Jewish tradition to which I also can no longer subscribe, namely that God is always right and we are always wrong, and whatever happens to us is the just desert of God's judgment. Again my rejection of all this stems from my understanding of the Shoah and God's role in it, because if I had to believe that the Shoah is another punishment by God, then my whole relationship to God, my whole belief structure, would be in collapse. So I need to totally reject the notion that Jewish history is the evidence of a just God. The very notion of God's accountancy of our failures and our trespasses and misdeeds is a powerful pedagogic tool, and one that I experienced in its depths when I was growing up and even into my adult life for a long time, but it has become an improper and insufficient way of seeing my relation to God today.

Except as a vision of the world redeemed, I no longer believe in the old kind of redemption. My ancestors' perception of the world was so limited, and the horizon was so circumscribed, that the notion of realistically achieving such an ultimate end, and of achieving it within a foreseeable time, made a lot more sense to them than it would for me today. In fact, if truth be told, though I still keep the vision alive, I have doubts about its realization. I return again to the saying from Pirke Abot that "it is not up to you complete the work, but neither are you free to desist from it." This has been my understanding of my own life and position in life, a motto for my own actions and my own commitment.

So while I do not think that redemption of the world is realistically projectable, the vision of it is still captivating and powerful, energizing and compelling. There is nothing wrong with that, because every life needs some kind of major outlook on ultimates, some kind of vision, hope. The vision is connected with one of the great achievements of the Jewish people and its tradition: the virtual infatuation with hope. Not just a commitment to hope, but an inescapable, powerful lure – the soul of the people totally suffused by hope.

This discussion leads to a corollary. Those who think of this life as limited and consistently project a different form of being, timelessness, eternity – whether in paradise, heaven, *olam habba*, the world to come – have a tendency, as a result, not to take this life too seriously. In fact, one of the almost unavoidable consequences of thought processes or belief stances of this kind is that life is ultimately devalued, made, as one rabbinic text says, a mere entryway, a foyer, of the real place where we will eventually be. This life is made merely a pass-through on the way to the timelessly real.

A second corollary is that this notion has the capacity, if not the necessity, of delaying and preventing involvement in moral issues and social change. It is not surprising that a good deal of Western civilization's current state is the product of this kind of thinking. The affairs of this world have really never had the prominent place of concern which they need in order to be addressed, because there has always been this anticipation, this promise, this expectation, of a much better nontemporal form of being. Think, for example, about the Muslim murder-bombers right now who are being inspired, even by their parents and family, to a "perfect life" that they cannot enjoy here? The whole construction about the end, while understandable in terms of both the physical and the intellectual environment as well as the beliefs of our ancestors, needs to be changed, to be discarded, and to be recognized as unwholesome.

Furthermore, that viewpoint is a horrible way of distorting what ultimately we would like to believe is implied by the original notion of God as Creator. After each stage of creation, the Bible says that God looks at creation and thinks of it as good. The creation of Adam, the human, is even judged to be "very good." This judgment is difficult to reconcile with the notion that it is meant to be good only for a little while and something much better is coming afterward. Such an interpretation is a serious distortion.

There is another consideration, a painful, disturbing sequel. If the current projection of the eventual extinction of all life on earth by the dying sun is correct, then all human life as we know it will end. Quite apart from the inherent possible contradiction to the Creatorship of God involved in that finality, we need also ask what will then happen to God. Who will bother about God, search for, worship, argue with, love, comfort God? What other partner does God have already now, or will God have then? What will be God's destiny in the absence of the human other? Can God be God without us? Did God not perhaps create cosmos and Adam to have an other, to break out of solipsism, out of total self-involvement?

Perhaps, in the future evolution of the human species, a capacity will develop to exist in a nonearth environment, and the dialogue between one of our far-off descendants and God will continue uninterruptedly. All I can say for sure now is that God and I, God and the human, are indispensable for each other, and are linked indissolubly.

Chapter Fifteen
The Mystery of Soul

"As the new heavens and the new earth that I make
will endure before me," declares the Lord, "so will your
name and descendants endure.

(Isaiah 66:22)

Soul is a lovely word that tries to say something about the mystery of what we might mean when we say that an individual has a personality, that everybody is different, that there is an indefinable something that sets each person apart from any other and, perhaps, from all other living things. But if anybody wants to talk about the soul as a recognizably separate substance, then I would have to demur, because I do not think it is true. Soul is another way of expressing part of my psychophysical being in a poetic and imaginative image for what I would unashamedly call the mystery of being human. Therefore, to me soul is not separable from physical being; it does not have an existence apart from the physical living being.

From my point of view, my being is an indissoluble element of life. I am a psychophysical entity that cannot be separated out into separate parts. In other words, the word "soul" is only a description of my living being. Once I am dead, there is no surviving soul, because the soul was an articulation of a mystery, of my "personality." Soul attempts to give an answer of some kind to the utterly shocking transitional distinction between a living, responding body and a corpse. I have had to be present when people died. The transition that occurs from someone who can still react to a pin prick or a feather held to her nose to catch some breath, to a corpse that is totally inert is profound, shocking, and radical. It is understandable that this change has proven to be so painful, puzzling, and complete that humans wanted to hope that something could survive, that something would continue beyond the moment of death.

According to traditional images, at the moment of death the soul leaves in a physically chartable departure. Thus there is a Jewish custom of covering the mirrors in the room in which death occurred, so that supposedly the soul is not arrested and therefore thwarted in its flight to wherever it is supposed to go. The underlying assumption is similar to that of the Greek myth of Narcissus, who looks into the water and is fixated by his own image. Such images are the result of a fascination with the notion that something animates us. Animation is derived from the Latin *anima*, which is usually translated as "soul." There are also all kinds of curious words like "ensoulment," which supposedly is the moment after conception, when the zygote changes from an assemblage of cells to a person. The way it is imagined, this is the moment of the juncture, the fusion, of the physical and the nonphysical, even in the earliest assemblage of cells in their multiplication process.

There is a medieval painting where the moment of death is represented by a little homunculus coming out the nostril of the corpse. The artist painted the soul as a tiny human. The concept of soul is how we have tried to deal with one of the great mysteries for any being that is consciously alive, sentient. All of the teachings we have about some existence after death, the soul being separated from the body in Western culture, are traceable in part to Plato and are not really biblical. Plato and Aristotle even purported to know the various layers and functions of the soul – three in each case. This is simply a striving to put some recognizable designation, a name, to functions that are inherently unnamable, ineffable.

Perhaps what we are really trying to say is that there is something divine in each of us. Because even as God is ineffable beyond the capacity of words to confine and define and express, so maybe this is also true of us, about what we then call "soul." But it should never be a definitive, substantive, traceably identifiable item. Precisely it is a word we use because we cannot really say anything else, because words often are incapable of giving the kind of description or designation for which we strive, but must concede that we cannot achieve. Once we understand soul to be ineffable, then the word "soul" becomes a convenient word, a rich word in terms of what we have begun to read into it, to cover what perhaps we ought not to probe any further.

I still remember Cardinal Bernardin's parting words to me. "Herman, I'm totally serene because I will be with my Lord."

But when I touched his cold hand as he lay in state in his residence, the hand that had always been so humanly warm and reassuring, I asked myself, "Joseph, where are you?" I knew this was not Joseph anymore, it was just a corpse. But I could not share his faith assertion that when he was dead, he would be with his Lord and therefore he had no fear of dying.

I do not believe there is anything after death that is identifiable as a given person. The body disintegrates into billions of components, some of which are totally indestructible. The body is made up of stuff that was most likely long used somewhere else in some other form. But I do not believe that anything considered as an identifiable continuance of me will exist. I am satisfied with that because I have had the extraordinary unmerited gift of life, which is my challenge to accept, to use, to understand, to fulfill to the extent that I am capable, even perhaps wise enough to try to do. Also, I can only be responsible, to some extent anyway, for my waking, conscious being.

Now I know how much comfort it is for people to think of themselves as somehow continuing beyond physical death, and I have hesitated to disavow or in any sense discourage their beliefs. A close relationship, bonding with a person, making the life of another a component of one's own life, has enormous power, joy, and fulfillment, but it comes at a high price. Like everything we humans seem to cherish, there is an underside to it. Of course, it is that when such people die, the void which is created, the wound that is struck, can sometimes not be filled or healed, sometimes even for a very long time.

There is no question that there are some people whose absence remains painful and represents an empty spot in one's life that cannot be filled. Autobiographically, I can say, in particular, that the death of my father has never ceased causing pain, albeit a diminishing pain. At my desk I have not only a picture of my late father, I also have a picture of the late Cardinal Bernadin, and for similar reasons. Just the other day, I watched the videotape of the visit to Israel I made with him and some others in 1994. After it was finished, I was deeply struck again by the sheer pain of the loss the cardinal's death created in my life. It still hurts, and I sat really quite stunned in grief for a while before I gathered myself up and let it fade away.

Like everyone, I have had other losses of a personal nature, of people who were central to my existence at one time or other. One of them was my then fiancé, who died in Palestine virtually on the eve of my trip there to marry her. So time and again, the searing pain of that loss surfaces, and I know it is the kind of a wound that just never heals totally. I do not expect it to heal totally. I understand that death causes any number of basic reactions so deeply felt that they need to be examined as well as to be addressed.

Nevertheless, there may be some real dangers in an imaginative treatment of death that asserts that it is not the end and that there will be, even as some have stated, reunions with the departed as well as a painless, everlasting, joyous "life." But can we really speak of life? Is not life what is precisely pre-mortem, prior to death, a fact beginning with conception and ending in death? Therefore, there cannot be life after death. It is a deeply inappropriate use of a word which has its own profound and definite meaning. These are fantasies that we humans have created to make it appear that death is not real, that it is just a transition from one form of being into another form of being.

There is one response to death, however, that seems to me to be really dangerous, and that is the one that tries to mask the loss as unreal. It is understandable how that can be very comforting, and how it can really somewhat soothe the pain of the loss. Is it, however, a method of facing the reality of death that is ultimately both honest and true and therefore valid? The danger arises in the way life as lived here and now, before death, is accepted as secondary in importance. In fact, very often, the consequence is that one is instructed to take life the way it comes; there is no need to struggle against what is, no incentive to improve the conditions of existence because this is merely the overture, the prelude. The real symphony is post-mortem. To me, this is a total denial of reality. Any attitude that does not want to confront reality, to the extent that we can understand it and interpret it, is a mistake. To me this is what it means to be human: to try to manage, interpret, understand, examine, review, the reality that confronts us and to attempt to live the most meaningful, creative, fulfilling existence of which we are capable and willing.

My own feeling is that many of the statements we make,

even in a liturgical way, particularly perhaps in a liturgical way, are intended to make those who are sorrow-stricken feel that their loss is really not as profound an insult to their own existence as they could consider it either in the first moment or upon reflection. So much in our attempt to ease the transition from participation in close relationships to their rupture in death is directed at telling the sufferers not to feel so deeply bereft and stricken, that the departed is in fact, as is often said, "in a better place," and is, therefore, relieved of some of the burden and difficulties that those who are alive have to continue to face and manage.

I will never forget an incident that happened when I was very young, about eight years old. My best buddy at the time was the only child of the janitor of the building in which we lived. Practically overnight, this young boy died. I was inconsolable, and I cried. My father suggested that I go down to the janitor's apartment to talk to his parents and comfort them. So I went down into the basement where they had their living quarters. I have never forgotten the father and mother sitting at the table, greeting me. They knew me, of course, I had been there other times, even though we usually played outside in the yard or on the street. When I wept and spoke of my loss at my friend's death, and expressed understanding of how they must also feel so bereft, the mother spoke up and said, "Herman, you've got to understand, he is now with Jesus. He doesn't have to live in this crummy apartment anymore. He doesn't have to endure all the things that are not good in this life, many of which we have to do. So do not cry. He is in a better world."

I could not understand it then, and as you can tell from this reference, this memory has made a permanent imprint on my own being. I must also say that I could not accept it then, and do not now. I understand the good intentions, as well the real comfort and soothing of hurt that such images and words bring to those in whose lives death has torn a wound. I just do not think that to paint such a picture and to create the anticipation that death is merely the portal to a better existence, to a more beautiful way of being, is the right way to seek comfort and manage loss.

It seems to me, and I have had to do it repeatedly myself, it is more real and honest to understand and accept the finality of death. Death is a radical discontinuity, a radical change in one's life, in one's relations, in the very texture of one's own being. I have found that when one undergoes the searing pain of trying to work this through, in addition to the actual removal of the beloved from one's own being, eventually there comes the acceptance of the total break, a different evaluation of the person who is gone, of the relationship that had existed, of the value of the bond. Then comes the readiness to face life as now reconstituted, reshaped, as a result of such an extraordinary and most painful experience.

I will never forget the death of a Jewish man who was, at the time, my best friend. His widow, who was not Jewish, surprised me with the statement that while her husband was comatose, she had her priest give him extreme unction. She believed she was preparing him for entry into "heaven," because she was totally convinced that this could not occur without the ministration of the rite. She said to me in the plainest words one could imagine, "I want to be reunited with him when I die." Now she was a deeply believing Christian, and I know that she spoke from the depths of her own belief and thought she was acting for the ultimate benefit of her dying spouse.

This is, of course, not the only such experience, even though I had never experienced it in so direct a way in my own personal life. I know that over and over again, maybe even preponderantly, this is how people treat death and are led to manage the pain of death.

Another danger is that such wishful thinking is a denial of one of the great events and realities with which we are confronted. Everything that lives, dies. Some forms of existence take millions or billions of years to disappear, but we as humans have a relatively short span of time. We just do not want to fully grasp and accept that we are the only creations that are timely. From the moment we are born, we are on the journey to death. We are also the only items in the created order, as far as we can tell, who know that we are getting older, who know that we are in time, that time is one of the most important identifying aspects of our being human. Other forms of life do not have a sense of time as far as we can tell. Flowers, for example, do not, even though they pass from birth to death, as do we. However, we humans know that we are going to die.

One could easily say that our whole intentionality toward ethics, toward achievement, toward fulfillment of anything we have planned, is based on our understanding that we have just a fixed amount of time allotted to us. Not only is this profoundly human, it is also threatening. Basically, the instinct to live seems to oppose or preclude the willingness to die. So perhaps one could say that life is a perpetual struggle to keep death at bay. We also know that this is only partially, temporarily successful. Ultimately we lose the battle.

Biblically this is told in the story of Adam and Eve in *Gan Eden*, a story that tells us something about what the sacred texts want us to hear as the ineluctable component and identify of our own selves. We are time-bound. The eating of the fruit gives the first couple the insight that they are sexually differentiated. This is the initiation of their understanding not only of sexuality, but implicitly and unavoidably of time. For obviously sexuality has to do with procreation, with birth and death. The eating of the fruit is the story-way of saying that to be human is to understand time. This is why Adam and Eve had to leave Paradise. In Paradise there is no time. It is only after eating the fruit that they become human. Before eating the fruit, they were creatures of a type not far different from other living things. It is only once they rebel and disregard the order not to eat the fruit that they become human through the fact that they now know time, that is to say, death. This experience is something that happens to them soon after they are expelled. It is not long thereafter that the first murder occurs – and among their sons. So the impact of time is radical, total, and, as the story is told, virtually immediate.

When it comes to comforting bereaved people, I have found that the only way I can do it in total honesty, and also to the best end-result, is simply to be there to share their grief, to be with them, perhaps to weep with them. I try, to whatever extent I can, to enter into their condition of being at that time. I do not come with some secret knowledge, learned or experienced formula, and I do not have a set of words I can apply to these terrible moments in the lives of those with whom I happen to be thrown into contact at a most difficult time. To me, the best I can to do is to try to share in the suffering, being present to those who suffer. Time and again I have found that this seems to help, and that it is not only the most honest approach, but also the one that reaches the deepest level of my capacity. So I studiously and deliberately avoid words that I cannot stand on with total integrity. I do not try to comfort people by pointing to the possibility or, as some would have it, the certainty of a form of being beyond death.

On a totally personal level, I do not expect anything of me to survive my death, except my DNA, or whatever atomic or sub-atomic particles of my physical body may continue on. There is a remarkable rabbinic statement that we were all standing at Sinai at the time of the first covenant with the Jewish community and God's descent onto the mountain. Today I accept that statement by assuming that someone whose DNA is now in me was there. So in a strange physical fashion, something of what I am today may have really been present then. I think there is something physical in all of us that retains its own identity,

290 HINENI – HERE I AM

but my self, my own specific being, I do not expect and do not believe will persist.

I must say that I am speaking in the context of my time, my culture, my striving to understand whatever there is. At the same time, I am fully conscious that qua human, we are in the earliest stages of our development. I totally deny that any human, any descendant of mine fifty thousand years from now, or five million years from now, or fifty million years from now, would not have a radically different understanding of life, of the cosmos, of nearly everything.

Recently I read a fascinating article that projects the notion that our universe may only be a tiny segment, a bubble, in an infinitely much more vast agglomeration of universes, and that Big Bangs occur continually, leading to the creation of other, parallel universes. This idea shakes the understanding that we live in the vastness of a cosmos that is thirteen billion light-years in the making and is some thirty billion light-years in diameter. This is such a vastness that we can only say the words but never really understand what we are saying. A billion is beyond comprehension, but in fact, as part of this projection concerning the universe, there was a figure mentioned of 10 to the power of 60. Such a number is, of course, unpronounceable as well as inconceivable.

There are theories, almost fantasies one might say, that in the first trillionth of a trillionth of a second after the Big Bang, certain "decisions" were made that were so refined and subtle that they led to the creation of the universe as we now know it, including this little complex we call earth and us as living conscious beings on it. It was clear in the telling of these great ideas that if there had been the tiniest, most minute change in the basic reactions, there would never have been the sort of universe we now are exploring, in which we find ourselves to be a tiny speck.

What I am saying, both with regard to death and to the

Messiah, is from the vantage point of my current understanding, fully conscious that it may someday be judged primitive in nature and condition. Although I no longer accept the reward-and-punishment construct of the human relationship with the mystery we call God, I believe we are responsible to, indebted to that Mystery. To speak, then, of God in accountancy fashion, keeping book on every individual human thereby to calculate and determine their fate is an unacceptable fantasy for me. It is part of the never-ending attempt by us believing human beings to interpret and thus understand the otherwise impenetrable ineffability of the divine. Yet, somehow, we believe and base our whole existence as believers on the proposition that somehow God "knows" us and therefore that mutual contact and relation are possible.

And so I am beset by questions and struggle to find answers, some of which may have prolonged validity, and others which are in flux and thus subject to slow or even rapid change. Such a position and condition of being is often troublesome and, at times, even painful, but it is also exhilarating, energizing, and steeped in unbreakable hope.

Postscript

After the completion of the manuscript which forms the content of this book, there are two related issues to which I want to address myself very briefly.

The first deals with the fundamental question of the future relationship between the Jews growing up in the State of Israel and the Jews living in the United States. Even a superficial glance cannot avoid noting a radical difference in the formation of the respective personae. A Jewish child growing up in Israel has a total, unquestioning, natural Jewish identity. He/she lives in a Jewish home and family. The first sounds heard are Hebrew. The lullabies are Hebrew. The words are Hebrew. With possibly a very few exceptions, all language which forms their identify is Hebrew. Their playmates and siblings are Jewish as are father and mother, uncles and aunts, etc. The street on which they live and play is Jewish. Their neighbors are Jewish, as is their teacher, mailman, grocer, policeman, President...They have practically, realistically, no choice.

Their American Jewish counterparts, however, live in a radically different mode. Everything about their Jewish identity needs continuous reinforcement. They are Jews by choice. Their

Jewishness is not automatic, natural, unquestioned. It needs continuous nurturing and often careful attention.

In sum, there is every prospect that there will be two different, probably even divergent types of Jews, and the likelihood by current wisdom is that the Israeli type may well become not only the more numerous, but also the more dominant. In this context, it is premature and irresponsible to speculate what the result of such disparity may be.

Added to all this is a certain strain in the relation between the Jewish communities in Israel and here. The old question of the validity and future of the diaspora already now persistent will grow in intensity. To me it is clear that in the last two and a half millennia, the diaspora was indispensable to the creativity and survival of the Jewish people. To my mind this is likely to remain true even in the future, precisely in the future. Diaspora is indispensable for a full flowering of the Jewish potential both intrinsically and extrinsically. Israel will only truly be Israel in concert with Diaspora Jews. They will always need each other. They will always need to be linked with each other.

The other issue, not totally unrelated, pertains to developments looming in the Jewish community here in the USA.

According to a recent poll, there was a finding that currently fifty percent of all Jewish children currently in the USA under age ten live in orthodox Jewish families. If this is a fairly accurate estimate, then it is possible to conclude that in twenty or thirty years hence, the majority of American Jews will be orthodox.

It is immediately apparent, if this assumption is more or less correct, that the composition of American Jewry will change radically from a now dominant position by non-orthodox Jews to its opposite. Nor will this be merely a shift in religious observance and perception. It will likely rearrange the whole cast of Jewish life here. Orthodox women and men will become the leaders of Jewish organizations far beyond their current numbers. Their views of some of the most current social issues and problems will undoubtably differ, sometimes sharply, from those now prevalent. Whatever political positions and trends a majority of Jews now favor most likely will change significantly. And one may well speculate that there will be many additional areas both of internal Jewish life and of public Jewish stances which will undergo major changes.

While such thoughts are speculative it is nonetheless or precisely because of this their nature necessary or, at least fascinating, to catch such a glimpse into the as-yet unformed future.

Acknowledgments

The publication of this book has been made possible by the generosity of Melvyn A. Abrams, Bernard and Sandra Meyers, and Bernard Rozran. Profound thanks.